About the WTO 2

Understanding the WTO	2	A global membership	8
How it all comes together	4	Welcoming new members	10
Joining the WTO	6	A brief history	12

A year in review 14

A message from WTO Director-General Pascal Lamy 14

Our year 16

Trade negotiations 20

Changes to the rules of trade require the agreement of all WTO members, who must reach consensus through rounds of negotiations. The most recent round began in 2001.

Implementation and monitoring 34

Various WTO councils and committees seek to ensure that WTO agreements are being properly implemented. All WTO members undergo periodic scrutiny of their trade policies and practices.

Dispute settlement 74

WTO members bring disputes to the WTO if they think their rights under trade agreements are being infringed. Settling disputes is the responsibility of the Dispute Settlement Body.

Building trade capacity 94

The WTO aims to help developing countries build their trade capacity and allows them a longer time to implement trade agreements. Hundreds of training courses are organized each year for officials from developing countries.

Outreach 110

The WTO maintains regular dialogue with non-governmental organizations, parliamentarians, other international organizations, the media and the general public to enhance cooperation and raise awareness of trade issues.

Secretariat and budget 132

The WTO Secretariat has over 600 regular staff and coordinates the activities of the WTO. Most of the WTO's annual budget consists of contributions by its 159 members.

Abbreviations 144

Further information 144

Understanding the WTO

There are a number of ways of looking at the World Trade Organization. It is an organization for trade opening. It is a forum for governments to negotiate trade agreements. It is a place for them to settle trade disputes. It operates a system of trade rules. Essentially, the WTO is a place where member governments try to sort out the trade problems they face with each other.

Who we are

The WTO was born out of negotiations aimed at progressively reducing obstacles to trade. The bulk of the WTO's current work comes from the 1986-94 negotiations called the Uruguay Round and earlier negotiations under the General Agreement on Tariffs and Trade (GATT). The WTO is currently the host to new negotiations, under the "Doha Development Agenda" launched in 2001.

Where countries have faced trade barriers and wanted them lowered, the negotiations have helped to open markets for trade. But the WTO is not just about opening markets, and in some circumstances its rules support maintaining trade barriers – for example, to protect consumers or prevent the spread of disease.

At its heart are the WTO agreements, negotiated and signed by the bulk of the world's trading nations. These documents provide the legal ground rules for international commerce. They are essentially contracts, binding governments to keep their trade policies within agreed limits. Although negotiated and signed by governments, the goal is to help producers of goods and services, exporters, and importers conduct their business, while allowing governments to meet social and environmental objectives.

The system's overriding purpose is to help trade flow as freely as possible – so long as there are no undesirable side effects – because this is important for economic development and well-being. That partly means removing obstacles. It also means ensuring that individuals, companies and governments know what the trade rules are around the world, and giving them the confidence that there will be no sudden changes of policy. In other words, the rules have to be "transparent" and predictable.

Trade relations often involve conflicting interests. Agreements, including those painstakingly negotiated in the WTO system, often need interpreting. The most harmonious way to settle these differences is through some neutral procedure based on an agreed legal foundation. That is the purpose behind the dispute settlement process written into the WTO agreements.

Virtually all decisions in the WTO are taken by consensus among all member countries. Equal treatment is one of the basic principles of the multilateral trading system.

What we stand for

The WTO agreements are lengthy and complex because they are legal texts covering a wide range of activities. But a number of simple, fundamental principles run throughout all of these documents. These principles are the foundation of the multilateral trading system.

Non-discrimination
A country should not discriminate between its trading partners and it should not discriminate between its own and foreign products, services or nationals.

Openness
Lowering trade barriers is one of the most obvious ways of encouraging trade; these barriers include customs duties (or tariffs) and measures such as import bans or quotas that restrict quantities selectively.

Predictability and transparency
Foreign companies, investors and governments should be confident that trade barriers should not be raised arbitrarily. With stability and predictability, investment is encouraged, jobs are created and consumers can fully enjoy the benefits of competition – choice and lower prices.

More competitive
Discouraging "unfair" practices, such as export subsidies and dumping products at below cost to gain market share; the issues are complex, and the rules try to establish what is fair or unfair, and how governments can respond, in particular by charging additional import duties calculated to compensate for damage caused by unfair trade.

More beneficial for less developed countries
Giving them more time to adjust, greater flexibility and special privileges; over three-quarters of WTO members are developing countries and countries in transition to market economies. The WTO agreements give them transition periods to adjust to the more unfamiliar and, perhaps, difficult WTO provisions.

Protect the environment
The WTO's agreements permit members to take measures to protect not only the environment but also public health, animal health and plant health. However these measures must be applied in the same way to both national and foreign businesses. In other words, members must not use environmental protection measures as a means of disguising protectionist policies.

What we do

The WTO is run by its member governments. All major decisions are made by the membership as a whole, either by ministers (who usually meet at least once every two years) or by their ambassadors or delegates (who meet regularly in Geneva). While the WTO is driven by its member states, it could not function without its Secretariat to coordinate the activities. The Secretariat employs over 600 staff, and its experts – lawyers, economists, statisticians and communications experts – assist WTO members on a daily basis to ensure, among other things, that negotiations progress smoothly, and that the rules of international trade are correctly applied and enforced.

Trade negotiations
The WTO agreements cover goods, services and intellectual property. They spell out the principles of liberalization, and the permitted exceptions. They include individual countries' commitments to lower customs tariffs and other trade barriers, and to open and keep open services markets. They set procedures for settling disputes. These agreements are not static; they are renegotiated from time to time and new agreements can be added to the package. Many are now being negotiated under the Doha Development Agenda, launched by WTO trade ministers in Doha, Qatar, in November 2001.

Implementation and monitoring
WTO agreements require governments to make their trade policies transparent by notifying the WTO about laws in force and measures adopted. Various WTO councils and committees seek to ensure that these requirements are being followed and that WTO agreements are being properly implemented. All WTO members must undergo periodic scrutiny of their trade policies and practices, each review containing reports by the country concerned and the WTO Secretariat.

Dispute settlement
The WTO's procedure for resolving trade quarrels under the Dispute Settlement Understanding is vital for enforcing the rules and therefore for ensuring that trade flows smoothly. Countries bring disputes to the WTO if they think their rights under the agreements are being infringed. Judgements by specially appointed independent experts are based on interpretations of the agreements and individual countries' commitments.

Building trade capacity
WTO agreements contain special provision for developing countries, including longer time periods to implement agreements and commitments, measures to increase their trading opportunities, and support to help them build their trade capacity, to handle disputes and to implement technical standards. The WTO organizes hundreds of technical cooperation missions to developing countries annually. It also holds numerous courses each year in Geneva for government officials. Aid for Trade aims to help developing countries develop the skills and infrastructure needed to expand their trade.

Outreach
The WTO maintains regular dialogue with non-governmental organizations, parliamentarians, other international organizations, the media and the general public on various aspects of the WTO and the ongoing Doha negotiations, with the aim of enhancing cooperation and increasing awareness of WTO activities.

How it all comes together

The WTO's top-level decision-making body is the Ministerial Conference, which usually meets every two years.

Below this is the General Council (normally ambassadors and heads of delegation in Geneva, but sometimes officials sent from members' capitals), which meets several times a year in the Geneva headquarters. The General Council also meets as the Trade Policy Review Body and the Dispute Settlement Body.

At the next level, the Goods Council, Services Council and Intellectual Property (TRIPS) Council report to the General Council.

Numerous specialized committees, working groups and working parties deal with the individual agreements and other areas such as the environment, development, membership applications and regional trade agreements.

Numerous specialized committees, working groups and working parties deal with the individual WTO agreements.

All WTO members may participate in all councils and committees, with the exceptions of the Appellate Body, dispute settlement panels and plurilateral committees.

Joining the WTO

Montenegro, Russia, Samoa and Vanuatu formally joined the WTO in 2012, raising the number of members (as of end-December 2012) to 157. Two other countries – the Lao People's Democratic Republic (Laos) and Tajikistan – completed their accession agreements during the year and joined in early 2013. This takes the WTO a step closer to its goal of universal membership. In 2012, the General Council adopted steps to ease the accession process for least-developed countries (LDCs). Measures were also taken to strengthen accession-related technical assistance for LDCs.

The General Council adopted the accession agreements of Laos on 26 October 2012 and of Tajikistan on 10 December 2012, meaning that both countries would formally become WTO members 30 days after notifying the WTO of the ratification of their accession protocols. Laos notified the WTO on 3 January 2013, and thus became the WTO's 158th member on 2 February. Tajikistan notified the WTO on 31 January 2013, and became the WTO's 159th member on 2 March.

As mandated by the Eighth WTO Ministerial Conference, the General Council formally approved in July 2012 new guidelines to enable LDCs to negotiate membership of the WTO more quickly and easily. The decision gives LDCs greater flexibility in goods and services commitments and on transition periods, and provides for additional technical assistance.

The Fourth Director-General's Annual Report on WTO Accessions, issued in December 2012, reviewed the empirical evidence on the benefits of WTO accession, based on the performance of Article XII members – i.e. countries that have joined since the WTO was established in 1995. It highlighted the fact that such countries had attracted higher than average inflows of foreign direct investment (FDI), with an average FDI increase of 15 per cent between 1995 and 2001. The report

Membership of the WTO (as of 31 December 2012)

Member[1]	Year of accession	Member	Year of accession	Member	Year of accession
Albania	2000	Czech Republic	1995	Jamaica	1995
Angola	1996	Democratic Republic of the Congo	1997	Japan	1995
Antigua and Barbuda	1995	Denmark	1995	Jordan	2000
Argentina	1995	Djibouti	1995	Kenya	1995
Armenia	2003	Dominica	1995	Korea, Republic of	1995
Australia	1995	Dominican Republic	1995	Kuwait	1995
Austria	1995	Ecuador	1996	Kyrgyz Republic	1998
Bahrain, Kingdom of	1995	Egypt	1995	Latvia	1999
Bangladesh	1995	El Salvador	1995	Lesotho	1995
Barbados	1995	Estonia	1999	Liechtenstein	1995
Belgium	1995	European Union	1995	Lithuania	2001
Belize	1995	Fiji	1996	Luxembourg	1995
Benin	1996	Finland	1995	Macao, China	1995
Bolivia, Plurinational State of	1995	France	1995	Madagascar	1995
Botswana	1995	Gabon	1995	Malawi	1995
Brazil	1995	The Gambia	1996	Malaysia	1995
Brunei Darussalam	1995	Georgia	2000	Maldives	1995
Bulgaria	1996	Germany	1995	Mali	1995
Burkina Faso	1995	Ghana	1995	Malta	1995
Burundi	1995	Greece	1995	Mauritania	1995
Cambodia	2004	Grenada	1996	Mauritius	1995
Cameroon	1995	Guatemala	1995	Mexico	1995
Canada	1995	Guinea	1995	Moldova, Republic of	2001
Cape Verde	2008	Guinea-Bissau	1995	Mongolia	1997
Central African Republic	1995	Guyana	1995	Montenegro	2012
Chad	1996	Haiti	1996	Morocco	1995
Chile	1995	Honduras	1995	Mozambique	1995
China	2001	Hong Kong, China	1995	Myanmar	1995
Colombia	1995	Hungary	1995	Namibia	1995
Congo	1997	Iceland	1995	Nepal	2004
Costa Rica	1995	India	1995	Netherlands	1995
Côte d'Ivoire	1995	Indonesia	1995	New Zealand	1995
Croatia	2000	Ireland	1995	Nicaragua	1995
Cuba	1995	Israel	1995	Niger	1996
Cyprus	1995	Italy	1995	Nigeria	1995

[1] Members are mostly governments but can also be customs territories.

also demonstrated that these members were more resilient to the global economic crisis, with FDI declining on average by 9 per cent between 2007 and 2008, compared with a 39 per cent drop globally.

Technical assistance is strengthened

Technical assistance continued to be strengthened. Acceding governments were invited to participate in over 100 technical assistance events.

The WTO Secretariat implemented components of the memorandum of understanding signed with the Government of China on accessions and LDCs. The China LDCs and Accessions Programme aims at strengthening LDCs' participation in the WTO and at assisting acceding LDCs. From 29 May to 1 June 2012, the first high-level roundtable was held in Beijing, focusing on best practices in WTO accessions for LDCs. The China Programme also set up an accessions internship scheme. The first two internships took place from January to October and two more began in October.

The International Trade Centre's Programme in Support of the Private Sector in Acceding Developing Countries and LDCs continued to be highly active. Further outreach activity took place through briefings to all regional groups at the level of heads of delegation. Some Working Party chairs undertook visits to acceding governments to meet with key domestic stakeholders. Briefings for new arrivals and workshops for parliamentarians and civil society were also organized. Several post-accession technical assistance activities took place, focusing on the implementation of the negotiated accession commitments and general membership obligations.

Transparency was further enhanced by regular meetings of the Informal Group on Accessions, the WTO Accessions Newsletter, the Fourth Director-General's Report on WTO Accessions and the launch of the Accession Commitments Database by the Director General in Beijing on 29 May 2012.

For 2013, the Director-General identified, in consultation with WTO members, three LDC and three non-LDC accessions, which, given their technical maturity, and depending on relevant progress in early 2013, could be completed this year. The LDCs are Afghanistan, Ethiopia and Yemen, while the non-LDCs are Bosnia and Herzegovina, Serbia and Kazakhstan.

Background on joining the WTO

The WTO is open to states or customs territories with full autonomy over their external commercial relations. To join the WTO, a government has to bring its economic and trade policies in line with WTO rules and principles, and negotiate with interested, individual trading partners on guaranteed minimum levels of access to their domestic markets for goods and services. It can take many years to become a WTO member because it requires the full support and consensus of the existing membership. However, the accession process is designed to ensure that new members are able to participate fully in the multilateral trading system from the outset.

159 members (as of 2 March 2013)

Member	Year of accession
Norway	1995
Oman	2000
Pakistan	1995
Panama	1997
Papua New Guinea	1996
Paraguay	1995
Peru	1995
Philippines	1995
Poland	1995
Portugal	1995
Qatar	1996
Romania	1995
Russian Federation	2012
Rwanda	1996
Saint Kitts and Nevis	1996
Saint Lucia	1995
Saint Vincent and the Grenadines	1995
Samoa	2012
Saudi Arabia, Kingdom of	2005
Senegal	1995
Sierra Leone	1995
Singapore	1995
Slovak Republic	1995
Slovenia	1995
Solomon Islands	1996
South Africa	1995

Member	Year of accession
Spain	1995
Sri Lanka	1995
Suriname	1995
Swaziland	1995
Sweden	1995
Switzerland	1995
Chinese Taipei	2002
Tanzania	1995
Thailand	1995
The Former Yugoslav Republic of Macedonia	2003
Togo	1995
Tonga	2007
Trinidad and Tobago	1995
Tunisia	1995
Turkey	1995
Uganda	1995
Ukraine	2008
United Arab Emirates	1996
United Kingdom	1995
United States of America	1995
Uruguay	1995
Vanuatu	2012
Venezuela, Bolivarian Republic of	1995
Viet Nam	2007
Zambia	1995
Zimbabwe	1995

States/customs territories seeking to join the WTO (as of 2 March 2013)
Afghanistan[2]
Algeria
Andorra
Azerbaijan
Bahamas
Belarus
Bhutan[2]
Bosnia and Herzegovina
Comoros[2]
Equatorial Guinea[2]
Ethiopia[2]
Iran
Iraq
Kazakhstan
Lebanese Republic
Liberia, Republic of [2]
Libya
São Tomé and Principe[2]
Serbia
Seychelles
Sudan[2]
Syrian Arab Republic
Uzbekistan
Yemen[2]

Countries that officially became WTO members in 2012

Montenegro	29 April 2012
Samoa	10 May 2012
Russian Federation	22 August 2012
Vanuatu	24 August 2012

Countries that ratified their accession packages in early 2013

	Date of approval of WTO accession package	Date of WTO membership
Laos[2]	26 October 2012	2 February 2013
Tajikistan	10 December 2012	2 March 2013

[2] Least-developed country.

Joining the WTO
www.wto.org/members

A global membership

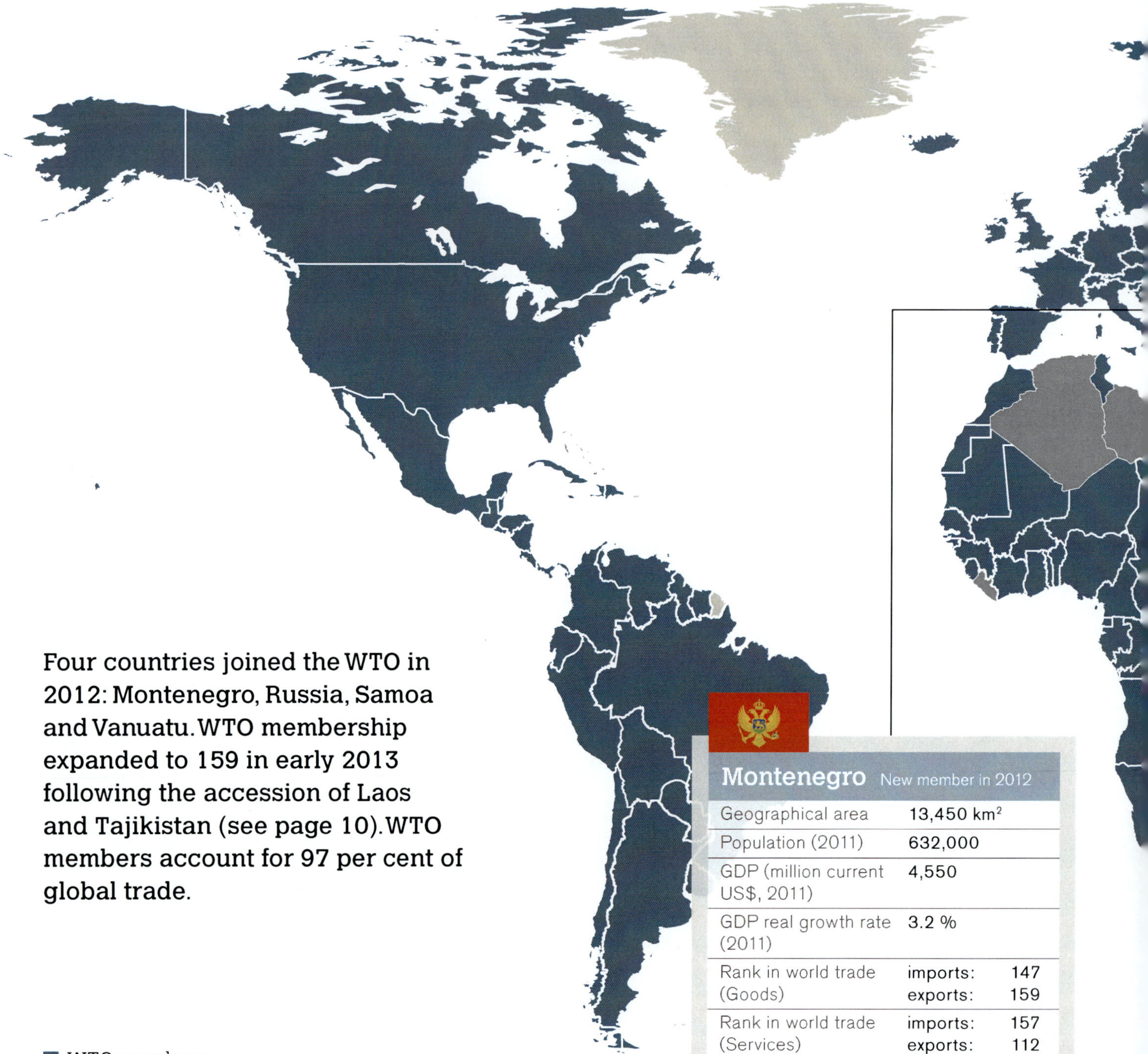

Four countries joined the WTO in 2012: Montenegro, Russia, Samoa and Vanuatu. WTO membership expanded to 159 in early 2013 following the accession of Laos and Tajikistan (see page 10). WTO members account for 97 per cent of global trade.

- WTO members
- New members in 2012
- Observers
- Non-members

Montenegro New member in 2012	
Geographical area	13,450 km^2
Population (2011)	632,000
GDP (million current US$, 2011)	4,550
GDP real growth rate (2011)	3.2 %
Rank in world trade (Goods)	imports: 147 exports: 159
Rank in world trade (Services)	imports: 157 exports: 112
Major trading partners	European Union, Serbia, Bosnia and Herzegovina

Russia New member in 2012

Geographical area	16,377,742 km²	
Population (2011)	141,930,000	
GDP (million current US$, 2011)	1,857,770	
GDP real growth rate (2011)	4.3 %	
Rank in world trade (Goods)	imports: exports:	17 9
Rank in world trade (Services)	imports: exports:	15 22
Major trading partners	European Union, China, Ukraine	

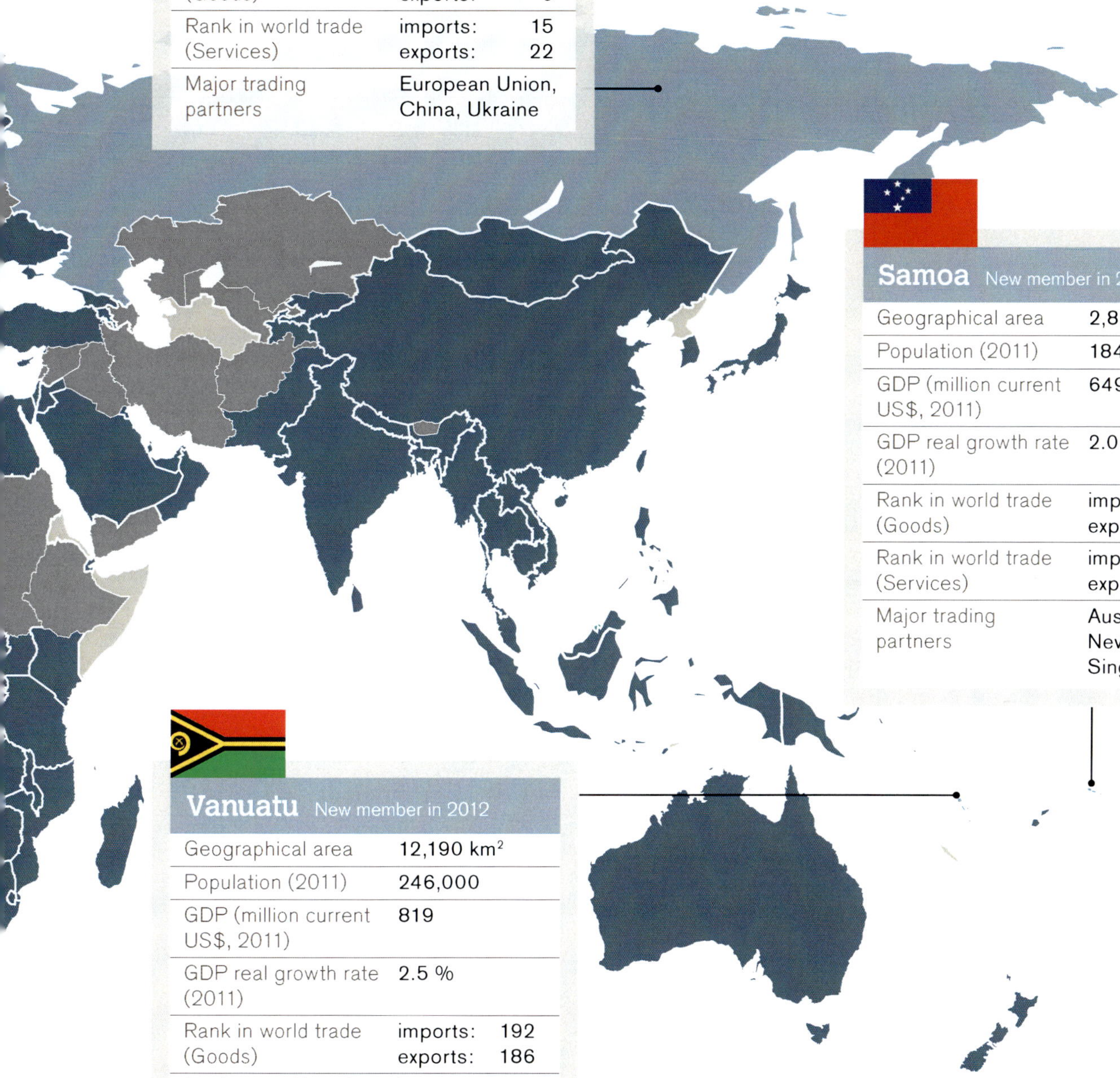

Samoa New member in 2012

Geographical area	2,830 km²	
Population (2011)	184,000	
GDP (million current US$, 2011)	649	
GDP real growth rate (2011)	2.0 %	
Rank in world trade (Goods)	imports: exports:	186 187
Rank in world trade (Services)	imports: exports:	186 164
Major trading partners	Australia, New Zealand, Singapore	

Vanuatu New member in 2012

Geographical area	12,190 km²	
Population (2011)	246,000	
GDP (million current US$, 2011)	819	
GDP real growth rate (2011)	2.5 %	
Rank in world trade (Goods)	imports: exports:	192 186
Rank in world trade (Services)	imports: exports:	176 155
Major trading partners	European Union, Australia, Philippines, New Zealand	

Source: WTO and World Bank

Welcoming new members

In 2012, the General Council approved the accession agreements of the Lao People's Democratic Republic (Laos) and Tajikistan. Both countries officially became WTO members in early 2013 after notifying the WTO that their parliaments had ratified the accords. The agreements contain commitments covering all WTO rules.

Laos and Tajikistan

The WTO accession process promotes the integration of new members into a global economy subject to enforceable trade rules. Laos and Tajikistan have undertaken to liberalize their trade regimes and accelerate their integration into the world economy. Their accession agreements contain commitments binding them to WTO rules, including, where necessary, specific transition periods which have been negotiated to respond to particular needs in a given area. They also include negotiated concessions and commitments on market access for goods and services.

The General Council approved Laos's package on 26 October 2012 after 15 years of negotiations. Over 90 laws and regulations were enacted over this period, including on trading rights, import licensing, customs valuation, investment, sanitary and phytosanitary measures, technical barriers to trade and intellectual property rights. Laos has agreed to accept "bound" rates, i.e. maximum ceiling levels, for all its import tariffs. Its average bound rate will be 18.8 per cent (19.3 per cent for agricultural goods and 18.7 per cent for non-agricultural goods). On services, Laos made specific commitments in 10 out of 12 sectors and 79 out of 160 sub-sectors.

Laos Deputy Prime Minister and Foreign Minister, H.E. Dr Thongloun Sisoulith, said that the conclusion of the accession negotiations marked a milestone in the history of Laos. He noted that "in a country like Lao PDR, the accession process was not limited to changing some laws and regulations. We had to change our way of doing business. Indeed, such a mind change is a difficult and time-consuming exercise. Given the progress we have made, both institutionally, legally and in our mind set, 15 years actually seem a very short time". The accession process has helped pave the way for Laos to meet the Millennium Development Goals by 2015 and graduate from least-developed country (LDC) status by 2020, he said. Over the past 10 years, Laos has experienced economic growth rates of over 7 per cent on average. Foreign direct investment has increased from USD 25 million in 2002 to almost USD 3 billion in 2011.

On 2 February 2013, Laos became the WTO's 158th member after formally notifying the WTO that it had ratified its membership agreement.

The General Council adopted Tajikistan's accession agreement on 10 December 2012. Tajikistan has agreed to bind all its import tariffs. The average final bound rate will be 8 per cent (10.4 per cent for agricultural goods and 7.6 per cent for non-agricultural goods). On services, Tajikistan made specific commitments in 11 out of 12 sectors and 111 out of 160 sub-sectors.

"For Tajikistan, a small and landlocked country, WTO accession is a road leading to the world economy", said WTO Director-General Pascal Lamy. Tajikistan's President, Emomali Rahmon, said that WTO membership "constitutes a landmark in Tajikistan's history and lays solid foundations for further promotion of sustainable social and economic growth. Applying for WTO membership 11 years ago was the right step forward for Tajikistan as it transforms itself into a market economy. Tajikistan will use its WTO membership as a means of fostering future economic growth and prosperity". He also said that Tajikistan will host a trade and investment conference in 2013 to reinforce the positive effects of market liberalization and send a clear signal that Tajikistan is now "open for business".

On 2 March 2013, Tajikistan became the WTO's 159th member after formally notifying the WTO that it had ratified its membership agreement.

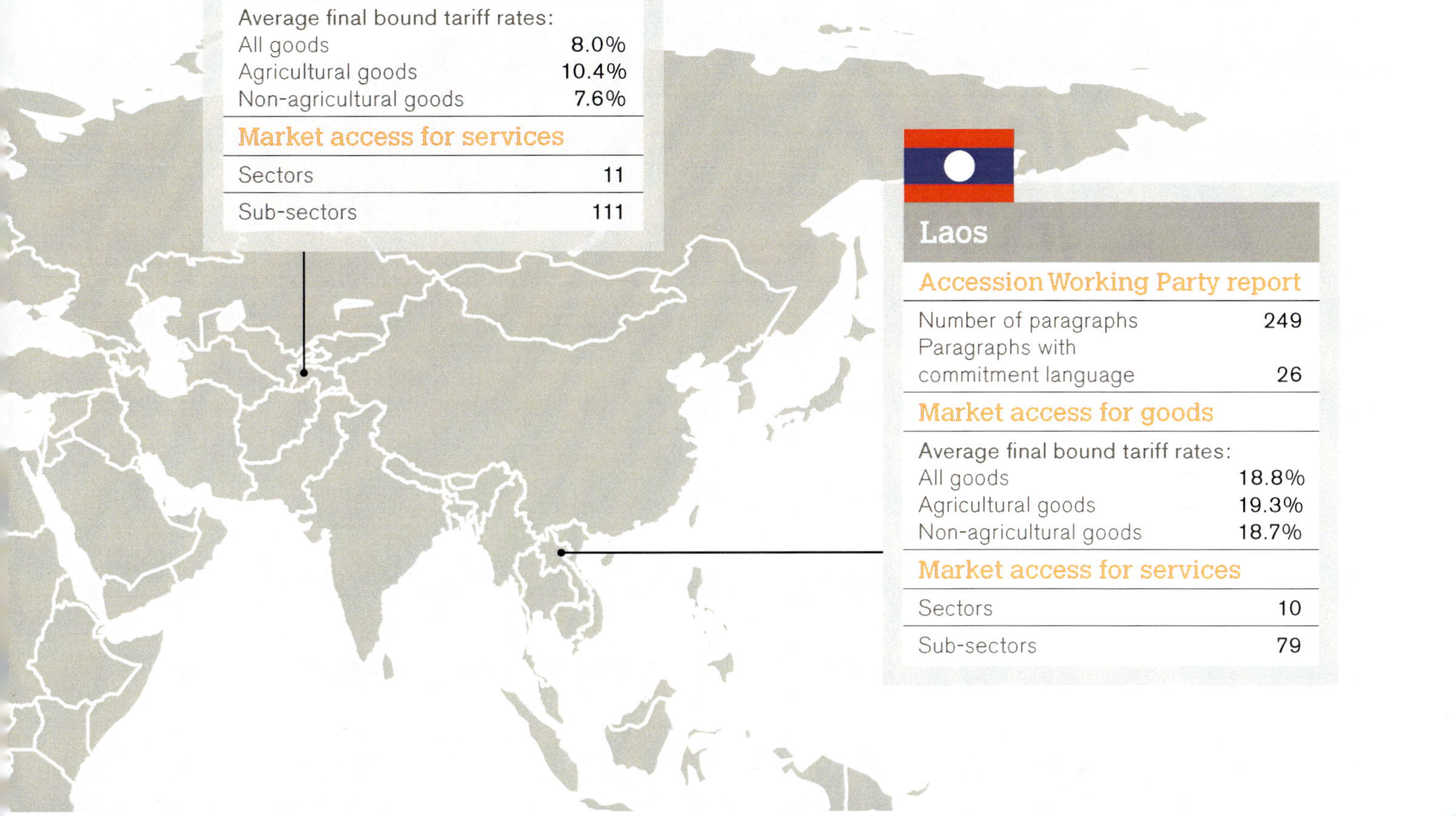

Tajikistan

Accession Working Party report	
Number of paragraphs	353
Paragraphs with commitment language	40
Market access for goods	
Average final bound tariff rates:	
All goods	8.0%
Agricultural goods	10.4%
Non-agricultural goods	7.6%
Market access for services	
Sectors	11
Sub-sectors	111

Laos

Accession Working Party report	
Number of paragraphs	249
Paragraphs with commitment language	26
Market access for goods	
Average final bound tariff rates:	
All goods	18.8%
Agricultural goods	19.3%
Non-agricultural goods	18.7%
Market access for services	
Sectors	10
Sub-sectors	79

159

The WTO has 159 members following the accession of Laos and Tajikistan in early 2013.

A brief history

The WTO began life on 1 January 1995 but its trading system is half a century older. Since 1948, the General Agreement on Tariffs and Trade (GATT) had provided the rules for the system. Whereas GATT had mainly dealt with trade in goods, the WTO and its agreements now cover trade in services, and in traded inventions, creations and designs (intellectual property).

'94

April
In April the Marrakesh Agreement establishing the WTO is signed.

World Trade Organization

'95

January
The WTO is born on 1 January.

May
Renato Ruggiero (Italy) takes office as WTO Director-General.

'96

February
WTO General Council creates the Regional Trade Agreements Committee.

December
First Ministerial Conference takes place in Singapore.

'97

December
70 WTO members reach a multilateral agreement to open their financial services sector.

'98

May
Second Ministerial Conference takes place in Geneva.

'99

September
Mike Moore (New Zealand) becomes WTO Director-General.

November
Third Ministerial Conference takes place in Seattle, US.

2000

January
Negotiations begin on services.

March
Negotiations begin on agriculture.

'01

November
Fourth Ministerial Conference in Doha, Qatar. Doha Development Agenda is launched.

'02

September
Supachai Panitchpakdi (Thailand) is elected WTO Director-General.

'03

September
Fifth Ministerial Conference takes place in Cancún, Mexico.

'04

July
Ministerial discussions on the Doha Round take place in Geneva.

'05

September
Pascal Lamy (France) becomes WTO Director-General.

December
Sixth Ministerial Conference takes place in Hong Kong, China. Aid for Trade Initiative is launched. Hong Kong Declaration is approved.

'06

June
Ministerial discussions on the Doha Round take place in Geneva.

September
First WTO Public Forum takes place in Geneva.

'07

January
Viet Nam becomes the WTO's 150th member.

November
First Global Review of Aid for Trade takes place in Geneva.

'08

July
Accession of the WTO's newest member, Cape Verde. Ministerial discussions on the Doha Round take place in Geneva.

'09

April
DG Pascal Lamy reappointed for second term of four years.

July
Second Global Review of Aid for Trade takes place in Geneva.

September
First WTO Open Day in Geneva.

November
Seventh Ministerial Conference begins in Geneva.

'10

January
New "Chairs Programme" launched to support developing country universities.

September
Second WTO Open Day in Geneva.

'11

July
Third Global Review of Aid for Trade takes place in Geneva.

December
Eighth Ministerial Conference takes place in Geneva.

'12

April
Montenegro joins the WTO.

May
Samoa joins the WTO.

August
Russia and Vanuatu become members of the WTO.

A message from WTO Director-General Pascal Lamy

In the early days of trade, seafarers relied on a combination of navigational skills, courage and good instincts to steer their way through turbulent waters. In more recent times, technology has transformed the way we circumnavigate the globe but the basic need to steer a steady course through stormy seas remains the same.

Over the past year, world trade has found itself tested by strong sea swells, with the global economy still buffeted by the lingering effects of the crisis of 2008-09. As a result, world trade growth fell to 2.0 per cent in 2012 – down from 5.2 per cent in 2011 – and is expected to climb only slightly in 2013, to around 3.3 per cent.

The need for a steady hand at the helm is greater now than ever before. The trade figures for 2012 highlight that, despite some progress, many of the structural flaws in the global economy are still to be addressed. Until governments rectify the policy shortcomings that have contributed to the crisis, protectionist pressures will continue to mount.

At this critical time, countries need to refocus their attention on reinforcing the multilateral trading system to enable trade to once again be an engine of growth and a source of strength for the global economy.

The upcoming WTO Ministerial Conference in Bali in December can contribute to reinforcing global trade by delivering a multilateral agreement on trade facilitation, some aspects of agriculture trade and important development issues. A trade facilitation agreement would make importing and exporting easier, less costly and more efficient. In a world increasingly defined by global supply chains, improvements to the flow of trade across borders would help developing countries in particular participate in these value chains and play a bigger part in world trade. An agreement in agriculture could create new exporting opportunities for developing country farmers while reinforcing governments' ability to source food for the needy. A development accord would offer reassurance to our poorest members, the least-developed countries.

The year 2012 marks the first time in world economic history that the GDP of developing countries surpassed that of developed economies. This is the product of the impressive growth registered by developing economies in recent decades. It has also been accentuated by the dismal growth rates experienced by advanced economies since the beginning of the crisis. In the years to come, developing countries, starting with Africa, are expected to grow three times faster than advanced economies. In short, the essence of future world growth will come from developing countries.

The geography of trade is also changing. Twenty years ago, 60 per cent of world trade was between developed countries, 30 per cent was between developed and developing countries and only 10 per cent was between developing countries. By 2020, trade between developing countries is expected to climb to one-third of world trade.

Through supply chains, developing countries have found an accessible means to insert themselves into the global economy. Trade is no longer about finished products or services. It is about adding value by contributing to a stage in the production of a finished product or by providing services. This is what prompted me to launch an international effort to look at the facts and figures of trade in value-added terms in the "Made in the World" initiative.

In January this year, the WTO and the OECD launched a first set of data that measures trade in value-added rather than gross terms. The preliminary results were surprising. First, services are traded internationally far more than we originally thought, comprising around 45 per cent of trade measured in value-added terms. Secondly, around 40 per cent of the value of exported goods is in fact imported inputs. Thirdly, bilateral trade balances, which are

Events of 2012

January

Director-General attends World Economic Forum in Davos, Switzerland.

February

WTO hosts workshop on "Aid for Trade, Sustainable Development and the Green Economy".

March

WTO launches new database on preferential trade arrangements.

Seminar on "Exchange Rates and Trade" held at WTO.

WTO and OECD sign accord to develop new database on trade in value-added terms.

April

Director-General announces members of "Panel for Defining the Future of Trade".

WTO welcomes Montenegro as its 154th member.

May

WTO marks 15th anniversary of Information Technology Agreement with two-day symposium.

WTO welcomes Samoa as its 155th member.

Workshop on "Aid for Trade and Trade Finance" held at WTO.

June

WTO celebrates 30th anniversary of Legal Affairs Division.

Director-General attends G20 Summit in Mexico and Rio+20 Earth Summit in Brazil.

Launch of WTO/ UNCTAD co-publication, *A Practical Guide to Trade Policy Analysis*.

often a source of tension among major trading partners, change when the full commercial value of imports is no longer attributed to the last link in the production chain. The geopolitical implications of using this measurement are therefore immediately plain to see.

Another change in the world trade scene is the increasing influence of non-tariff obstacles to trade. Successive WTO negotiating rounds, bilateral trade agreements and unilateral trade opening have significantly reduced the relative weight of tariffs in global trade but it is becoming clear that creating new trade opportunities and reducing the cost of trading will require addressing non-tariff barriers (NTBs). This was the topic of our flagship publication, the *World Trade Report*, in 2012.

A clear trend is emerging where NTBs are less about shielding producers from import competition and more about protecting consumers. In many cases, these measures are important and necessary. The new NTBs typically address concerns over health, safety, environmental quality and other social considerations. The danger is that these measures may sometimes be misused for protectionist purposes. Even when not used for protectionist reasons, the use of NTBs may result in differences between regulatory systems that can substantially raise trade costs and reduce or distort trade flows.

So, what can policy-makers do about these new trends? Better cooperation remains a priority. The trade-opening agenda remains even more relevant today than it was in the pre-crisis period, and the most effective way to do this is through the multilateral route. I see four priorities for a successful global trade opening agenda.

The first is to recognize that imports are an essential ingredient of a country's export competitiveness. So the key is not how to export more but how to add more value and to use trade to expand a country's economy more quickly. The second priority is to reduce the impact of non-tariff barriers by achieving regulatory cooperation and by avoiding the use of NTBs for discriminatory purposes. Thirdly, a global effort is needed to develop a common framework for investment. Fourthly, for many poor countries, trade opening cannot translate into growth, development and jobs without trade capacity building. Moving forward, we have to see how to better leverage the contribution of the private sector to support this.

At a time when commitments to the Aid for Trade initiative are on the decline, it is important to find new ways of bringing support to developing countries so that they can continue to increase their share in world trade. South-South partnerships are key in this endeavour. Increasing the role of the private sector is another one. The focus of the Fourth Global Review of Aid for Trade in July 2013 in Geneva will therefore be on showcasing the partnerships which exist between public and private sector actors focused on helping our poorest members to integrate better into value chains.

An important ingredient towards this goal is ensuring the availability and affordability of trade finance. While the picture in trade finance has improved since the collapse we saw at the beginning of the crisis in 2008, there remain concerns that small and medium-sized enterprises, especially those in low-income countries, do not have adequate access to the guarantees they need to enter fully into the global marketplace. Multilateral development banks have a very important role to play here so I particularly welcome the recent launch of a trade finance programme by the African Development Bank whose initiative complements the efforts of other regional players.

Further guidance on the future of world trade has been provided by the panel of stakeholders that I constituted in April 2012. Their report, published this year, emphasizes that WTO members need to strive for the alignment of their trade regimes and for "convergence" between preferential trade agreements and the multilateral trading system. The report also calls for greater coherence between trade and other domestic policies, such as education, and between trade and public policy non-tariff measures. The role of the WTO is to seek out new initiatives that can bring about these aims in cooperation with other international agencies and non-governmental organizations. There is plenty of "food for thought" in this short report which I hope WTO members will now use as they re-think their multilateral trade policy agendas.

Finally, on a personal note, it has been a great honour for me to serve as the Director-General of the WTO for the past eight years. As I approach the end of my mandate, I would like to thank the Secretariat for its outstanding work during my tenure. I would also like to encourage them to continue challenging our members with new ideas, high-quality research and sharp analysis, all of which are trademarks of the WTO Secretariat. I would also like to wish every success to Mr Roberto Carvalho de Azevêdo, who will be tasked with steering the WTO in the years to come.

Pascal Lamy
Director-General

July

WTO hosts workshop on "Aid for Trade and Services".

Launch of *World Trade Report 2012* on non-tariff measures.

August

WTO welcomes entry of Russia and Vanuatu, bringing total membership to 157.

September

WTO Public Forum takes place in Geneva.

October

General Council approves WTO membership for Laos.

November

EU and Latin American countries sign agreement ending 20-year banana disputes.

December

General Council approves WTO membership for Tajikistan.

General Council announces next Ministerial Conference to be held in Bali in December 2013.

Nine candidates are nominated for post of Director-General to succeed Pascal Lamy.

Our year

In 2012, WTO membership grew to 157 following the accession of Montenegro, Russia, Samoa and Vanuatu. The General Council also approved the membership of Laos and Tajikistan, paving the way for their accession in early 2013. WTO members continued to seek to break the deadlock in the Doha Round negotiations and were unanimous in their desire to deliver a positive outcome for the Ninth Ministerial Conference, which will be held in Bali, Indonesia, from 3 to 6 December 2013.

Trade negotiations

In 2012, negotiators responded to a call by the Eighth Ministerial Conference in December 2011 to seek to break the deadlock in the Doha Development Agenda, with some progress made in a number of areas, notably trade facilitation, agriculture and dispute settlement.

The Trade Negotiations Committee (TNC) meeting in December 2012 provided an opportunity to weigh up the work undertaken in each area of the negotiations and to map the way forward for 2013. The chairs of the TNC subsidiary bodies provided reports on the activities in their respective committees. The Director-General, as Chair of the TNC, gave his own assessment of the state of play and his view of the path to follow, and WTO members had an opportunity to voice their needs and expectations for the year ahead.

Members were unanimous in their desire to deliver a positive outcome at the Ninth Ministerial Conference in Bali, Indonesia, in December 2013 and agreed to continue working in a timely, pragmatic and constructive manner towards identifying some accords to deliver to the ministerial meeting.

The Director-General encouraged members to work towards what is reasonably doable, strive to build consensus around such proposals and avoid being confrontational. Members also stressed that any early package would not be the end of the line, but rather a milestone to gather momentum for the full conclusion of the Doha Round.

See pages 20-33

9 The WTO will hold its Ninth Ministerial Conference in Bali in December 2013.

9 The Doha Round is the ninth round of trade negotiations.

Implementation and monitoring

Following the offer by the Government of Indonesia to host the WTO's Ninth Ministerial Conference, the General Council agreed that it would be held in Bali, Indonesia, on 3-6 December 2013.

In July, the General Council approved improved guidelines that will provide a simpler framework for the entry of least-developed countries into the WTO family. The Council also approved the membership of Laos and Tajikistan in the latter part of 2012, clearing the way for them to join the WTO in early 2013.

Other WTO councils and committees continued to monitor the implementation of WTO agreements in 2012. The Information Technology Agreement celebrated its 15th anniversary with a two-day symposium that reviewed trade liberalization and the evolution of global trade in information and communications technology since 1996.

The WTO also maintained its trade monitoring role. The reports on global trade developments prepared by the WTO Secretariat in 2012 showed that WTO members and observers had by and large continued to resist domestic protectionist pressures and kept markets open overall. However, they also warned of potential dangers in the near future because of uncertainties in the global economy, persistently high levels of unemployment, and increasing trade tensions.

The number of regional trade agreements (RTAs) between WTO members continued to increase. By the end of 2012, WTO members had notified 546 RTAs to the WTO. All WTO members except Mongolia are members of one or more, with some belonging to as many as 30. The WTO received 37 new notifications in 2012, a considerable increase over the 25 received in 2011.

See pages 34-73

20 The WTO conducted 20 Trade Policy Reviews of WTO members in 2012.

15 The WTO marked the 15th anniversary of the Information Technology Agreement with a two-day symposium.

159 The WTO has 159 members following the accession of Laos and Tajikistan in early 2013.

Dispute settlement

There was a sharp increase in dispute settlement activity in 2012, with both developed and developing countries active in bringing disputes to the WTO for resolution. Some WTO members, including Russia, participated for the first time.

The Dispute settlement Body (DSB) received 27 notifications of requests for consultations, the first stage in the WTO's dispute settlement process. This is the highest number of requests in the last ten years. By the end of 2012, 456 disputes had been filed since the WTO's creation in 1995. Of the 27 new requests for consultations, Latin American members launched nine, with Argentina the most active with three complaints.

The DSB established 11 new dispute settlement panels. The recent trend of increasing numbers of disputes in the trade remedies area continued in 2012. The DSB set up seven panels to examine complaints in this area, covering anti-dumping measures, countervailing duties (subsidies) and safeguard actions (to guard against import surges). Trade remedies allow governments to take remedial action in situations where the domestic industry is being injured.

The DSB adopted 18 panel reports and 11 Appellate Body reports. Of the reports issued in 2012, four addressed claims under the Technical Barriers to Trade Agreement and three addressed export restrictions. A long report dealt with subsidies relating to large civil aircraft (often referred to as the Boeing dispute).

The 20-year EU-Latin America banana disputes reached a major milestone in 2012 when the European Union and Latin American countries formally settled their claims.

In June 2012, the WTO's Legal Affairs Division held a conference to mark the 30 years since its predecessor, the GATT Office of Legal Affairs, was created. The DSB appointed Mr Seung Wha Chang (Republic of Korea) to serve for four years as Appellate Body member commencing on 1 June 2012.

See pages 74-93

WTO members most involved in disputes 1995 to 2012

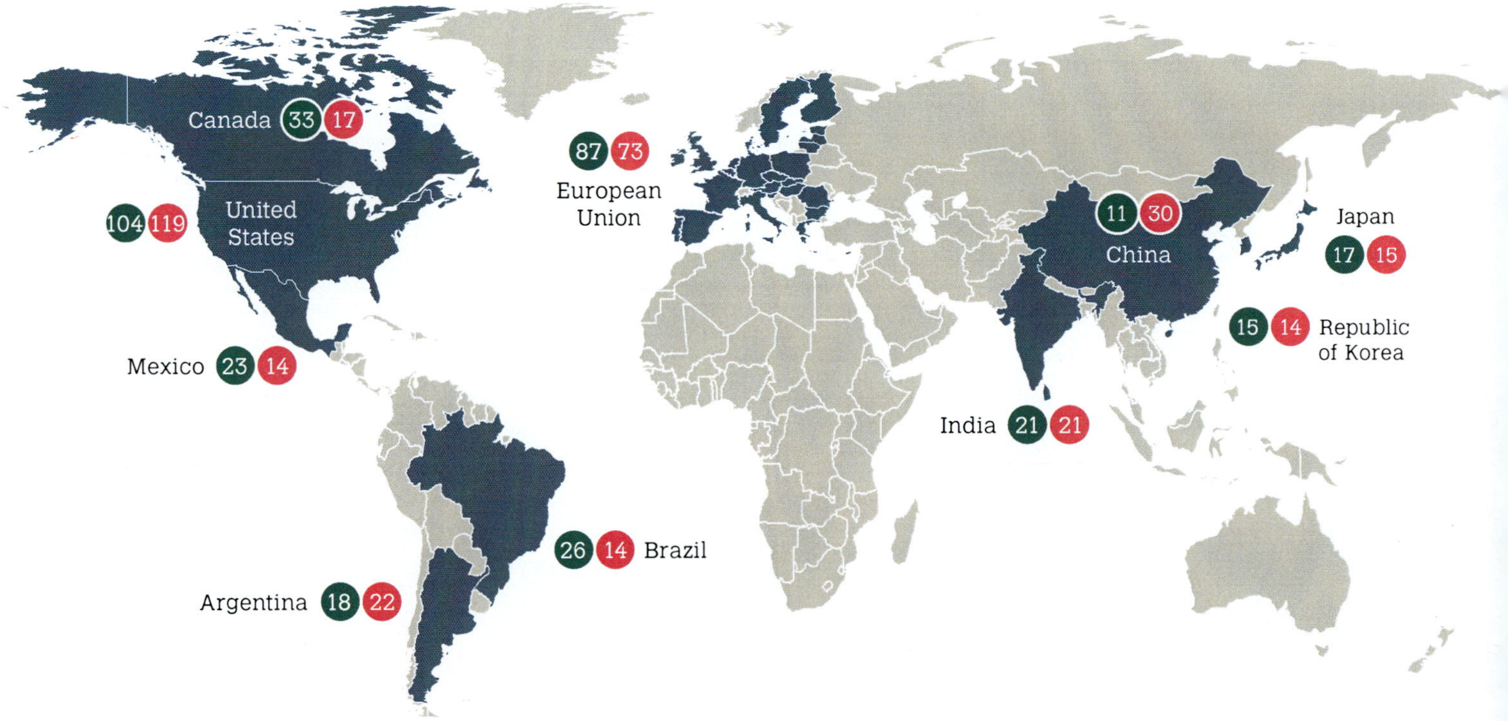

Complainant Respondent

456 By the end of 2012, WTO members had filed 456 disputes since the WTO was created in 1995.

27 WTO members filed 27 new disputes in 2012.

Building trade capacity

New guidelines were introduced in 2012 to streamline the accession process of least-developed countries (LDCs). "These improved guidelines provide a simpler framework for the entry of LDCs into the WTO family. It is another example of positive action in favour of the world's poorest countries", said WTO Director-General Pascal Lamy.

In 2012, Aid for Trade continued to mobilize resources. Commitments rose in 2010 to USD 45 billion, according to the latest figures, up from some USD 40 billion in 2009. The Director-General announced that the Fourth Global Review of Aid for Trade will take place on 8-10 July 2013. With a focus on private sector development, the review will cover the role that Aid for Trade can play in helping connect developing countries to national, regional and global value chains. Underpinning the review is a monitoring and evaluation exercise conducted by the WTO and the Organisation for Economic Co-operation and Development (OECD). Four workshops on Aid for Trade were held in 2012.

After four years of negotiations and a year of work by WTO members on implementation measures and data collection, the WTO launched in March 2012 a new publicly available database on preferential trade arrangements (PTAs) – schemes under which developed countries grant preferential tariffs to imports from developing countries.

In 2012, the WTO undertook 343 technical assistance activities, both in Geneva and in various WTO member countries, to help government officials from developing countries gain a better understanding of the multilateral trading system. The programme continued to place particular emphasis on providing assistance to Africa and LDCs, with activities for Africa constituting 24 per cent of the annual total.

The WTO e-learning programme continued to grow in 2012, with a total of 33 online courses in English, French and Spanish available on the e-learning website and through the WTO website. Over 6,500 people applied for enrolment in these courses, including more than 1,110 from LDCs.

See pages 94-109

Outreach

The WTO maintained regular dialogue with non-governmental organizations (NGOs), parliamentarians, other international organizations, journalists and the general public in 2012. The major outreach event of the year was the Public Forum, which attracted about 1,200 participants from a wide variety of backgrounds and organizations to discuss "Is Multilateralism in Crisis?".

The WTO organized two regional technical assistance events in Ghana and Colombia for African and Latin-American NGOs. It also organized four training activities for journalists and two regional workshops for parliamentarians in Singapore and Laos.

The WTO website attracted almost 1.4 million visits a month in 2012 and the WTO made increased use of social media. It also further expanded its publications programme, in particular its co-publications with other international organizations.

The WTO participated in the Rio+20 Earth Summit in Brazil and the UNCTAD Ministerial Conference in Doha, Qatar. The Director-General also attended the G20 Summit in Los Cabos, Mexico, in June 2012. Earlier in the year, he established a panel of eminent individuals to analyse challenges to global trade opening in the 21st century.

In 2012, the WTO took a number of initiatives to bring the WTO and the business community closer together. Over 300 businesses replied to a survey asking for their views on the work of the WTO and on how to improve cooperation between business and the WTO.

The WTO named its first two Youth Ambassadors, students Ankita Mishra from India and Karina Hehs from Brazil, who were appointed after winning a contest to produce the best essay and video on the theme of "How can trade promote development?". The WTO also continued to develop its Chairs Programme for academic institutions from developing countries.

The WTO and the Organisation for Economic Co-operation and Development (OECD) developed a database on bilateral trade flows measured in value-added terms rather than the traditional customs value. The database was launched in Paris in January 2013.

See pages 110-131

1,200

The WTO Public Forum 2012 attracted about 1,200 participants.

Trade negotiations

- In 2012, negotiators continued to seek to break the deadlock in the Doha Development Agenda, with some progress made in a number of areas, notably trade facilitation, agriculture and dispute settlement.

- WTO members were unanimous in their desire to deliver a positive outcome at the Ninth Ministerial Conference in Bali, Indonesia, in December 2013 and agreed to continue working towards identifying some accords to deliver to the ministerial meeting.

- Members stressed that any early package would not be the end of the line, but rather a milestone to gather momentum for the full conclusion of the Doha Round.

Doha Development Agenda 22

Doha Round negotiations in 2012	22
Agriculture	23
Market access for non-agricultural products	24
Services	25
Trade-related aspects of intellectual property rights (TRIPS)	26
Trade and development	28
Trade and transfer of technology	29
Trade and environment	30
Trade facilitation	30
WTO rules	31
Dispute Settlement Understanding	32
Government Procurement Agreement	32

Background on trade negotiations

Changes to the rules of trade require the agreement of all WTO members, who must reach consensus through rounds of negotiations. The most recent round began in 2001.

Doha Development Agenda

At the Fourth Ministerial Conference in Doha, Qatar, in November 2001, WTO member governments agreed to launch a new round of trade negotiations. They also agreed to work on other issues, in particular the implementation of the current WTO agreements. The entire package is called the Doha Development Agenda (DDA) or the Doha Round. The negotiations take place in the Trade Negotiations Committee (TNC) and its subsidiaries, which are usually regular councils and committees meeting in special session or specially created negotiating groups. The chairs of the nine negotiating bodies report to the TNC, chaired by the WTO Director-General, which coordinates their work.

Doha Round negotiations in 2012

In 2012, negotiators responded to a call by the Eighth Ministerial Conference in December 2011 to seek to break the deadlock in the Doha Development Agenda (DDA), with some progress made in a number of areas, notably trade facilitation, agriculture and dispute settlement. Work is expected to intensify in 2013 in an attempt to deliver a package of agreements to take to the Ninth Ministerial Conference in Bali in December 2013.

The 2011 Ministerial Conference acknowledged that, despite full engagement and intensified efforts, the Doha negotiations were at an impasse and that it was unlikely that all elements of the Doha Round could be concluded simultaneously in the near future. However, ministers were not ready to give up on the Doha mandate and decided to give new impetus to the trade talks by instructing negotiators in Geneva to explore different approaches. In particular, they told them to seek to advance the negotiations in areas where progress could be achieved while at the same time intensifying efforts to overcome the stalemates in those areas where substantial differences remained, all of this while respecting the principles of transparency and inclusiveness, and in accordance with the DDA mandate, especially its development component.

In line with these instructions, work in the negotiating groups focused on the identification of those areas that could be delivered earlier than the conclusion of the "single undertaking" (nothing is agreed until everything is agreed), which is the full DDA. Work got off to a slow start, but the pace picked up in the second half of the year. The TNC meeting in December 2012 provided an opportunity to weigh up the work undertaken in each area of the negotiations and map the way forward for 2013. The chairs of the TNC subsidiary bodies provided reports on the activities in their respective committees. The Director-General, as Chair of the TNC, gave his own assessment of the state of play and his view of the path to follow, and WTO members had an opportunity to voice their needs and expectations for the year ahead.

Some encouraging developments

The meeting showed that although progress had not been even across the board, some encouraging developments had been recorded in the areas of trade facilitation, agriculture and development as well as in dispute settlement. The message that emerged was one of commitment and determination.

Members were unanimous in their desire to deliver a positive outcome at the Ninth Ministerial Conference (MC9) and agreed to continue working in a timely, pragmatic and constructive manner towards identifying some accords to deliver to the ministerial meeting. Delegations expressed overall support for the guidelines suggested by the Director-General for the handling of the negotiations in the run-up to MC9.

The Director-General encouraged members to work towards what is reasonably doable, strive to build consensus around such proposals and avoid being confrontational. Besides resolving to ensure a successful and meaningful outcome of the 2013 ministerial gathering, WTO members also stressed that any early package would not be the end of the line, but rather a milestone to gather momentum for the full conclusion of the Doha Round.

As Chair of the Trade Negotiations Committee, Pascal Lamy reported regularly on the state of play in the Doha Round negotiations.

Agriculture

In 2012, agriculture negotiators responded to the political guidance provided by the WTO's Eighth Ministerial Conference in December 2011 to explore different negotiating approaches, with a view to a successful conclusion of the Doha Development Agenda. While work during the first part of the year proceeded relatively slowly, in the second half discussions accelerated. By the end of 2012, negotiators had identified several issues on which to intensify work in preparation for the Ninth Ministerial Conference in December 2013.

Recognizing that a comprehensive conclusion of the Doha Round was unlikely in the near future, the Eighth Ministerial Conference (MC8) in December 2011 urged WTO members to explore different negotiating approaches. In response, agriculture negotiators focused on identifying issues for which there might be a reasonable chance of achieving agreement. Regular consultations on cotton were also held, in line with guidance given by MC8.

The first half of 2012 provided a period of reflection on how to move negotiations forward. The Chair, New Zealand Ambassador John Adank, met informally with delegations to discuss their views. Delegations also exchanged views during a meeting of the Special Session on Agriculture in March on how its work could progress. However, these consultations did not lead to significant movement, either in terms of process or substance.

In the second half of the year, the momentum picked up with WTO members putting forward several proposals. One proposal called for the WTO Secretariat to circulate updated information on the administration of tariff rate quotas (TRQs) and export competition (export subsidies and other export measures that could contain subsidies). Under tariff rate quotas (or simply tariff quotas), imports within an agreed quota are charged lower duties than those outside (these can be high).

Two other papers put forward by developing country groups proposed text for an understanding on TRQ administration and on public stockholding for food security purposes. The latter would let governments buy food for stockholding from poor farmers at supported prices that would be excluded from subsidy limits. Both of these suggest an early agreement on the relevant paragraphs of the December 2008 draft outline deal known as the draft "modalities".

Agriculture negotiators began discussions on these issues to determine whether agreement could be reached ahead of the Ministerial Conference in Bali, Indonesia, in December 2013.

Background on agriculture

The agriculture negotiations began in 2000 under a commitment that WTO members made in the 1986-94 Uruguay Round to continue farm trade reforms. They were brought into the Doha Round when it was launched in 2001. Broadly, the objective is to reduce distortions in agricultural trade caused by high tariffs and other barriers, export subsidies and domestic support. The negotiations, conducted by the WTO Committee on Agriculture meeting in special session, also take into account social and political sensitivities in the sector and the needs of developing countries.

While initial consultations revealed a range of sensitivities about the extent to which a selective approach can achieve the overall balance necessary in agriculture, the tone of the discussions was constructive and pragmatic.

At the end of the year, the Secretariat issued a paper on TRQ administration methods and fill rates (the extent to which quotas are filled). The Secretariat also initiated work on export competition using information notified by WTO members as well as information collected through a questionnaire. In addition, the Chair requested that members implementing programmes of public stockholding for food security purposes and domestic food aid provide background information on these programmes. This information will inform the work of the agriculture negotiating group in 2013.

Market access for non-agricultural products

In early 2012, the Negotiating Group on Market Access for Non-Agricultural Products (NAMA), at the suggestion of then Chair Luzius Wasescha of Switzerland, resumed discussions on tariffs, which in the past few years had been side-lined in favour of discussion of non-tariff issues. However, there was little progress either on tariffs or on non-tariff barriers (NTB) during the year. New Chair Remigi Winzap of Switzerland said members must intensify their efforts in 2013, noting a successful NAMA negotiation is especially important for members who want to enhance the participation of their companies in, or become part of, a regional or global value chain.

In his final report before stepping down, Chair Wasescha said in July that in spite of his best efforts to prod members into thinking of new approaches, the tariff negotiations remain at a standstill. It is clear, he said, that for some members the current draft NAMA modalities (blueprint) do not provide a suitable basis for progress. At the same time, it is equally apparent that other members are not willing to discard a text they have spent ten years negotiating.

Nevertheless, there are options that members might pursue. These include the possible introduction of safety valves, which could give members the confidence to be more ambitious on tariff-cutting because they would be assured of some respite in difficult times, Ambassador Wasescha said. Another option is the timeframe for tariff cuts. Rather than having a blanket timeframe, as in the current draft modalities, it could be possible to extend or shorten the timeframe of cuts on individual items. This might help achieve a necessary balance between ambition and flexibility, the ambassador said.

Over the past three years, the Negotiating Group has mainly spent time on the various non-tariff barrier (NTB) proposals and on conducting a text-based negotiation on some of them. However, since the beginning of 2012 some members have declared work cannot continue in isolation from the tariff negotiation. As a result, the deadlock in tariffs has spread to NTBs.

Background on market access for non-agricultural products

Non-agricultural products are products not covered by the Agreement on Agriculture. These range from manufactured goods to fuels and fisheries. Collectively they represent more than 90 per cent of world merchandise trade. The negotiations aim to reduce or, as appropriate, eliminate tariffs, as well as non-tariff barriers (NTB) such as import licensing systems and technical barriers to trade particularly on goods of export interest to developing countries. The negotiations are conducted in the Negotiating Group on Market Access for Non-Agricultural Products (NAMA).

The Negotiating Group, working in three small groups, had drafted three working texts, covering the so-called horizontal mechanism, textile labelling and transparency.

The horizontal mechanism aims at achieving flexible and expeditious procedures, involving a facilitator, to assist members to address concerns regarding NTBs. It establishes step-by-step procedures and timetables and provides suggestions for the role of the facilitator. On labelling of textiles, clothing, footwear and travel goods, the proposal seeks to provide clarity and definitions to labelling requirements under the present Technical Barriers to Trade (TBT) Agreement. Finally, on transparency in the adoption of new technical regulations, the text proposes more clarity and transparency in the elaboration and implementation of technical regulations.

Textile labelling has seen the most progress, notably on its scope, with members of the small negotiating group agreeing that intermediate products would be covered. Subsequently, discussion revolved around the differentiated treatment for these products, Ambassador Wasescha said. There was also significant advance in transparency issues, with delegations beginning work on improving the availability of information on the regulatory lifecycle of measures.

At a meeting on 29 November 2012, the NAMA Group confirmed Ambassador Winzap as the new Chair.

Services

Negotiations to lower barriers to trade in services made little headway in 2012 and the Council for Trade in Services held no special sessions. The Working Party on Domestic Regulation held a good information exchange on existing regulatory practices but the Working Party on the GATS Rules remained at an impasse.

Market access

Chair Fernando de Mateo (Mexico) told the Trade Negotiations Committee in December that he had continued to consult WTO members on market access issues. In line with guidance given at the 2011 Ministerial Conference, members also explored informally different negotiating approaches, striving to advance the services negotiations where progress could be achieved. But there was no progress, and in 2012 Mr de Mateo did not convene any special sessions of the Council, which is where negotiations formally take place. In large part, the paralysis reflects the impasse in the overall Doha Development Agenda negotiations.

Domestic regulation

In 2012, the Working Party on Domestic Regulation pressed ahead with addressing technical questions that have arisen in the negotiations. On the basis of 93 questions submitted by members, discussions focused on how certain domestic regulation concepts and principles are implemented at the national level.

The information exchange helped to shed light on existing regulatory practices. Some WTO members also used this exercise to reflect on possible implications for the horizontal disciplines under consideration. The mandate of the Working Party is to develop disciplines to ensure that licensing and qualification requirements and procedures, and technical standards, do not constitute unnecessary barriers to trade in services.

Background on services

Services are the most important economic activity in many countries when measured as a share of overall production, and they are the single largest source of employment. The General Agreement on Trade in Services (GATS) mandates WTO members to progressively liberalize trade in services through successive rounds of negotiations. At the Doha Ministerial Conference in November 2001, the services negotiations became part of the "single undertaking" under the Doha Development Agenda. The negotiations are overseen by the Council for Trade in Services, meeting in special session, and its subsidiary bodies, in particular the working parties on domestic regulation and on GATS rules.

Services negotiations
www.wto.org/servicesnegs

To support the discussions, members tasked the WTO Secretariat with two major background notes. The note on "Regulatory Issues in Sectors and Modes of Supply" provides an overview of how regulation can affect trade in services in individual sectors and modes. A second note – "Technical Standards in Services" – seeks to clarify how standards are formulated and implemented in service sectors.

GATS rules

The Working Party on GATS Rules carries out the negotiating mandates contained in Articles X (emergency safeguard measures), XIII (government procurement) and XV (subsidies) of the GATS. As in previous years, however, WTO members did not engage in any text-based negotiations as there was no common vision of what could constitute an acceptable outcome in any of the three areas.

On emergency safeguard measures, members saw the need to pause and take stock of the concepts and options discussed in the negotiations since the inception of the Working Party in 1995. Emergency safeguards, based on the principle of non-discrimination, would permit a member temporarily to suspend commitments in the event of an unforeseen surge in imports of services that caused, or threatened to cause, injury to a domestic service industry.

Based on a series of dedicated discussions on the broader economic and developmental importance of government procurement in services, conducted in late 2010 and 2011, several initial suggestions for future work had emerged. However, in 2012, members made no headway on any of the issues raised.

Concerning subsidies in services, members could not agree on whether they would first need to identify concrete evidence of trade-distortive effects before entering into negotiations on multilateral disciplines to avoid such effects.

Trade-related aspects of intellectual property rights (TRIPS)

Negotiations remained deadlocked on notifying and registering geographical indications (GI) for wines and spirits. In December, Yonov Frederick Agah of Nigeria, the new chair of the TRIPS Council special sessions, which handle the negotiations, said the biggest stumbling block is differences of opinion over the mandate – including whether talks should only be about wines and spirits, as originally mandated, or whether other products could be added. Delegations are also divided on, among other things, the consequences of registration and whether the register applies to all members or only those agreeing to it.

Negotiations on a GI register

The register for wines and spirits is intended to facilitate the protection of geographical indications (GI). These are place names (or sometimes other terms or signs associated with a place) used to identify products as originating from a location that gives them particular qualities, their reputation or other characteristics. Bordeaux and Tequila are well-known examples. The TRIPS Agreement mandates negotiations on establishing a register and work has continued since 1996.

The three main proposals under consideration are:

- a 2003 proposal by Hong Kong, China
- the so-called "Joint Proposal" of 2005, revised in 2011, from a group of countries that want the register to be essentially a source of information about national protection of registered GIs
- the "W/52" proposal put forward in 2008 by a group of over 100 countries as part of a package also covering other TRIPS issues. This proposal is considered to create a stronger expectation of protection for GIs entered on the register.

Background on TRIPS

The Doha Development Agenda mandates negotiations on a multilateral system for notifying and registering geographical indications (GIs) for wines and spirits. The Council for Trade-Related Aspects of Intellectual Property Rights (TRIPS) carries out the negotiations in special session. In its regular sessions, the TRIPS Council implements other relevant ministerial decisions, notably those relating to technology transfer and dispute settlement. The Hong Kong Ministerial Declaration mandates the Director-General to consult on certain TRIPS-related implementation issues identified in the Doha Declaration.

Intellectual property
www.wto.org/tripsnegs

In April 2011, the then Chair, Darlington Mwape of Zambia, circulated a "Draft Composite Text". It was the first time a single text had been produced in draft treaty language reflecting members' positions on the three above-mentioned proposals and other issues, such as special and differential treatment. During 2012, Chair Agah held informal consultations on how to meet a call by the Eighth Ministerial Conference to advance negotiations where progress could be achieved and seek some "early harvest". Positions are entrenched on product coverage and whether, as the initial negotiating mandate says, the register should be confined to GIs for wines and spirits, or whether it should extend to other products (such as food and agricultural products). Other stumbling blocks are the consequences of registration and whether the register would apply to all WTO members or only those electing to take part. Some delegations opposed restarting work unless the mandate was firmly anchored in the Draft Composite Text. For others, it was not acceptable to work on the draft text just to discuss the mandate.

Another difficulty relates to the linkage made by some delegations to two TRIPS-related implementation issues, namely the extension of the protection of GIs for wines and spirits (GI extension) and the relationship between the TRIPS Agreement and the Convention on Biological Diversity (TRIPS-CBD). It was suggested during informal consultations that the three issues – the register, TRIPS-CBD and GI extension – be unbundled and addressed in separate tracks. There was no consensus on this.

Consultations on outstanding implementation issues

The 2005 Hong Kong Ministerial Declaration called for consultations by the Director-General on TRIPS-related "outstanding implementation issues". The first issue concerns the possible extension to other products of the "higher" or "enhanced" level of protection that is currently only required for GIs for wines and spirits. Members continued to differ on whether such an extension would help their trade in such products, or whether increasing the level of protection would create an unnecessary legal and commercial burden. The other issue concerns the relationship between the TRIPS Agreement and the Convention on Biological Diversity (CBD): whether – and, if so, how – TRIPS should do more to promote the CBD objective of equitably sharing the benefits that arise when genetic resources are used in research and industry. The main focus has been on proposals to amend the TRIPS Agreement to require patent applicants to disclose the source or the country providing genetic resources and associated traditional knowledge. No further consultations have been held since the Director-General presented a written report covering the period from March 2009 to April 2011.

Incentives for technology transfer

In November 2012, the TRIPS Council, in regular session, undertook its tenth annual review of the incentives given to companies by developed countries to transfer technology to least-developed countries (LDCs). Developed countries provided detailed information on the incentives they make available. The LDC Group presented a paper with further questions in relation to the 2011 reports.

The TRIPS Agreement requires incentives for technology transfer to LDCs, and the mechanism was set up by a Council decision in 2003 detailing the information to be supplied by developed countries on how their domestic technology transfer incentives function.

The WTO Secretariat organized a fifth annual workshop for LDC and developed-country delegations to discuss the operation of the incentives. Based on an LDC proposal, delegations explored the possibility of a harmonized reporting format to assist analysis and understanding of the reported measures.

Disputes over intellectual property protection

In general, disputes can be brought under the WTO Dispute Settlement Mechanism not only if an agreement or commitment has been violated, but also if an expected benefit under an agreement has been nullified without violating the letter of the agreement. For disputes over intellectual property protection, the TRIPS Agreement prescribed a five-year moratorium on initiating such "non-violation and situation complaints" and this moratorium has been extended by a series of Ministerial Conferences.

The Eighth Ministerial Conference in December 2011 directed the Council to continue examining the scope and modalities for these disputes and to make recommendations to the next Ministerial Conference in 2013. It also agreed that, in the meantime, members would not initiate such complaints under the TRIPS Agreement. In 2012, the TRIPS Council continued to consider the scope and modalities for such complaints. For the purpose of facilitating the Council's work, the Secretariat updated, at the Council's request, a summary of the points made in earlier discussions, and organized a briefing session.

Trade and development

In 2012, the special session of the Committee on Trade and Development, which handles the negotiations, made some progress in the three specific areas, or clusters, in which it is working. These are the 28 Agreement-specific proposals agreed in principle at the 2003 ministerial meeting, another six proposals on enhancing special and differential treatment and the mechanism for monitoring the use and implementation of the special rights.

Over the first half of the year, the Committee met every Friday under a work plan mapped out by Chair Fook Seng Kwok of Singapore in consultation with WTO members. Each meeting was devoted to one of the clusters. Thereafter, meetings were held every two weeks to allow more time for preparation. The schedule generated renewed momentum in the work of the special session.

The informal consultations in the Committee were complemented with regular bilateral and plurilateral informal meetings between the Chair and various stakeholders, including monthly meetings with the African and least-developed country (LDC) groups. The Committee also continued coordinating with other WTO bodies to which other Agreement-specific proposals – so-called "Category II" proposals – were referred.

28 Cancún Agreement-specific proposals

In line with instructions from the WTO's Eighth Ministerial Conference, the CTD special session began a stocktaking exercise involving the 28 Agreement-specific proposals agreed in principle at Cancún, Mexico, in 2003. The objective is their formal adoption. To help them, WTO members asked the Secretariat to prepare a factual assessment of what has happened over the intervening years that might affect adoption of these proposals in their current form.

The Secretariat identified six proposals as having been affected by developments since 2003. Initial discussion among members focused on the scope of the stocktaking and whether it should be limited to the six affected proposals or whether the remaining 22 should also be included. Members agreed to commence work on the six, with the understanding that the rest would be considered in informal meetings among members outside the special session process. The option to revisit these 22 proposals after completion of work on the initial six was not excluded.

Background on trade and development

Many WTO agreements contain provisions that give developing countries special rights and that allow developed countries to treat them more favourably than other WTO members. As part of the Doha Round of negotiations, the special session of the Committee on Trade and Development is reviewing these special and differential treatment provisions, with a view to making them more precise, effective and operational.

Six other agreement-specific proposals

Separate from the 28 (Cancún) agreement-specific proposals is another set of six agreement-specific proposals that have been the subject of negotiations in the special session for some time. Three relate to the Agreement on Sanitary and Phytosanitary Measures (SPS) and the other three to the Agreement on Import Licensing. In 2012, members held a series of consultations on the proposals relating to the SPS Agreement (Articles 10.2 and 10.3 regarding "special and differential treatment"), on occasion inviting the Secretariat to make some technical clarifications. The year saw notable progress, particularly on the proposal relating to Article 10.3.

Category II proposals

The Chair held meetings on the Category II proposals with the secretaries of the relevant WTO bodies in October 2012, with a view to getting a sense of the status of work and how best progress could be expedited on these proposals. In his report to the Trade Negotiations Committee (TNC) in December, he described progress as mixed.

Monitoring mechanism

In 2012, the Committee continued its work on advancing and developing the monitoring mechanism. Initially, work commenced on the basis of a non-paper (unofficial document) drawn up by the previous Chair, Thawatchai Sophastienphong. Sensing a lot of divergence among members, the Chair invited all members to provide their textual suggestions, which he incorporated into a consolidated text. Consultations have since focused on bridging remaining gaps.

Trade and transfer of technology

In 2012, the Working Group on Trade and Transfer of Technology held three formal sessions at which it continued to analyse the relationship between trade and technology transfer as well as ways to increase the flow of technology to developing countries. Work was largely based on presentations by the Organisation for Economic Co-operation and Development (OECD), the WTO and the United Nations Conference on Trade and Development (UNCTAD) on topics related to innovation and technology transfer.

Relationship between trade and transfer of technology

The OECD presentation entitled "Knowledge Transfer and Global Value Chains" highlighted OECD's work on global value chains (GVCs), which cover the full range of activity in production networks. The presentation underscored broad conceptual issues in the context of GVCs and technology transfer and identified five types of governance models in GVCs. These range from governance by the market, where individuals or firms buy and sell products between themselves, to a hierarchical model in which transactions take place within a single firm or group.

It found that the extent of knowledge transfer varied and depended on the choice of model. The relational model, the third of the five types, was found to be the most beneficial for technology transfer as it envisaged face to face interactions and high opportunity for mutual learning, as in the case of apparels in East Asia and computers in Chinese Taipei. Knowledge transfer was mainly taking place through market transactions both as intended transfer through, among others, international trade, foreign direct investment (FDI), licensing and movement of staff as well as unintended transfers (including through demonstration effects, increased competition, vertical linkages – upstream and downstream – as well as through patent applications).

The presentation by the WTO focused on the impact of fragmentation of production on international competitiveness. It highlighted the fact that services and manufacturing firms operate increasingly across regions and multiple network production chains, and that participation in GVCs through FDI also results in technology transfer and increased exports. Goods and services are frequently produced in production networks spreading across various countries, according to each firm's comparative advantage. This new way of organizing production and trade, resulting in global value chains, is often referred to as "trade in tasks".

These presentations raised a number of issues, including how GVCs affect the economic development and trade prospects of developing countries. The role of governments in promoting participation of local firms in GVCs and technology transfer, and how lowering trade barriers in intermediate goods can benefit developing countries were other issues, along with what policy steps could be appropriate to enhance trade flows and technology transfer.

UNCTAD made a presentation on the impact of bilateral investment treaties, regional trade agreements and non-equity modes (NEMs) on transfer of technology. Non-equity modes refer to contractual relationships that international corporations have with host country firms that do not involve any equity stake. Based on two UNCTAD publications – *The World Investment Report 2011* and *Local Production of Pharmaceuticals and Related Technology Transfer in Developing Countries*, the presentation showed that NEMs, a middle ground between FDI and trade, are most common in the pharmaceuticals, automotive components, information technology services and electronics sectors. NEMs play a crucial role in helping the diffusion of technology and skills to local partners. However, upgrading of local skills and training primarily depend on domestic capacity to absorb and assimilate as well as on the nature and content of the contractual agreement.

Increasing the flow of technology to developing countries

WTO members considered a communication from Colombia, Costa Rica, Mexico and Peru proposing a workshop in Geneva on trade and transfer of technology under the auspices of the Working Group.

Background on trade and transfer of technology

The Working Group on Trade and Transfer of Technology was established by the Doha Ministerial Conference in 2001 to examine the relationship between trade and transfer of technology and to make recommendations on steps that might be taken, within the mandate of the WTO, to increase flows of technology to developing countries.

During 2012, members also continued their discussion of an earlier submission by India, Pakistan and the Philippines entitled "Facilitating Access to Information on Appropriate Technology Sourcing". Members reiterated their view that experience sharing by countries that have undergone rapid technological development and sharing of important lessons drawn in the development process could constitute an important aspect of the work in the Working Group. Such experience sharing would allow developing countries to make more informed choices without "re-inventing the wheel".

Trade and environment

In 2012, the Committee on Trade and Environment in Special Session (CTESS) focused its discussion on ways to take the work of the CTESS forward, in particular on the reduction and elimination of barriers to trade in environmental goods and services.

In 2012, under the chairmanship of Ambassador Hiswani Harun (Malaysia) and then Ambassador Selim Kuneralp (Turkey), who took over the chair of the CTESS in November, discussions with delegations were dedicated to the environmental goods part of the negotiations as good progress had already been made on the two negotiating items relating to the relationship between multilateral environmental agreements (MEAs) and the WTO.

In environmental goods and services, members had worked previously on the identification of environmental goods as well as on the approaches to be used to reduce or eliminate tariff and non-tariff barriers to environmental goods. The goods discussed so far in the negotiations fall within a broad range of environmental categories, such as air pollution control, renewable energy, waste management and water treatment, environmental technologies, and carbon capture and storage. The consultations and meetings organized by both chairs focused on identifying ways to resume work on environmental goods and to move the discussion forward in the CTESS.

Background on trade and environment

The negotiations on trade and environment, part of the Doha Development Agenda (DDA), address two main themes: the relationship between the WTO and multilateral environmental agreements (MEAs); and the elimination of barriers to trade in environmental goods and services. The negotiations take place in special sessions of the Committee on Trade and Environment. The negotiations aim to ensure that trade and environmental policies are mutually supportive.

Trade facilitation

The trade facilitation negotiations advanced in 2012, under the chairmanship of Eduardo Sperisen-Yurt of Guatemala, with a reduction in the number of outstanding questions in the draft negotiating text. The WTO Secretariat hosted two symposia on the implementation of the trade facilitation measures being negotiated. Donors continued to support a technical assistance project that enables officials from African, Caribbean, Pacific and least-developed countries to attend negotiations in Geneva.

Delegations revised various articles of the draft consolidated negotiating text, streamlining the language and reducing the number of outstanding questions, which are indicated by square brackets in the text. Negotiations took place in a variety of formats, led by Chair Eduardo Sperisen-Yurt of Guatemala. Aside from the negotiating group meetings, delegates facilitated a series of other working sessions. All meetings were carried out in a bottom-up, member-driven, inclusive and transparent manner.

Background on trade facilitation

Negotiations on a new Trade Facilitation Agreement, formally launched in July 2004 as part of the Doha Development Agenda, are conducted in the Negotiating Group on Trade Facilitation. They aim to expedite the movement, release and clearance of goods, including goods in transit, as well as to ensure effective cooperation between customs and other appropriate authorities. Particular attention is paid to developing and least-developed countries, which stand to benefit from far-reaching flexibilities and considerable technical assistance and capacity-building support.

Trade and environment
www.wto.org/environmentnegs

Trade facilitation negotiations
www.wto.org/facilitationnegs

The WTO Secretariat conducted two symposia on the implementation of the trade facilitation measures being negotiated. The first was conducted for the entire membership and included presentations from members on implementation costs, best practices and lessons learned. The second was held in Kenya for all African countries. The latter was co-hosted by the African Development Bank and included the participation of many regional economic communities, Africa-based technical assistance projects, national aid agencies and international organizations.

Support from donors allowed the continuation of a technical assistance project that provides funding for the participation of capital-based officials from developing countries in meetings of the negotiating group in Geneva. A total of 120 officials from African, Caribbean, Pacific and least-developed countries participated in two meetings of the negotiating group in 2012. Donor governments have indicated their willingness to continue this programme in 2013.

WTO rules

In 2012, the Negotiating Group on Rules continued to seek a way forward on the issues within its mandate – anti-dumping, subsidies and countervailing measures, fisheries subsidies and regional trade agreements. Bilateral and open-ended consultations by the Group's new Chair showed that delegates are reluctant to resume negotiations until the overall situation of the Doha Development Agenda changes. The Group has, however, continued technical activities, most notably in the context of the Technical Group, which exchanges information about the anti-dumping practices of WTO members.

Background on WTO rules

WTO members agreed at the Doha Ministerial Conference in 2001 to launch negotiations to clarify and improve WTO rules on anti-dumping, subsidies and countervailing measures, and regional trade agreements. In the context of the subsidies negotiations, there was specific mention of disciplines on fisheries subsidies, and at the Hong Kong Ministerial Conference in 2005 there was broad agreement on strengthening those disciplines, including through a prohibition of certain forms of fisheries subsidy that contribute to overcapacity and over-fishing. With regard to regional trade agreements, the General Council established in December 2006, on a provisional basis, a transparency mechanism for regional trade agreements.

Following his election in February, the new Chair, Wayne McCook of Jamaica, invited interested delegations to bilateral consultations to seek their views regarding the work of the Group, and in October 2012 called open-ended informal consultations to allow an exchange of views among delegations. He concluded that there was little appetite for resuming active negotiations. He did note, however, an interest in continuing some technical work.

One area where such technical work has continued is in the Technical Group, which is a forum in which delegations can exchange information about their anti-dumping practices. The Technical Group met in April and in October and exchanged information about the institutional structures of members' anti-dumping authorities, training and resource issues, investigation time-lines, and a range of issues relating to injury to domestic industry determinations in anti-dumping investigations. Another area in which certain delegations saw some scope for technical activity was fisheries subsidies, although at the initiative of particular delegations rather than in the Negotiating Group. In addition, it appeared that some further technical work on regional trade agreements also might be useful.

Rules negotiations
www.wto.org/rulesnegs

Dispute Settlement Understanding

In 2012, the Dispute Settlement Understanding negotiations focused on issues that had not been fully discussed the previous year. The Chair of the special sessions noted significant progress in a number of areas and said that the next objective will be to issue a revised Chair's text.

WTO members completed the review of the 12 issues that have been in discussion since 2008 on the basis of a Chair's text by focusing in 2012 on those questions that had not been deeply discussed the previous year.

Reporting to the Trade Negotiations Committee in December, Chair Ambassador Saborío Soto of Costa Rica said that the level of engagement had remained solid throughout the year and that proposed improvements to the proposals had often been the result of intense efforts among participants themselves, including efforts to take on board the comments heard from other participants. As a result, significant progress had been achieved in a number of areas, and where gaps remain, these have been identified and narrowed down as much as was feasible at this stage.

The Chair saw the need to move to a more horizontal negotiation-oriented stage in order to finalize the work and reach agreement on clarifications and improvements to the Dispute Settlement Understanding. With this in mind, the next objective will be to work towards a revised Chair's text to take stock of the progress made, consolidate it and pave the way for a final agreement.

The 12 issues identified in the 2008 text are developing-country interests (including special and differential treatment), effective compliance, member-control and flexibility, mutually agreed solutions, panel composition, post-retaliation, remand, sequencing, strictly confidential information, third-party rights, time-savings, and transparency and amicus curiae briefs.

Half of these issues had been considered in 2011, so work in 2012 focused on the other six, namely developing-country interests, member-control and flexibility, panel composition, remand, strictly confidential information and third-party rights. As in 2011, the work was conducted around group meetings in various formats, depending on the subject to be discussed.

On the question of developing-country interests, a number of developing countries have identified certain issues of interest to them relating to timeframes, promoting prompt compliance, participation and access to dispute settlement. Member-control and flexibility involves issues such as whether to allow the parties to a dispute to jointly seek deletion of parts of a panel or Appellate Body report while remand covers the question of whether the Appellate Body can send cases back to panels for further action.

Background on Dispute Settlement Understanding

In November 2001, at the Doha Ministerial Conference, WTO members agreed to negotiate to improve and clarify the Dispute Settlement Understanding (DSU) – the rules and procedures governing the settlement of WTO disputes. These negotiations, which take place in special sessions of the Dispute Settlement Body, are part of the Doha Development Agenda but are not part of the "single undertaking". This means they are not legally tied to the success or failure of the other Doha negotiations.

Government Procurement Agreement

On 30 March 2012, the parties to the WTO Government Procurement Agreement (GPA) formally adopted the revised text of the accord after a final review required by the "political conclusion" that was reached in December 2011.

The revised GPA, apart from its new and improved text, will lead to a significant expansion in market access and brings a commitment to new work programmes relating to the administration and further evolution of the pact. The new agreement comes into force as soon as two-thirds of the parties have ratified it and submitted their instruments of acceptance. Parties have collectively pledged themselves to provide the required instruments and to implement the revised GPA promptly.

Background on Government Procurement Agreement

The Government Procurement Agreement (GPA), adopted in 1994, ensures that signatories do not discriminate against the products, services or suppliers of other parties to the Agreement with respect to the government procurement opportunities that are opened to foreign competition. It sets minimum standards for the transparency of procurement, which are based on internationally recognized best practices. The GPA is a "plurilateral" agreement, which means that it applies only to those WTO members that have agreed to be bound by it. The Committee on Government Procurement administers the GPA.

Director-General Pascal Lamy and Nicholas Niggli, then Chair of the Committee on Government Procurement, witnessed the formal adoption of the revised Government Procurement Agreement on 30 March 2012.

The market access gains from the renegotiation are valued at USD 80 billion to USD 100 billion or more annually. The additional market access commitments include:

- the extension of coverage to approximately 600 additional procuring entities, including local governments and sub-central entities
- for the first time, coverage by three major parties of build-operate-transfer arrangements (BOTs), a form of public-private partnership that is increasingly used for infrastructure development (these are contracts under which a firm builds an infrastructure project, for example, and runs it for an agreed time before transferring ownership to the government)
- additional coverage of services procurement by the majority of parties, particularly with respect to telecommunications
- the reduction of applicable thresholds by four of the parties
- the elimination by several parties of miscellaneous restrictions on market access or reciprocity requirements that were previously applied.

The new rules update the GPA text to take into account developments in government procurement practice, notably the widespread use of electronic tools. They better ensure fairness in the award of government contracts. New transitional measures have been adopted to facilitate accession to the GPA by developing countries (see page 70). The revised text also aims at fighting corruption.

The Committee's new work programmes include discussions on facilitating participation by small and medium-sized enterprises in government procurement, improving available statistical data, and promoting sustainable procurement practices.

Implementation and monitoring

- The General Council agreed that the Ninth Ministerial Conference would be held in Bali, Indonesia, on 3-6 December 2013.
- The Council approved improved guidelines that provide a simpler framework for the entry of least-developed countries into the WTO family.
- The Council approved the membership of Laos and Tajikistan, clearing the way for them to join the WTO in early 2013.
- The WTO's trade monitoring reports showed that WTO members and observers had by and large continued to resist domestic protectionist pressures in 2012.
- The WTO received 37 new notifications of regional trade agreements between WTO members in 2012, a considerable increase on the 25 received in 2011.

General Council 36

Trade in goods 39

Market access 40
Agriculture 41
Sanitary and phytosanitary measures 42
Technical barriers to trade 44
Subsidies and countervailing measures 45
Anti-dumping practices 46
Customs valuation 47
Rules of origin 48
Import licensing 49
Safeguards 49
Trade-related investment measures 50
Information technology 51
State trading enterprises 53
Trade in civil aircraft 53

Trade in services 54

Trade-related aspects of intellectual property rights (TRIPS) 56

Trade and environment 58

Regional trade agreements 60

Trade Policy Reviews 62

Trade monitoring reports 66

Trade, debt and finance 68

Government Procurement Agreement 70

Integrated Trade Intelligence Portal (I-TIP) 72

Background on implementation and monitoring
Various WTO councils and committees seek to ensure that WTO agreements are being properly implemented. All WTO members undergo periodic scrutiny of their trade policies and practices.

General Council

In 2012, the General Council agreed that the Ninth Ministerial Conference will be held in Bali, Indonesia. It oversaw the progress of the Doha Round negotiations on the basis of reports from the Director-General in his capacity as Chair of the Trade Negotiations Committee. It heard the Director-General's annual report on accessions and on the development assistance aspects of cotton. In July, it adopted recommendations on the accession of least-developed countries (LDCs) as mandated by the Eighth Ministerial Conference. It also reviewed progress in the Work Programme on Electronic Commerce.

Ninth Ministerial Conference

Following the offer by the Government of Indonesia to host the Ninth Ministerial Conference (MC9), the General Council agreed that it would be held in Bali, Indonesia, on 3-6 December 2013. The General Council also took note of the following guiding principles to be applied to both the preparatory process and to the Conference itself:

- the "FIT" principle – full participation, inclusiveness and transparency
- any issue for action or decision by ministers proposed by WTO members should be developed by them in line with the normal consensus principle
- issues for action or decision by ministers should be agreed well before MC9.

Accessions

Further to the MC8 decision on the accession of least-developed countries (LDCs), the General Council in July adopted the recommendations of the Sub-Committee on LDCs designed to further streamline and facilitate the accession process. The decision sets benchmarks for acceding LDCs on goods, services, transparency in accession negotiations, special and differential treatment and transition periods as well as technical assistance (see page 6). The Director-General said that the improved guidelines provide a simpler framework for the entry of LDCs into the WTO family.

The General Council approved the accession agreements of the Lao People's Democratic Republic and Tajikistan, in October and December respectively, clearing the way for them to join 30 days after notifying the WTO that they had ratified the accords.

Background on the General Council

The General Council is entrusted with carrying out the functions of the WTO and taking actions necessary to this effect between meetings of the Ministerial Conference in addition to carrying out the specific tasks assigned to it by the Agreement establishing the WTO.

Notifications were received in early 2013, resulting in Laos joining the WTO on 2 February and Tajikistan joining on 2 March.

Appointment of officers to WTO bodies

At its February meeting, the General Council agreed that the Chair would initiate a process of consultations to review the guidelines for the appointment of officers to WTO bodies. At its July meeting, following the consultations carried out by the Chair, the General Council approved a number of practical steps to improve the implementation of the guidelines. Among other recommendations, the General Council said that the appointment process should be set in motion more carefully and allow sufficient time. More comprehensive information about the process should be provided to delegations, in particular to group coordinators, at an early stage, including through early meetings.

TRIPS-related matters

In December, the General Council received a report from the Council on Trade-related Aspects of Intellectual Property Rights (TRIPS) on its review of the implementation of Paragraph 6 of the Doha Declaration on the TRIPS Agreement and Public Health (see page 56). This relates to special provisions, currently contained in a waiver to the TRIPS Agreement, permitting generic versions of patented medicines to be exported to developing countries with no manufacturing capacity of their own, and which cannot otherwise use TRIPS flexibilities to issue compulsory licences on public health grounds.

Waivers under Article IX of the WTO Agreement

In 2012, the General Council considered and granted a number of requests for waivers from obligations under the WTO Agreement, as set out in Table 1. It also reviewed the following multi-year waivers:

- Least-developed countries (LDCs) – Article 70.9 of the TRIPS Agreement with respect to pharmaceutical products, granted on 8 July 2002 until 1 January 2016
- Preferential tariff treatment for LDCs, granted on 27 May 2009 until 30 June 2019
- European Union – Application of autonomous preferential treatment to Moldova, granted on 7 May 2008 until 31 December 2013

Elin Østebø Johansen (right) chaired the General Council in 2012.

- United States – Former Trust Territory of the Pacific Islands, granted on 27 July 2007 until 31 December 2016
- United States – Caribbean Basin Economic Recovery Act, granted on 27 May 2009 until 31 December 2014
- United States – African Growth and Opportunity Act, granted on 27 May 2009 until 30 September 2015
- United States – ANDEAN Trade Preference Act, granted on 27 May 2009 until 31 December 2014
- Preferential treatment to services and service suppliers of least-developed countries, granted on 17 December 2011 until 17 December 2026
- Kimberley Process Certification Scheme for rough diamonds, granted on 15 December 2006 until 31 December 2018
- Canada – CARIBCAN, granted on 30 November 2011 until 31 December 2013
- European Union – Application of autonomous preferential treatment to the West Balkans, granted on 30 November 2011 until 31 December 2016.

Other issues

The General Council heard concerns expressed by Cuba about the intellectual property rights of the holder of the Havana Club Cuban rum brand in the United States. A large number of members raised questions about Ukraine's resort to Article XXVIII to raise duties on over 350 tariff lines. Ukraine says that it was pushed to act by the economic situation. Members expressed concerns about the scope of the move and its systemic implications.

The General Council also heard updates concerning the Chair's consultations on improving the guidelines for granting intergovernmental organizations permanent observer status in the WTO. On e-commerce, Deputy Director-General Harsha Singh gave an overview in July of work taking place and noted that overall there was more substantive engagement on this matter than in the past. He drew attention to a proposal by Ecuador and Cuba on a Workshop on E-Commerce, Development and Small and Medium-sized Enterprises (SMEs).

As part of its overall oversight function, the General Council also conducted a year-end review of WTO activities on the basis of annual reports from all its subsidiary bodies. The Director-General provided regular updates to the Council on the measures taken to streamline the conduct of meetings and the production of documents.

In addition, the General Council reviewed other matters relating to the WTO budget, the building renovation project for the Centre William Rappard and the WTO pension plan, and considered two reports from the Joint Advisory Group of the International Trade Centre (ITC). The Joint Advisory Group is the policymaking body of the ITC, the trade promotion agency for developing countries jointly sponsored by the WTO and the United Nations Conference on Trade and Development (UNCTAD).

Table 1: Waivers under Article IX (Decision-Making) of the WTO Agreement

In 2012, the General Council granted the following waivers from obligations under the WTO agreements.

Member(s)	Type	Decision of	Expiry	Decision
Australia; Brazil; Canada; China; Costa Rica; Dominican Republic; El Salvador; European Union; Guatemala; Honduras; Hong Kong, China; India; Israel; Republic of Korea; Macao, China; Malaysia; Mexico; New Zealand; Norway; Pakistan; Russian Federation; Singapore; Switzerland; Separate Customs Territory of Taiwan, Penghu, Kinmen and Matsu; Thailand; and United States	Introduction of Harmonized System 2012 changes into WTO schedules of tariff concessions	11 Dec 2012	31 Dec 2013	WT/L/875
Argentina; Australia; Brazil; Canada; China; Costa Rica; Croatia; Dominican Republic; El Salvador; European Union; Guatemala; Honduras; Hong Kong, China; India; Israel; Republic of Korea; Macao, China; Malaysia; Mexico; New Zealand; Nicaragua; Norway; Pakistan; the Philippines; Singapore; Switzerland; Thailand; United States; and Uruguay	Introduction of Harmonized System 2007 changes into WTO schedules of tariff concessions	11 Dec 2012	31 Dec 2013	WT/L/874
Argentina; Australia; Brazil; China; Croatia; European Union; Iceland; India; Malaysia; and Uruguay	Introduction of Harmonized System 2002 changes into WTO schedules of tariff concessions	11 Dec 2012	31 Dec 2013	WT/L/873
Australia; Botswana; Brazil; Canada; Croatia; European Union; India; Israel; Japan; Republic of Korea; Mexico; New Zealand; Norway; the Philippines; Russian Federation; Singapore; Chinese Taipei; Thailand, Turkey, United States; and Bolivarian Republic of Venezuela	Kimberly Process Certification Scheme for Rough Diamonds - Extension of Waiver	11 Dec 2012	31 Dec 2018	WT/L/876
Cuba	Article XV:6 – Extension of waiver	14 Feb 2012	31 Dec 2016	WT/L/850
European Union	Preferences for Pakistan	14 Feb 2012	31 Dec 2013	WT/L/851

Trade in goods

Over the course of four meetings held in 2012, the Council for Trade in Goods approved a number of waiver requests, individual and collective, such as the extension of the waiver on the Kimberley Process Certification Scheme (KPCS), the on-going harmonization of tariff schedules and the European Union duties on certain goods from Pakistan. It also discussed a range of trade concerns raised by members.

The collective requests on the changes to schedules of tariff concessions to be applied under the Harmonized System (HS), referred to the extension of the deadlines to update the tariff schedules of the requesting members so as to reflect changes in the HS they apply. The other collective waiver request related to the KPCS for Rough Diamonds, which was set to expire at the end of 2012. This waiver gives legal cover to trade measures adopted by the Kimberley Process participants, which aim at breaking the link between armed conflict and trade in rough diamonds. The Goods Council agreed to extend the waiver by six years or until 31 December 2018 and, forwarded the draft decision to the General Council for adoption. The extension was requested by 21 members and coordinated by the United States.

The Council also approved a waiver requested by the European Union (EU) on EU duties on certain products from Pakistan to help the country recover from massive floods in 2010. The EU reiterated that it was asking for a waiver for an exceptional measure in exceptional circumstances, and would not set a precedent in the WTO. Some members, notably textile exporters, had previously expressed concerns about granting the duty waiver. The Council also approved a further extension for Cuba to its waiver concerning Article XV:6, which refers to WTO members who are not members of the International Monetary Fund (IMF).

Members raised a number of specific trade concerns during the year. In November Australia introduced a joint statement by 23 delegations urging Ukraine, in the interest of the multilateral trading system and the global economy, to withdraw its notification to re-negotiate its tariffs on a large number of products. Concerns referred to the large number of tariff lines covered by Ukraine's notification, the extent to which Ukraine would be able to compensate other members, as required by Article XXVIII of GATT 1994 and, the lack of transparency on this matter. In reply, Ukraine indicated that it was following the established procedures in a transparent manner, that its notification was a normal practice in the WTO and that it should not be seen as a protectionist measure.

Other trade concerns related to Chinese Taipei's subsidies applied to the purchase of domestic electronic appliances; the EU restrictive measures on bio-diesel imports; Russia's implementation of WTO accession commitments; and Ukraine's recycling fee draft law. Other concerns, previously discussed included Argentina's import restricting policies and practices; Ukraine's implementation of customs valuation legislation; and Brazil's increase of the industrial product tax on the automotive sector, along with the ruling of the EU Court of Justice on the detection in honey of pollen containing DNA from genetically modified maize.

Note was taken of the consultations held by the Philippines concerning its request for a waiver relating to special treatment for rice and of the notifications made by the Chinese Taipei and the Republic of Korea concerning their duty-free market access schemes for least-developed countries (LDCs).

Finally, on notifications, the Chairperson, Ambassador Tom Mboya Okeyo (Kenya), invited delegations to explore ways of finding the right balance between transparency and the cost-saving recommendations endorsed by the General Council at its meeting in November 2011.

Background on trade in goods

The Council for Trade in Goods (Goods Council or the Council) is responsible for the workings of all WTO Agreements on trade in goods. It consists of the full WTO membership and reports to the WTO General Council. The Goods Council has 11 subsidiary committees dealing with specific subjects, such as agriculture, market access, subsidies, technical barriers to trade, sanitary and phytosanitary measures, import licensing and customs valuation. All these committees also comprise all WTO members. Also reporting to the Goods Council are a working party on state trading enterprises and the Information Technology Agreement (ITA).

Market access

In 2012, the Committee on Market Access pressed ahead with updating members' schedules to bring them into line with the four amendments – HS1996, HS2002, HS2007 and HS2012 – made to the Harmonized System (HS).

In two formal meetings, in April and in October, it approved a new format for notifications of quantitative restrictions and agreed to procedures for eventually making public negotiating material of the Dillon Round, together with some additional material from the four earlier GATT rounds. Most of the negotiating material of the earlier GATT rounds is now derestricted and is available on the WTO website. Ukraine's announcement that it would raise tariffs on over 350 lines triggered intense debate at the October meeting.

The Committee has been focusing on the various transposition exercises and approved several collective waivers for HS2002, HS2007 and HS2012. With regard to HS96, Chairman Bipin Menon of India informed members that he had consulted with four of the five members whose schedules remained uncertified with a view to seeing how progress could be made.

The HS2002 exercise is well advanced with 99 schedules certified and a further four schedules in the process of certification. For HS2007, the Committee agreed on the methodology to be used to transpose schedules and work began, with 21 HS2007 files being released for multilateral review. A further 26 draft files were completed and sent to members for a first review and eight members made submissions. The subject of non-consensus correlated HS2007 lines was also discussed. These are lines on which the Harmonized System Committee at the World Customs Organization has yet to reach a common view. The Secretariat also received the first HS2012 submission from the United States.

Background on market access

The Committee on Market Access provides a forum for consultation and supervises the implementation of tariff and non-tariff concessions that are not covered by any other WTO body. It also seeks to ensure that schedules of commitments are kept up to date, including changes required by amendments to the Harmonized System (HS). This is crucial for surveillance purposes (i.e. to be able to compare tariffs in the schedules of commitments with those applied in practice by WTO members). The HS, developed by the World Customs Organization, allows countries to classify trade goods on a common basis. It has been updated three times since 1996.

The Committee agreed to a proposal by Chair Menon to hold informal consultations on discontinuing the waiver reports that the Committee sends to the Council for Trade in Goods (CTG) twice a year. The information is already in the annual report to the CTG.

Notifications of quantitative restrictions

A big step was taken in respect of the timeliness and completeness of notifications when, after four years of discussion, the Committee approved the draft Decision on Notification Procedures. The Council for Trade in Goods subsequently adopted it. The decision requires members to make complete notifications of all quantitative restrictions in force by 30 September 2012 and at two-yearly intervals thereafter. Members should also notify changes to quantitative restrictions no later than six months from their entry into force. The information will be stored in a database, which will be made available to the public in 2013. The Secretariat will circulate an annual report listing, among other things, the WTO members making notification and the type of notification made.

Databases

The Secretariat reported on development of the Integrated Data Base (IDB) and the Consolidated Tariff Schedules (CTS) database, their use, the status of software development and technical assistance. The IDB compiles information on applied tariffs and imports, as notified by members, while the CTS collates information on members' schedules of concessions. The databases are used – among other things – for the calculation of "ad valorem" equivalents (duties expressed as a percentage of the value of an item) of tariffs based on quantity or weight. The Secretariat plans to integrate into the IDB historical tariff and import information for 29 countries covering years 1988 to 1995. It also intends to put together a consolidated document on IDB notification for ease of reference.

Other developments

Negotiating records from the first four GATT rounds were posted on the WTO public website, so concluding a process that had taken three years. The Committee also approved procedures for the proposed publication of material from the fifth – Dillon Round – and some additional negotiating material of the four earlier rounds. This material will be a rich source of information for academics, students and others.

Ukraine's declaration of intent to raise duties on over 350 tariff lines triggered intense debate at the October meeting, with a number of members raising objections and seeking further information. Ukraine said it was making the move under Article XXVIII of the GATT and that the move had been dictated by evolving global and internal factors.

Agriculture

Besides pursuing its core activity of reviewing WTO members' compliance with their commitments under the Agreement on Agriculture, the Committee on Agriculture continued to review the implementation issues for which it has responsibility under the Doha Development Agenda. These include developing disciplines on export credits and other export financing measures and ensuring transparency in the administration of tariff quotas. Consultations on members' participation in the normal growth of world agricultural trade were also held within the framework of the export subsidy disciplines.

At its four meetings in 2012, the Committee reviewed progress in the implementation of WTO members' commitments on the basis of their notifications and matters specifically raised under Article 18.6 of the Agreement on Agriculture (which allows members to raise any matter relevant to implementation).

Approximately 180 notifications were subject to detailed review. A total of 391 questions were raised, 85 per cent of which related to individual notifications. Figure 1 gives a snapshot of the nature and number of concerns raised by subject area, i.e. market access, domestic support, export competition and export prohibitions and restrictions.

As notifications are the principal source of information for monitoring compliance, the Committee closely supervised these with respect to members' reporting obligations. In this context, specific concerns were raised regarding long overdue notifications, in particular in the domestic support and export subsidy areas.

Background on agriculture

The Agreement on Agriculture aims to reform trade and make WTO members' policies more market-oriented. The rules and commitments apply to the areas of market access, domestic support and export competition as well as export restrictions and prohibitions. The Committee on Agriculture meeting in regular session oversees the implementation of the Agreement. The Committee is also entrusted with monitoring the follow-up to the Marrakesh Ministerial Decision regarding net food-importing developing countries, which sets out objectives on the provision of food aid and other assistance to the beneficiary countries.

Figure 1: Concerns raised in the Committee on Agriculture in 2012, by subject area

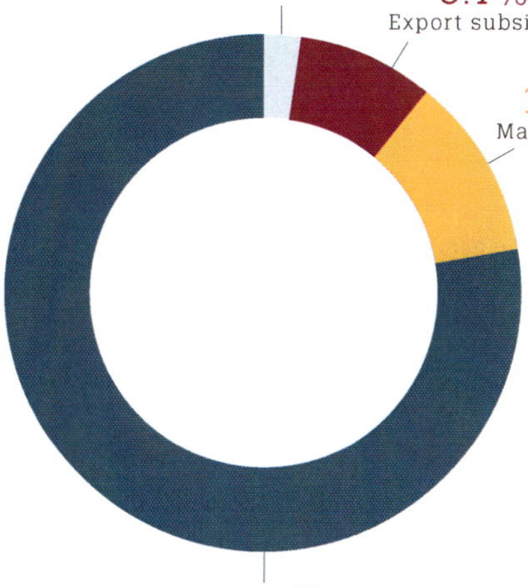

Net food-importing developing countries

In March 2012, the WTO list of net food-importing developing countries (NFIDCs) was further extended to include Antigua and Barbuda and El Salvador. As in previous years, the Committee had a dedicated discussion on the implementation and monitoring of the Marrakesh decision on NFIDCs.

Based on the notifications received and with the assistance of the United Nations Food and Agricultural Organization, the International Monetary Fund and the Inter-American Institute for Cooperation on Agriculture, WTO members considered food aid levels to least-developed countries (LDCs) and NFIDCs as well as the technical and financial assistance made available by donor members and multilateral institutions to improve their agricultural productivity and infrastructure.

"Significant exporters"

Building on discussions held since 2010, the Committee intensified its work on updating the 1995 list of "significant exporters" within the framework of notification requirements on export subsidies. There was constructive engagement with a number of delegations tabling additional contributions, bringing the discussions to a more technical level.

A list that takes account of current agricultural trade will improve the Committee's ability to monitor potential subsidization of exports and evasion of commitments. Significant exporters were defined in 1995 as countries whose share of total world exports in particular products exceeds 5 per cent and who, in addition to members with export subsidy reduction commitments, are required to notify total export volumes for such products.

Looking ahead

In 2013, the Committee will continue to strengthen its monitoring tools and functions by, among other things, seeking further engagement from WTO members on updating the list of "significant exporters" established in 1995, and capitalizing on the technical assistance and outreach sessions organized by the WTO Secretariat. A new database that documents the review process undertaken by the Committee since 1995 will provide useful input to the Committee's work.

Sanitary and phytosanitary measures

The Committee on Sanitary and Phytosanitary (SPS) Measures granted observer status to another four organizations, bringing to 25 the number that have regular or ad hoc observer status. The Committee continued to work on guidelines to facilitate the use of the "good offices" of the Chair in resolving trade concerns and on the development of a working definition of SPS-related private standards. A workshop on the transparency provisions of the SPS Agreement provided training on using the SPS Information Management System and the online system for submission of notifications as well as information on the online tools of the SPS standard-setting bodies.

In 2012, the Committee granted observer status on an ad hoc basis to the African Union, the Common Market for Eastern and Southern African States (COMESA), the Economic Community of Central African States (ECCAS/CEEAC) and the Gulf Cooperation Council Standardization Organization in recognition of the important role that observer organizations can play in assisting WTO members to fully benefit from, and comply with, the SPS Agreement. The Committee also agreed to invite all organizations with ad hoc observer status to participate in all of the SPS Committee meetings during 2013.

The Committee continued to address issues arising from the third review of the operation and implementation of the SPS Agreement. An informal working group was established to advance work on guidelines to facilitate the implementation of Article 12.2 of the SPS Agreement on "ad hoc consultations and negotiations" to resolve specific trade concerns.

The Committee considered a proposed revision to the procedure for monitoring the use of international standards. It also considered further encouragement of joint work by the WTO, the Codex Alimentarius Commission, the International Plant Protection Convention (IPPC) and the World Organization for Animal Health (OIE) on cross-cutting issues, such as certification and inspection, and recommendations to improve

Background on sanitary and phytosanitary measures

The Agreement on the Application of Sanitary and Phytosanitary (SPS) Measures establishes the rights and obligations of WTO members regarding measures taken to ensure food safety, protect human health from plant- or animal-spread diseases, protect plant and animal health from pests and diseases, or prevent other damage from pests. Governments must ensure that their SPS measures are based on scientific principles.

SPS coordination at the national and regional levels. The Committee continued to discuss the effects of SPS-related private standards on trade, on the basis of the actions agreed by the Committee. Discussions focused in particular on the development of a working definition of SPS-related private standards.

A workshop in October on the transparency provisions of the SPS Agreement provided interactive training on the use of the SPS Information Management System and on the new online SPS Notification Submission System (NSS). Those attending included a large number of officials from developing and least-developed countries with direct responsibility as SPS national notification authorities and enquiry points.

A growing number of members are making use of the NSS to submit notifications online since it became operational at the beginning of 2012. Representatives from the Codex, the IPPC and the OIE also provided information on their online information tools. During 2012, 1,219 notifications (including corrections and revisions) were submitted, compared with 1,388 in 2011. This brings the total number of notifications submitted since the entry into force of the Agreement in 1995 to 14,869. Over 48 per cent of all SPS notifications submitted during 2012 were submitted using the NSS.

The Committee considered a wide range of "specific trade concerns" at each of its three meetings in 2012. Sixteen new specific trade concerns were raised and other previously raised concerns were discussed again. New issues included Indonesia's closure of certain ports of entry, China's testing measures for food additives, US measures on fresh lemon imports, modifications to EU testing procedures for pesticide residues, Japan's rejection of shrimp consignments due to certain residues and Russia's import ban on live animals.

Two trade concerns were reported to have been resolved. One related to Chinese Taipei's maximum residue levels for ochratoxin A in coffee and the other to the US prohibition of certain ornamental plants from Costa Rica. A total of 344 specific trade concerns were raised between 1995 and the end of 2012 (see Figures 2 and 3).

Figure 2: Number of new SPS trade concerns raised per year

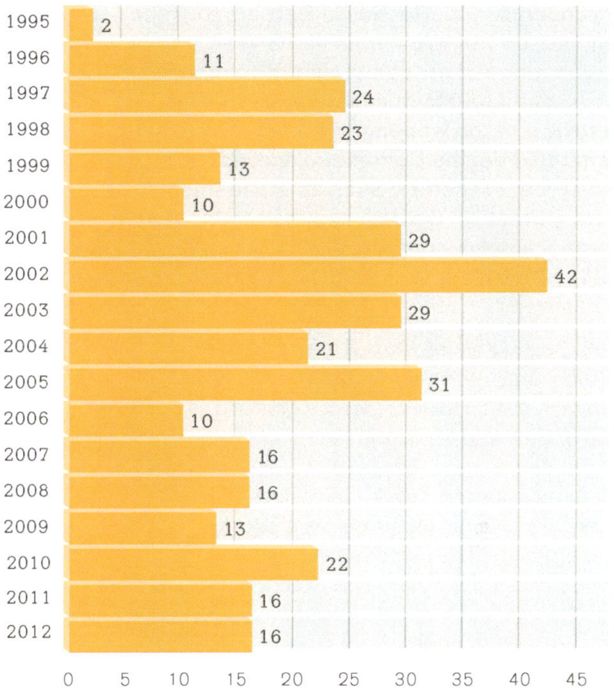

Figure 3: SPS trade concerns by subject, 1995 to end 2012

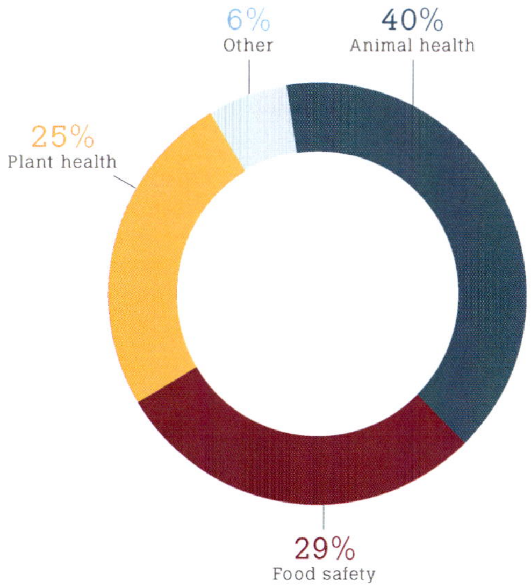

IMPLEMENTATION AND MONITORING

Technical barriers to trade

In 2012 WTO members raised a record 94 specific trade concerns in the Technical Barriers to Trade (TBT) Committee, up from 76 the previous year, covering trade in a broad range of products. Health-related concerns, however, continued to dominate the agenda. Following the latest review of the working of the Agreement on Technical Barriers to Trade, the Committee agreed to shift its focus towards broader themes, such as standards and good regulatory practice, that are common to the specific trade concerns that have dominated its work. The hope is that this will enable the specific concerns to be addressed more easily.

The TBT Committee discussed 35 new trade concerns and 59 existing ones during the year. Matters relating to public health, such as alcohol and tobacco labelling, were extensively discussed. Between 1995 and the end of 2012, over 360 specific trade concerns were raised in the TBT Committee (see Figure 4). Among new issues discussed in 2012 was New Zealand's plan to introduce plain packaging legislation for tobacco products. The proposal comes after Australia's plain packaging tobacco legislation became a legal dispute at the WTO. Although health-related issues were prominent in debate, concerns related to environmental measures were also raised. These included questions about bio-fuels, solar panels, energy labelling and carbon footprints, among others.

Background on technical barriers to trade

The Agreement on Technical Barriers to Trade tries to ensure that regulations, standards, testing and certification procedures followed by WTO members do not create unnecessary obstacles to trade. The number of regulations adopted by countries has continued to grow in response to consumers' demands for safe, high-quality products, the protection of health and the need to curb pollution and environmental degradation. In an effort to curb the growing number of specific trade concerns brought before the Technical Barriers to Trade Committee, members have agreed to shift their focus to address broader cross-cutting themes – such as the application of standards, conformity assessment procedures and good regulatory practice.

Most of the measures discussed are mandatory governmental regulations (i.e. technical regulations or conformity assessment procedures), but standards (and frequently, international standards) are also discussed to the extent that they are used as references for mandatory measures. The range of products discussed is broad, as are the nature of measures – covering product safety specifications, toxicity limits, energy and health labelling, environmental performance requirements, compatibility of electronic products, quality and health testing requirements, product registration requirements, amongst many others.

With the aim of settling specific trade concerns more easily, members decided to give more time to discussing the underlying themes that recur in these issues. The decision was taken in November as part of the review the Committee conducts every three years into how well the TBT Agreement is working. Ultimately, trade in goods ranging from food, medicines and cosmetics to toys, telephones and tyres may flow more easily. In March 2013 back-to-back sessions will be set aside for discussing good regulatory practice and standards, while transparency will be taken up in June. Other themes will follow. The report of the 6th Triennial Review covers all key areas, including enhancing transparency by improving information sharing and consultation on draft measures. The Committee has also put more emphasis on those disciplines that deal with the particular challenges of developing countries. The main purpose of this work is to improve the practices, processes, institutions and infrastructures that members put in place to implement the TBT Agreement, thereby avoiding unnecessary barriers to trade.

Disputes

Since 1995, 45 WTO disputes have cited the TBT Agreement in the formal dispute settlement consultations. In 2012, three Appellate Body reports were circulated in respect of cases that dealt mainly with the Agreement. These disputes concerned challenges related to three US measures: country of origin labelling (COOL) requirements; the production and sale of clove cigarettes; and measures affecting the importing, marketing and sale of tuna and tuna products. Two further TBT-related disputes are in the pipeline: one concerning a European Union measure prohibiting the importing and marketing of seal products, and another concerning an Australian measure affecting plain packaging requirements applicable to tobacco products.

Observers

Representatives of various observer organizations – the FAO/WHO Codex Alimentarius Commission, the International Electrotechnical Commission, the International Organization for Standardization (ISO), the International Trade Centre (ITC), the OECD, the International Organization for Legal Metrology, the United Nations Economic Commission for Europe (UNECE), the United Nations Industrial Development Organization (UNIDO), the International Telecommunication Union (ITU) and the World Health Organization (WHO) – updated the TBT Committee on activities relevant to its work, including on technical assistance. The Committee agreed, in 2012, to extend ad hoc observer status to the Bureau Internationale des Poids et Mesures (BIPM).

Figure 4: Specific trade concerns raised in the TBT Committee

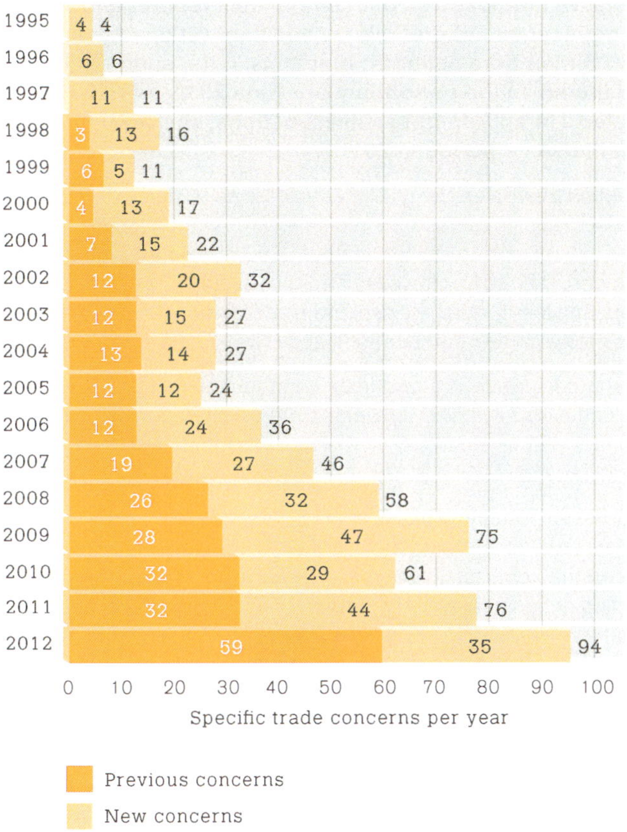

Subsidies and countervailing measures

The Committee on Subsidies and Countervailing Measures (SCM) focused in 2012 on encouraging more WTO members to notify their subsidy programmes and on improving the timeliness and completeness of notifications. A significant number of members have still to make new and full notifications. The Committee decided to further extend the transition period for the elimination of export subsidy programmes of 19 developing countries.

In 2012, the SCM Committee reviewed members' notifications of specific subsidies, notifications of countervailing duty legislation, semi-annual reports of countervailing actions and ad hoc notifications of preliminary and final countervailing measures taken. At the Committee's regular meeting in April, the then Chair Andreas Krallmann (Germany) expressed serious concern about the state of subsidy notifications. New Chair Sam C. S. Hui (Hong Kong, China) returned to the theme at the October meeting and invited the 73 members (down from 80 in April) that had not yet made their 2011 new and full subsidy notifications to explain the reasons for that.

The SCM Agreement requires members to notify their specific subsidies each year. Members are asked to give priority to submitting new and full notifications every two years, while the Committee gives less emphasis to reviewing updated notifications. In 2012, the Committee continued its consideration of 2009 and 2011 new and full subsidy notifications. At both its April and October meetings, the Committee discussed ways to improve the timeliness and completeness of notifications and other information flows on trade measures under the SCM Agreement.

The Committee also reviewed the annual updating notifications by developing country members granted an extended transition period for the elimination of certain export subsidy programmes. On the basis of the review, the Committee agreed to renew the transition period for a further year to the end of 2013. The 19 members are Antigua and Barbuda, Barbados, Belize, Costa Rica, Dominica, Dominican Republic, El Salvador, Fiji, Grenada,

Background on subsidies and countervailing measures

The Subsidies and Countervailing Measures (SCM) Agreement regulates the use of subsidies by WTO members as well as the use of countervailing measures (usually in the form of increased duties) by members where subsidized imports of a product are causing or threatening to cause injury to the domestic industry. The SCM Committee provides WTO members with the opportunity to discuss any matters relating to the operation of the SCM Agreement.

Subsidies and countervailing measures
www.wto.org/scm

Guatemala, Jamaica, Jordan, Mauritius, Panama, Papua New Guinea, Saint Kitts and Nevis, Saint Lucia, Saint Vincent and the Grenadines, and Uruguay. The programmes involved are mainly related to free trade zones or to tax incentives for exporters.

In addition, certain developing members are listed in the SCM Agreement as exempt from the general requirement to eliminate export subsidies as long as they remain low-income countries. To qualify for exemption, a listed member must have a per capita gross national product (GNP) of less than USD 1,000, as reported by the World Bank. Listed members in 2011 were Bolivia, Cameroon, Congo, Côte d'Ivoire, Ghana, Guyana, Honduras, India, Indonesia, Kenya, Nicaragua, Nigeria, Pakistan, Senegal, Sri Lanka and Zimbabwe. Least-developed country (LDC) members are also exempt from the prohibition on export subsidies.

The Committee also reviewed notifications related to countervailing duty legislation. In the 12 months to 30 June 2012, eight members notified the Committee of 29 new countervailing duty investigations, including nine initiated by the United States and seven by Canada. At the end of June, there were 82 notified countervailing measures in force (definitive duties and price undertakings), of which 50 were maintained by the United States, 11 by Canada and ten by the European Union.

Anti-dumping practices

The Committee on Anti-Dumping Practices reviewed new legislative notifications, the semi-annual reports and ad hoc notifications of preliminary and final actions taken by WTO members at its two meetings in the spring and the autumn. In the period January-June 2012, members initiated 114 anti-dumping investigations, sharply up from 69 in the same period in 2011.

Argentina, Australia, Brazil, Canada, Indonesia, Malaysia and Chinese Taipei increased their initiations of anti-dumping investigations during the first half of 2012 compared with the same period in 2011. However, frequent users such as the European Union, India, Mexico, Pakistan, Ukraine and the United States slowed their anti-dumping activity.

The sharp increase in anti-dumping in the first six months of the year, compared with 2011, reversed a recent trend towards fewer actions. In the whole of 2011, 153 anti-dumping actions were initiated against 213 in 2008.

WTO members taking anti-dumping actions have been using the revised report format, adopted in 2008, to submit their semi-annual reports. Furthermore, many members taking anti-dumping actions have been using the minimum information format as revised in 2009 to provide their ad hoc notifications of such actions, and it has been observed that compliance with this notification obligation has improved. Following the creation of a more specific automated reply to electronic notifications, most members have been providing all their notifications electronically.

Background on anti-dumping practices

WTO members are allowed to apply "anti-dumping" measures on imports of a product where the exporting company exports the product at a price lower than the price it normally charges in its home market and the dumped imports cause or threaten to cause injury to the domestic industry. The Committee on Anti-Dumping Practices provides WTO members with the opportunity to discuss any matters relating to the Anti-Dumping Agreement.

Anti-dumping
www.wto.org/ad

The Working Group on Implementation discussed papers on other known causes of injury to domestic industry, the accuracy and adequacy test, and sunset reviews at its spring and autumn meetings. The other known causes of injury are those known factors, other than the dumped imports, which the authorities in the importing country should examine to ensure that the injuries caused to the domestic industry by these factors are not attributed to the dumped imports. The adequacy and accuracy test is what anti-dumping authorities use to assess whether there is sufficient evidence to launch an anti-dumping investigation. Finally, the sunset review refers to the review that may be conducted by the authorities before a definitive anti-dumping duty lapses to determine whether to extend that duty or lift it.

Customs valuation

The Committee on Customs Valuation continued to review national legislation, as well as responses to the checklist of issues raised by members. New or further notifications of national legislation were received from eight members, bringing to 16 the number of notifications that the Committee has under review. Training events on customs valuation were held in Africa, Asia and Latin America, some of which were delivered jointly with the World Customs Organization.

In 2012, the Committee received new or further notifications of national legislation from the Kingdom of Bahrain, Cape Verde, Ecuador, Nicaragua, Russia, Rwanda, Uruguay and Ukraine. At its May and October meetings, the Committee continued its examination of the legislation of Belize, Cambodia, China, Costa Rica, Nigeria, Saint Vincent and the Grenadines, Thailand, and Tunisia. The review of Thailand was concluded during the year and progress was made in the reviews of Cambodia and China. However, the notification record remains poor: 42 of the 157 members have never sent any notification and 70 members have not provided responses to the checklist, which is a questionnaire that facilitates review of national legislation.

The 2012-2013 WTO biennial technical assistance plan envisages regional training activities on market access issues, which include customs valuation. Two such activities were delivered in 2012, in the Republic of Korea in June (Asian region) and in Chile in August (Latin American region). The regional workshop planned for English-speaking Africa had to be postponed, but will take place in 2013. National training can also be provided on customs valuation. Four national activities were delivered in 2012. The first one took place in The Gambia and was delivered by the WTO Secretariat. The WTO and the World Customs Organization jointly organized three other events in Honduras, the Kyrgyz Republic and Peru.

Background on customs valuation

The value of a good plays a critical role in the calculation of import duties. Although the customs value is indispensable for the calculation of ad valorem duties, which are the most common type, it is often also required for the calculation of other duties (e.g. compound and mixed), as well as other border taxes. The WTO Agreement on Customs Valuation seeks to protect the value of tariff concessions by establishing a fair, uniform and neutral system for the valuation of goods for customs purposes, which precludes the use of arbitrary or fictitious values. The Committee on Customs Valuation manages the Agreement along with the Agreement on Preshipment Inspection.

Customs valuation
www.wto.org/customsvaluation

New notifications on preshipment inspections were received from Ecuador and Russia. Preshipment Inspection (PSI), a standing item on the agenda of the Committee, is the practice of employing private companies to check shipment details such as price, quantity and quality of goods ordered overseas. The Agreement on PSI recognizes that the principles of the GATT Agreement apply to such activities. The purpose is to safeguard national financial interests (prevention of capital flight and commercial fraud, as well as customs duty evasion, for instance) and to compensate for inadequacies in administrative infrastructures.

The Committee received a request for observer status from the International Chamber of Commerce (ICC). The ICC expressed the desire to cooperate with the Committee, particularly on problems that could arise from the eventual misuse of customs valuation databases to set minimum or reference prices. Members are currently considering the request.

Rules of origin

The Committee on Rules of Origin began the work of transposing draft, harmonized rules of origin into more recent versions of the Harmonized System for classifying traded goods as part of its technically complex and long-running discussions on the harmonization of non-preferential rules of origin. It also reviewed notifications by WTO members.

In two meetings in 2012, the Committee pursued its work on harmonizing non-preferential rules of origin. It completed the first steps of the work to transpose rules of origin that were initially negotiated for the 1996 version of the Harmonized System (HS) to later versions. Developed by the World Customs Organization, the system provides a common basis for classifying traded goods. The system was revised in 2002 and 2007 and the Committee reviewed the results of the harmonization work to correct them according to these revisions. The Secretariat is conducting the work in collaboration with the World Customs Organization and WTO members.

Rules of origin are important in implementing such trade policy instruments as anti-dumping and countervailing duties, origin marking and safeguard measures. However, with the growth of global value chains, it is becoming increasingly difficult to determine where a product comes from.

The committee also reviewed notifications by WTO members. In 2012, 11 new notifications under Article 5 and paragraph 4 of Annex II of the Agreement were received. They brought the total number of members having notified non-preferential rules of origin to 85 and the total number of members having notified preferential rules of origin to 127. The latter number reflects both notifications made to the Committee as well as to other bodies of the WTO.

Technical assistance on rules of origin was delivered in regional and national workshops, as well as in the context of the WTO's regional and advanced trade policy courses.

Background on rules of origin

Rules of origin are the criteria used to determine the country in which a product was made. They are used in the implementation of many trade measures, including trade statistics, the determination of customs duties, origin labelling, and the application of anti-dumping measures. The main objective of the Agreement on Rules of Origin is to harmonize the rules so that all WTO members use the same criteria to determine origin in their non-preferential trade. This work is conducted by the Committee on Rules of Origin in the WTO and the Technical Committee under the auspices of the World Customs Organization in Brussels.

Import licensing

During 2012, members submitted 74 notifications to the Committee on Import Licensing for review under various provisions of the Agreement. Four members submitted notifications for the first time under different articles of the Agreement. Currently, only 17 members have never submitted any notification.

Import licences are permits granted before a product is imported. The administrative procedures for obtaining the licences should be simple, neutral, equitable and transparent.

The Committee has provided a regular forum for the discussion of specific notifications submitted by members. At the two meetings held in 2012, 15 members submitted 17 notifications under Articles 1.4(a) and/or 8.2(b) covering publications and/or legislation on import licensing procedures, and seven members submitted 17 notifications under Article 5, which refers to the institution of licensing procedures or changes in these. In addition, 39 members made 40 notifications under Article 7.3, which relates to responses to the annual questionnaire on import licensing procedures.

The Committee also considered specific questions and answers concerning the import licensing systems notified/applied by some members and took note of the trade concerns regarding the import licensing regimes applied/notified. Amongst issued raised were Argentina's non-automatic licences and related measures on a range of imports that continued to cause concern among a number of delegations. Also discussed were India's licensing for boric acid and Indonesia's licensing for livestock, animal products, and fruit and vegetables.

Background on import licensing

The Agreement on Import Licensing Procedures establishes disciplines on members' import licensing systems, with the principal objective of ensuring that the procedures applied for granting import licences do not in themselves restrict trade. The Agreement says import licensing should be simple, transparent and predictable, and administered in a neutral and non-discriminatory way.

Safeguards

Notifications of new investigations rose during 2012 to 25 from 11 the year before. The Chair of the Safeguards Committee submitted a factual report on a request regarding Article 13.1 of the Agreement on Safeguards. It was the first use of this article, which deals with whether the procedural requirements of the Agreement have been complied with in connection with a safeguard measure.

At its two meetings in 2012, the Safeguards Committee reviewed notifications by WTO members of their safeguards rules and actions. The 25 notifications of new investigations made in 2012 were more than double the number of new investigations initiated in 2011. By contrast, the number of final measures taken during 2012 fell to six from 11 in 2011 (see Figure 5). Russia, which acceded to the WTO in 2012, notified that safeguard investigations were initiated for three products. These notifications were made on behalf of the Eurasian Economic Commission. By the end of 2012, the Committee had received and discussed notifications from five members regarding their new or revised domestic legislation and/or regulations on safeguards.

Figure 5: Summary of safeguard investigations by year (for all members)

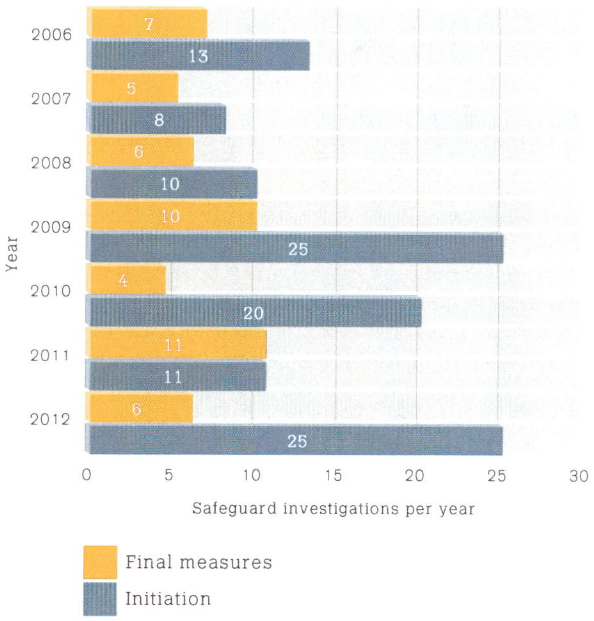

Import licensing
www.wto.org/importlicensing

Safeguards
www.wto.org/safeguards

At the October meeting, a new ten-delegation grouping called "Friends of Safeguards Procedures" expressed concern about "procedural, transparency, and due process issues" related to certain safeguard investigations. Speaking on behalf of the group of mainly developed countries, the United States said there has been an alarming increase in safeguard actions in recent years, and members must work together to deal with systemic concerns about safeguard proceedings.

With regard to Colombia's request presented on 3 May 2011 under Article 13.1(b) about Ecuador's safeguard measures on glass windshields, a factual report was submitted by the Chair of the Safeguards Committee to the Council on Trade in Goods in April 2012. Colombia has argued that Ecuador has committed clear violations, while Ecuador maintained that its measure was consistent with the Safeguards Agreement.

Background on safeguards

WTO members may take "safeguard" actions (temporarily restrict imports of a product) to protect a specific domestic industry from an increase in imports of any product that is causing, or threatening to cause, serious injury to the industry. In these circumstances, they have the right to restrict imports of the product from all sources (but not from a specific member or group of members). The Agreement on Safeguards provides detailed rules concerning the investigation that must be conducted and the application of safeguard measures.

Trade-related investment measures

At its two meetings in 2012, the Committee on Trade-Related Investment Measures (TRIMs) discussed six new investment measures taken by WTO members and continued debate on four measures previously raised in 2011. In addition, it reviewed compliance with members' notification obligations under the TRIMs Agreement.

Three new investment measures were placed on the agenda at the May 2012 meeting. The first, at the request of the European Union, Japan and the United States, concerned Argentina's informal "trade balancing" policy, whereby companies seeking to import products should agree to export goods of an equal or greater value, or to establish production facilities in Argentina. The second, at the request of the European Union and the United States, concerned certain Brazilian local content requirements in the telecommunications sector, and the third, raised at the request of the European Union and the United States, concerned certain Indian local production requirements for government procurement of electronic goods.

Another three new investment measures were raised at the October 2012 meeting. The first, raised by Australia and the European Union, concerned what they said were Brazilian tax advantages for domestically manufactured automotive vehicles. The second, raised by the United States, concerned certain Chinese investment measures relating to the steel sector and the third, raised by the European Union, concerned certain local content provisions in a Ukrainian draft law related to the electric power industry.

During the year, discussion continued on four issues previously raised in 2011, including India's mandatory local content requirements in project guidelines for the Jawaharlal Nehru national solar mission, Indonesia's local content requirements in the telecommunications sector and in the energy (mining, oil and gas) sector and Nigerian measures for the development of local content in its oil and gas industry.

The Committee took note of four new notifications under Article 6.2 of the TRIMs Agreement. Members who had not provided notifications to date were urged to do so promptly. Article 6.2 of the TRIMs Agreement requires members to notify the Committee of all publications in which TRIMs may be found, including those applied by regional and local governments and authorities within their territory. The United States indicated that it was looking forward to Russia's notification under Article 5.1 of the Agreement of its trade-related investment measures not in conformity with the Agreement, pursuant to Table 38 of the Working Party Report on Russia's accession.

Background on trade-related investment measures

The Agreement on Trade-Related Investment Measures (TRIMs) recognizes that certain investment measures can restrict and distort trade. It states that WTO members may not apply any measure that discriminates against foreign products or that leads to quantitative restrictions, both of which violate basic WTO principles. A list of prohibited TRIMs, such as local content requirements, is part of the Agreement. The TRIMs Committee monitors the operation and implementation of the Agreement and allows members the opportunity to consult on any relevant matters.

Information technology

Colombia and Montenegro joined the Information Technology Agreement (ITA) in 2012, taking membership to 75. Russia took a step closer to membership by presenting its draft ITA schedule. On 16 November 2012, Tajikistan's ITA schedule was also approved. Tajikistan will become a participant to the ITA upon the date of its accession to the WTO. The ITA celebrated its 15th anniversary with a two-day symposium that reviewed trade liberalization and the evolution of global trade in information and communications technology since 1996. The Committee continued work on non-tariff measures (NTMs), including the electromagnetic compatibility (EMC) and electromagnetic interference (EMI) pilot project, and agreed to include a review of product coverage as a regular agenda item.

During the year, ITA membership rose to 75 with the admission of Colombia and Montenegro, and Tajikistan said it would join on its accession to the WTO, which took effect in early 2013. Russia presented its draft ITA schedule together with the Secretariat's verification sheet and began work on addressing comments received from participants. Several delegations urged Russia to complete these procedures as soon as possible in order to become a full participant to the ITA at an early date.

Background on information technology

The Information Technology Agreement (ITA) was launched in December 1996 in Singapore as a plurilateral agreement. It requires participants to provide duty-free treatment to IT products, including computers, telecommunication equipment, semi-conductor manufacturing equipment, and software and scientific instruments. The Committee of the Participants on the Expansion of Trade in Information Technology Products (or the ITA Committee) oversees the Agreement.

Participants to the ITA represent around 97 per cent of world trade in information technology products. The ITA provides for participants to completely eliminate duties on IT products covered by the Agreement on a most-favoured nation (MFN) basis. Thus, the benefits of this plurilateral agreement are extended to all WTO members.

The Committee continued its deliberations on non-tariff measures (NTMs). It noted that the response to a survey on conformity assessment procedures for electromagnetic compatibility (EMC) and electromagnetic interference (EMI) was still slow. Two more participants provided answers over the year, taking the number of responses to-date to 28. However, this leaves 20 participants still to reply. The Committee urged those that have not yet given the information to do so as quickly as possible. In considering ways to advance and expand its work on NTMs other than EMC/EMI, the Committee also heard reports and updates by participants on their contributions to work on NTMs, including in other bodies of the WTO and informally.

Expanding product coverage

At the Committee meeting in November, the Republic of Korea reported some progress in technical discussions it hosted on expanding the current product coverage of the ITA. It said that the 17 participating members were moving towards more substantial discussions and that it planned to circulate a revised consolidated list of products proposed for inclusion. Delegates had agreed at the Committee's first meeting in May to make reviews of product expansion a regular agenda item. The European Union told the May meeting that it would no longer insist on a review of the ITA based on its proposal tabled in 2008, which linked ITA expansion with negotiations on non-tariff barriers.

Anniversary celebrations

The ITA marked its 15th anniversary with a two-day symposium on 14-15 May. The gathering was open to all WTO members and observers, the private sector, IT industry representatives, academic experts in IT technologies, international inter-governmental organizations, non-governmental organizations (NGOs) and journalists. It reviewed the evolution and liberalization of global trade in information and communication technology (ICT) products since 1996, and their impact, including on developing countries. It also looked at the latest developments in the ICT sector, the socio-economic benefits, including as an enabler of sustainable development, and the prospects for, and challenges to, the continued expansion of trade in ICT products. WTO Director-General Pascal Lamy told the meeting that the ITA was one of the most successful trade agreements ever.

In addition, the WTO published *15 Years of the Information Technology Agreement,* which charts the history of the Agreement and the effect it has had on the global trade in IT products. Details of the latest trends in IT trade and discussions on the future of the ITA make this publication a useful source of information for government officials and policy-makers as well as academics, students and all those involved in the IT sector.

State trading enterprises

In 2012, the Working Party on State Trading Enterprises reviewed 71 notifications and approved a recommendation to extend indefinitely the current frequency of notifications.

In an effort to reduce the notification burden on members and help improve compliance with their obligations, the Working Party on State Trading Enterprises adopted, in 2003, a recommendation to modify the frequency of notifications. According to this recommendation, new and full notifications are submitted every two years rather than every three years, with updating notifications in the intervening years. The recommendation for the new frequency took effect as of 2004 for a trial phase of four years, and this trial phase was extended in 2008 and 2010 until 30 June 2012. Following a series of consultations, members agreed at a formal meeting in June 2012 to extend the current frequency of notifications on an indefinite basis.

At its regular meeting in October 2012, the Working Party reviewed 59 new and full notifications and 12 updating notifications from 30 WTO members covering different review periods. For comparison purposes, in 2011 the Working Party reviewed 12 new and full notifications and seven updating notifications from eight members.

Background on state trading enterprises

State trading enterprises are defined as governmental or non-governmental enterprises, including marketing boards, which have been granted exclusive or special rights or privileges to deal with goods for export and/or import. They are required to act in a manner consistent with the WTO principle of non-discriminatory treatment. The Working Party on State Trading Enterprises reviews notifications by WTO members on their state trading activities.

Trade in civil aircraft

In 2012, the Trade in Civil Aircraft Committee held one meeting, where signatories continued to discuss their work to bring the annex to the Agreement relating to product coverage into line with the 2007 update of the Harmonized System, used for classifying goods for customs purposes.

During the year, Montenegro acceded to the Agreement, bringing the total number of signatories to 32, of which 20 are member states of the European Union.

Background on trade in civil aircraft

The Trade in Civil Aircraft Agreement aims to achieve maximum freedom of world trade in civil aircraft, parts and related equipment by eliminating tariffs, promoting fair and equal competitive opportunities for civil aircraft manufacturers, and regulating government support for civil aircraft development, production and marketing. The Committee on Trade in Civil Aircraft provides signatories with an opportunity to consult on any matters relating to the operation of the Agreement.

State trading enterprises
www.wto.org/statetrading

Trade in civil aircraft
www.wto.org/aircraft

Trade in services

In 2012, the Council for Trade in Services continued to focus on issues surrounding information and communication technologies (ICT), particularly e-commerce and international mobile roaming. Transparency was another issue that figured prominently on the agenda, with members discussing how compliance with the notification process might be improved. Jamaica became the latest member to ratify the General Agreement on Trade in Services (GATS) Fifth Protocol, covering trade in financial services.

Throughout 2012, the Council continued work on electronic commerce as mandated by the 2009 Ministerial Conference. This included, among other things, communications on trade-related ICT principles, mobile applications and cloud computing services as well as the e-commerce activities of small and medium-sized enterprises (SMEs). Members contributed with their experiences in these areas. The Council also addressed a proposal to organize a workshop focusing on the services aspects of electronic commerce. E-commerce will thus continue to figure prominently on the Council's agenda in 2013.

The Council carried on with dedicated discussions on international mobile roaming and its status under the GATS. Several members shared information on their national roaming markets, including at a symposium organized by Australia. Members also benefitted from the updates provided by a representative of the International Telecommunication Union (ITU) on its work on international mobile roaming.

In accordance with the GATS' transparency provisions, the Council received 46 notifications of new or revised measures deemed by the members concerned to significantly affect trade in sectors they had subjected to commitments. Another 16 notifications dealt with new economic integration agreements covering services trade, and a further one concerned recognition measures. For the first time, a WTO member made a notification about a measure taken by another member that the notifying member considered to affect the operation of the GATS.

The Council also resumed discussions on how compliance with the GATS' notification requirements might be improved in order to further enhance transparency. Deliberations were held against the backdrop of a Swiss communication on the issue and a WTO Secretariat note providing an updated statistical record of notifications. Consultations on this topic are scheduled to be held in early 2013.

Financial services

Following a request by Jamaica, which had completed its domestic ratification process, the Council re-opened the Fifth Protocol to the GATS. Jamaica accepted the Protocol on 16 October 2012, thus giving legal effect to the commitments on financial services it had undertaken as part of the extended negotiations on this sector concluded in December 1997.

The Committee on Trade in Financial Services, a standing body under the Council, continued its consideration of classification issues in financial services, based on inputs provided by WTO members.

As a follow-up to a previous discussion, the Committee organized a workshop on trade in financial services and development. Speakers came from academia, national governments and international organizations, including the International Monetary Fund, the Financial Stability Board and the United Nations Conference on Trade and Development (UNCTAD). The purpose of the workshop was to deepen discussion on the link between financial services trade and development initiated last year by the Committee, and to promote dialogue and information sharing among members on different regulatory, trade and policy aspects surrounding this issue. The Committee will continue exploring the relationship between trade in financial services and development, focusing on specific aspects.

Background on trade in services

The General Agreement on Trade in Services (GATS) defines trade in services as consisting of four types of transactions: mode 1 – cross-border supply (a supplier in one WTO member provides services to a consumer in another member's territory); mode 2 – consumption abroad (a consumer from one member consumes services in another member's territory); mode 3 – commercial presence (a foreign company provides services by establishing an operation in another member's territory); and mode 4 – presence of natural persons (individuals move to supply services in another member's territory). The Council for Trade in Services, which is open to all WTO members, oversees the operation of the GATS.

The Committee also considered a proposal by Ecuador to discuss the relationship between macro-prudential regulation and GATS disciplines. Macro-prudential regulation aims at reducing the risk and the macroeconomic cost of financial instability. Members agreed to hold a dedicated discussion on this issue in 2013.

Specific commitments

The Committee on Specific Commitments oversees and examines the implementation of GATS commitments and most-favoured nation (MFN) exemptions as well as the procedures for the modification of schedules of commitments. The Committee aims to improve the technical accuracy and coherence of WTO members' services commitments and the operation of the GATS. With this in view, it regularly discusses classification and scheduling issues and their implications for the scope and content of specific commitments.

With regard to classification, the sectors examined included computer and related services, telecommunications services, audiovisual services, environmental services, energy services, postal and courier services, distribution services and legal services. To facilitate the exchange of views, discussions took place in informal mode with input from the WTO Secretariat. Key contributions are reflected in informal, non-attributable summaries circulated under the Chair's responsibility.

At the request of delegations, the Committee also started reviewing the operation of the procedures for the modification of schedules of specific commitments. The Secretariat presented a factual report on the application of these procedures, and delegations shared their views and experiences. It was agreed that the exercise would not lead to a re-opening of the procedures.

Trade-related aspects of intellectual property rights (TRIPS)

The TRIPS Council continued its discussion on topics such as access to medicines for the poorest countries, promotion of transparency and least-developed countries' needs for assistance as part of its regular review of intellectual property (IP) matters. The Council also exchanged information on and debated a number of policy issues raised by individual countries, such as national innovation strategies and the role of IP in fostering market-based innovation.

Promoting transparency

Transparency of national intellectual property systems is a key principle of TRIPS. It reduces trade tensions and builds productive trading relationships in knowledge products and technology. In 2012, the Council gave further consideration to ways of improving the timeliness and completeness of notifications under the TRIPS Agreement and other relevant information flows. It took note of the material still required to complete the pending reviews of TRIPS implementing legislation of three members, initiated the review of the legislation of Maldives, and agreed on the arrangements for the review of the legislation of Russia.

TRIPS and public health

In 2003, members agreed on the "Paragraph 6" system of special compulsory licences for export, which gives poor countries additional flexibility under the TRIPS Agreement to gain access to affordable medicines. The system allows generic versions of patented medicines to be produced under compulsory licence (that is, without the consent of the patent holder) for export to countries that cannot manufacture the medicines themselves. The TRIPS Agreement originally only permitted compulsory licensing predominantly to serve the domestic market (unless remedying anti-competitive practices).

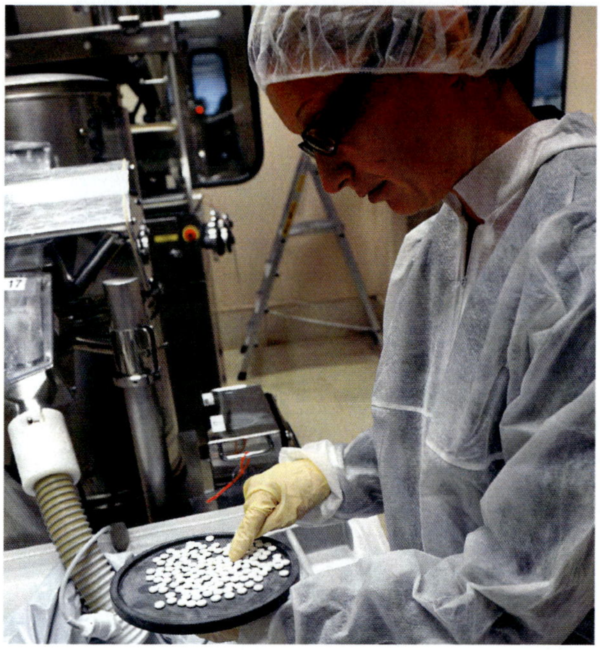

The new system changed this, first through a set of waivers and then through an amendment in 2005 creating a new kind of compulsory licence for the export of medicines. The Council held its annual review of the functioning of the system at its November meeting. Three more countries accepted the amendment, which will come into force when two-thirds of members have accepted it. As of 31 December, 44 countries had done so (counting the European Union as one).

Issues relating to TRIPS and public health were addressed in many of the Secretariat's technical cooperation activities aimed at assisting members to understand the rights and obligations, including the available options, which flow from the TRIPS Agreement and relevant decisions of WTO bodies. For example, 27 developing-country officials took part in the eighth workshop on the TRIPS Agreement and Public Health in October designed to help their countries assess the implications of flexibilities for pharmaceuticals in the TRIPS Agreement and, when needed, to make effective use of such flexibilities. The workshop was organized by the Secretariat in close collaboration with the World Health Organization (WHO) and the World Intellectual

Background on trade-related aspects of intellectual property rights

Intellectual property rights have become an important element in international trade and a key part of the debate over economic development and broader public policy questions, such as public health and the environment. The Agreement on Trade-Related Aspects of Intellectual Property Rights (TRIPS) is the most comprehensive international treaty governing the protection, administration and enforcement of intellectual property rights. The Council for TRIPS, a body open to all WTO members, administers the TRIPS Agreement, provides a forum for debate on policy issues relating to TRIPS and reviews the intellectual property legislation of individual members.

Property Organization (WIPO) as part of well-established trilateral cooperation on building capacity on issues arising when intellectual property rights and public health are linked. A particular emphasis was laid on pricing and procurement policies as a key element in securing access to medicines, and experts from major procurement initiatives shared their practical experiences with participants. Among the other issues covered were licensing policies adopted by the private sector, the safety, efficacy and quality of medicines, the role of competition policy, and intellectual property rights provisions in regional or bilateral free trade agreements, and their link with public health.

Plants, animals, biodiversity and traditional knowledge

The Council continued to address a cluster of subjects related to biotechnology, biodiversity, genetic resources and traditional knowledge, as instructed by the 2005 Hong Kong Ministerial Declaration. These discussions cover the review of the TRIPS provisions dealing with the patentability of plant and animal inventions and the protection of plant varieties, the relationship between the TRIPS Agreement and the Convention on Biological Diversity (CBD), and the protection of traditional knowledge and folklore.

Technical cooperation and capacity building, and LDC general transition period

The Council reviewed the available technical cooperation in the area of intellectual property on the basis of information it received from developed countries, other intergovernmental organizations and the WTO Secretariat. The 2005 decision that extended to 1 July 2013 the transition period for least-developed countries (LDCs) to apply their TRIPS obligations also requested them to identify their priority assistance needs so that these could be effectively addressed. In 2012, Mali reported in detail on its needs, taking the number of countries to report by the end of the year to seven. Following the decision of the Eighth Ministerial Conference to invite the Council to consider requests from LDC members for a further extension of the transition period, Haiti on behalf of the LDC group presented such a request in November.

As part of an intensifying coordination process, the Secretariat again organized, at the request of the LDC group and with the support of the Swedish Government, a three-day symposium with officials from LDCs, donor countries and intergovernmental organizations to promote dialogue and coordination on assessing and responding to priority assistance needs.

Other issues

No new proposals emerged from the reviews, mandated under the TRIPS Agreement, of the Agreement as a whole (the "71.1 review") and of the application of the provisions on geographical indications (the "24.2 review").

The Council's work on the incentives for technology transfer to LDCs and on "non-violation and situation complaints" is described on page 27.

Issues raised by individual members

The Council considered a number of policy issues raised by individual members. At the request of the Dominican Republic, it continued its discussion from the previous year on Australia's proposed tobacco plain-packaging legislation. While some delegations raised concerns about its compatibility with the TRIPS Agreement, some others asserted countries' rights to use flexibilities in the Agreement for public health purposes, including tobacco control.

Counterfeiting

At the request of Australia, Canada, the European Union, Japan, the Republic of Korea, Mexico, New Zealand, Singapore, Switzerland and the United States, the Council again discussed trends relating to the enforcement of intellectual property rights. These members, participants to the Anti-Counterfeiting Trade Agreement (ACTA), said their main aim was to strengthen enforcement against proliferation of counterfeit goods. They stressed that ACTA does not target generic medicines, and nor would it interfere with legitimate access to the Internet. However, others expressed concerns that the provisions of ACTA go beyond the TRIPS provisions. Some LDCs said that despite what ACTA members said they were worried that the agreement could limit LDC access to generic medicines. Some developed and advanced developing countries saw counterfeiting and piracy as one of the most serious problems to be discussed by the Council because of the economic loss and because products can be dangerously sub-standard. However, some developing countries said intellectual property rights violations should not be confused with sub-standard products. They argued that the discussion should take place in agencies such as the World Customs Organization (WCO), because customs officers are responsible for tackling internationally traded counterfeit goods, and the WHO, whose work includes tackling sub-standard medicines.

Innovation

Innovation is essential for raising living standards, and intellectual property has an important role to play provided an appropriate balance is struck and governments act to help smaller players, the Council heard at its meeting in November. The two-hour exchange of information and ideas, put on the agenda by Brazil and the United States, was the first time the Council had discussed innovation. Members agreed that the topic, which is broader than the usual discussions in the TRIPS Council, is important and most accepted that a balanced intellectual property system has a role to play in spurring innovation, a term which is not defined in the TRIPS Agreement. However, speakers differed in their emphasis. Some developing countries argued that the system gives advantages to richer countries and larger corporations, and stressed the need to use flexibilities.

Brazil and the United States also briefed the Council on the on-going negotiations at WIPO on limitations and exceptions for the benefit of visually impaired persons.

Trade and environment

In 2012, the Committee on Trade and Environment (CTE) received information on and debated a range of environmental policy developments, from climate change mitigation and fisheries to environmental technology dissemination. The WTO Secretariat issued the 2009 Environmental Database in electronic format and held the first advanced course on trade and the environment.

Climate change mitigation measures

Members discussed two national measures aimed at mitigating greenhouse gas emissions, the Republic of Korea's emission trading scheme and Norway's carbon tax. Some members supported these initiatives, but others raised a number of issues, including the extent to which such measures contribute to sustainable development, the risk that they might affect developing countries' trade and the appropriateness of the WTO as a forum to discuss climate change. Some members also stressed the need to perform impact assessments before implementing carbon emission reduction schemes, so as to avoid disguised restrictions to trade. The importance of addressing global environmental problems multilaterally rather than through unilateral measures was also emphasized.

Product carbon footprint and labelling schemes continue to be a concern for many developing countries, particularly with respect to the development of international standards. Discussions highlighted the complexity of the methodologies used and the importance of transparency and inclusiveness in the standard-setting process. Several developing countries said that such schemes should take into account developing country needs and difficulties to avoid creating unnecessary market barriers.

At the United Nations Framework Convention on Climate Change (UNFCCC) conference in Doha in December, the WTO Secretariat co-organized with the International Monetary Fund (IMF) a side event on carbon policies. The event gathered together key stakeholders and policy-makers, and discussed the design, trade impact and environmental effectiveness of carbon policies.

Background on trade and environment

Sustainable development and protection and preservation of the environment are fundamental goals of the WTO. The Committee on Trade and Environment is responsible for examining the relationship between trade and the environment.

Fisheries

The European Union presented a regulation on combating illegal, unreported and unregulated (IUU) fishing. While members welcomed this initiative, some concerns were also raised, including the importance of avoiding barriers to trade affecting products from developing countries, the need to address this global problem multilaterally and the difficulty of defining illegal fishing. Several members also stressed the importance of providing technical assistance to developing countries in order to facilitate implementation. A representative of the Organisation for Economic Co-operation and Development (OECD) briefed the CTE on a recent meeting of the OECD Committee for Fisheries.

Environmental technologies

Russia and Australia introduced Annex C of the APEC 2012 Leaders' Declaration of September 2012 – Asia-Pacific Economic Co-operation (APEC) List of Environmental Goods – which endorses reductions of applied tariff rates to 5 per cent or less on 54 environmental goods by the end of 2015. While many members acknowledged APEC's achievement, several others cautioned against the transposition of the APEC list to the WTO negotiations on the opening of markets in environmental goods and services.

The CTE held a workshop on environmental technology dissemination (12 November 2012), where experts from members, international organizations, academia and the private sector explored the main developments in environmental technologies. They discussed the economic, technological and policy factors that can either promote or hamper the diffusion of environmental technology, including the absorptive capacity in developing countries, and the role of intellectual property rights for the generation, dissemination and transfer of technology. Particular attention was given to carbon capture and storage (CCS) technologies, low emission technologies, and waste management and water treatment technologies.

Green economy

During the Rio+20 United Nations Conference on Sustainable Development (20-22 June), the WTO Secretariat organized a high-level side event (20 June), entitled "Multilateral Cooperation Towards Inclusive Green Growth", with the participation of the WTO Director-General, Peter Poschen, Director of the Job Creation and Enterprise Development Department of the International Labour Organization (ILO), Han Seung-soo, Board Chair of the Global Green Growth Institute in Seoul, Republic of Korea, Achim Steiner, Executive Director of the United Nations Environment Programme (UNEP) and with Josette Sheeran, Vice Chair of the World Economic Forum (WEF), as moderator. The event explored ways to ensure that multilateral cooperation supports countries' efforts to promote inclusive green growth and sustainable development.

A UNEP representative briefed the CTE on its activities aimed at implementing the Rio+20 call for the development of green economy policies. A representative of the United Nations Conference on Trade and Development (UNCTAD) highlighted in the CTE the potential of developing countries and economies in transition to strengthen the capacity and competitiveness of green sectors and enhance exports of green goods and services in world markets.

Transparency

In order to enhance the transparency of environmental measures and requirements, the WTO Secretariat circulated the 2009 Environmental Database, which compiles the environment-related measures notified in 2009 under all WTO agreements, as well as the environment-related measures and programmes mentioned in Trade Policy Reviews released in 2009. The database is now being circulated in two parts: a brief description of the environment-related notifications and Trade Policy Reviews; and an electronic table providing the underlying data used for analysis to facilitate usage of information.

Technical assistance

In addition to national workshops organized in Angola (28-29 March) and Paraguay (5-6 November), the WTO Secretariat held the first Advanced Course on Trade and Environment (16-27 April) at WTO headquarters in Geneva. The two-week course benefited from the participation of 26 government officials from least-developed countries, developing countries and economies in transition. The main objective was to consolidate participants' knowledge of trade and environmental issues and facilitate their participation in the work of the CTE and the environment chapter of the Doha Development Agenda negotiations. A large spectrum of environment-related trade topics, such as environmental requirements and market access, WTO disputes involving environmental issues, environmental technologies, climate change and green economy, were discussed through lectures, case studies and a round table, with contributions from experts from the WTO, other international organizations and non-governmental organizations. The course was also an opportunity for participants to exchange national experiences and enhance dialogue between trade and environment officials.

Regional trade agreements

In 2012, the WTO received 37 new notifications, a considerable increase over the 25 received in 2011. The notifications involved 23 regional trade agreements (RTAs). Eight of the RTAs were between developed partners, with another eight involving developed and developing partners. The remaining seven were between developing country partners. The Americas was the region with the highest number of notifications – ten, followed by the Commonwealth of Independent States (CIS) region with eight.

Of the 546 RTA notifications received by the WTO as of 31 December 2012, 354 were in force (see Figure 5). RTAs include free trade agreements and customs unions. Under WTO rules, the goods and services aspects of RTAs have to be notified separately, so they are counted separately. However, putting the two together, the 546 notifications involve 414 individual RTAs, of which 235 are currently in force.

A key feature of modern RTAs is that they are broadening and, in many cases, deepening their coverage. While some agreements are limited to reducing barriers to trade in goods, the agreements are becoming increasingly more comprehensive, with provisions on market opening in services and in other areas, such as investment, competition policy, trade facilitation, government procurement, intellectual property, electronic commerce and, in some cases, labour and the environment.

Most agreements are bilateral, giving rise to an increasingly complex regime of different trade regulations. Critics argue that these overlapping regional trade regimes make international trade more complex and undermine WTO non-discrimination principles. However, proponents of RTAs say they can lay the groundwork for future multilateral trade rules. The consolidation of existing RTAs, for instance, through accession by non-parties can also reduce the degree of discrimination they cause.

Of the 23 individual RTAs notified to the WTO in 2012 (counting goods and services components as one), 14 included both components. The trend towards agreements between developing and developed trading partners appears to have been maintained. The number of agreements between developed partners rose slightly compared to previous years. Countries from the Americas region were involved in ten RTAs, and the rest involved members in the Commonwealth of Independent States (CIS) region (eight agreements), the Asia Pacific (five), Europe (four) and Africa (two agreements). Six of the agreements covered members from two different regions.

Monitoring RTAs

All RTAs, regardless of whether they are notified under Article XXIV of the General Agreement on Tariffs and Trade (GATT) 1994, the Enabling Clause between developing countries (for trade in goods), or the General Agreement on Trade in Services (GATS) Article V (for trade in services), are subject to the provisions and procedures of the Transparency Mechanism for Regional Trade Agreements. Established by a decision of the General Council in December 2006, and applied provisionally from 2007, the mechanism provides specific guidelines on when a new RTA should be notified to the WTO Secretariat and the related information and data to be provided. It also requires the Secretariat to prepare a factual presentation on each RTA, and for each RTA to be reviewed by members.

Agreements notified under Article XXIV of the GATT 1994 and Article V of the GATS are considered by the Committee on Regional Trade Agreements (CRTA), while agreements notified under the Enabling Clause are considered by a dedicated session of the Committee on Trade and Development (CTD). The General Council decision requires WTO members to inform the WTO Secretariat in the event of any subsequent changes to a notified agreement and to provide a report once an agreement is fully implemented. In the interests of transparency, WTO members are also encouraged to inform the Secretariat of any agreements being negotiated or those that have been signed but are not yet in force ("early announcements").

Notified agreements already in force are considered by the CRTA or by the CTD, normally within a year of the date of notification. The consideration is based on a "factual presentation" prepared by the Secretariat on the basis of information and data provided by the parties to the agreement. The factual presentation describes the main provisions of the agreement and the degree of trade liberalization to be achieved between the parties during its implementation period.

Background on regional trade agreements

The Committee on Regional Trade Agreements (CRTA) is responsible for monitoring all regional trade agreements (RTAs) notified to the WTO, except those notified under special provisions for agreements between developing countries (the Enabling Clause), which are considered by the Committee on Trade and Development. The CRTA's two principal duties are to examine individual RTAs and to consider their systemic implications for the multilateral trading system and the relationship between them. The overall number of RTAs in force has been increasing steadily; all WTO members except Mongolia are members of one or more (some belonging to as many as 30), creating what has been described as a tangled "spaghetti bowl" of overlapping trade regulations.

In 2012, the CRTA held four meetings and considered 20 notifications of RTAs, counting goods and services separately (or 13 RTAs counting goods and services notifications together), compared with 20 in 2011 and 28 in 2010.

The Transparency Mechanism also requires the WTO Secretariat to prepare "factual abstracts" on RTAs examined by the CRTA prior to the 2006 General Council decision. By the end of 2012, 75 factual abstracts had been prepared in consultation with the relevant RTA parties and posted on the RTA database.

In addition, three "early announcements" were received from members in 2012, two for RTAs under negotiation and one for newly signed RTAs not yet in force. As of December 2012, the WTO had received 78 "early announcements", 30 involving RTAs that had been signed but were not yet in force and 48 involving RTAs under negotiation. Forty-two of these early announcements have subsequently been notified following entry into force of the agreements.

As called for by the General Council decision on transparency, all the information on RTAs notified to the WTO is contained in a publicly accessible RTA database, which can be consulted at http://rtais.wto.org. The database, which became available to the public in January 2009, contains textual information on all RTAs notified to the WTO, including links to the official texts and annexes of each agreement as well as information on the examination or consideration process in the WTO. For those RTAs that have already been the subject of a factual presentation, the database also contains the relevant trade and tariff data.

For the Transparency Mechanism to be adopted on a permanent basis, WTO members need to review, and if necessary, modify it as part of the overall results of the Doha Round. Members are also required to review the legal relationship between the mechanism and relevant WTO provisions on RTAs. In December 2010, members decided to commence the review (see Negotiating Group on Rules on page 31).

For information on preferential trade arrangements (PTAs), see page 96.

Table 2: Regional trade agreements considered in 2012

Turkey – Chile (goods)	EFTA states – Serbia (goods)
Hong Kong, China – New Zealand (goods and services)	European Union – Egypt (goods)
Colombia – Mexico (goods and services)	European Union – South Africa (goods)
European Union – Republic of Korea (goods and services)	Turkey – Jordan (goods)
Peru – Republic of Korea (goods and services)	Peru – Chile (goods and services)
Canada – Colombia (goods and services)	New Zealand – Malaysia (goods and services)
EFTA states – Albania (goods)	

Note: The table refers to 13 individual agreements, of which seven covered both goods and services and six covered only goods.

Figure 6: All RTAs notified to the GATT/WTO (1949 to 2012) by year of entry into force

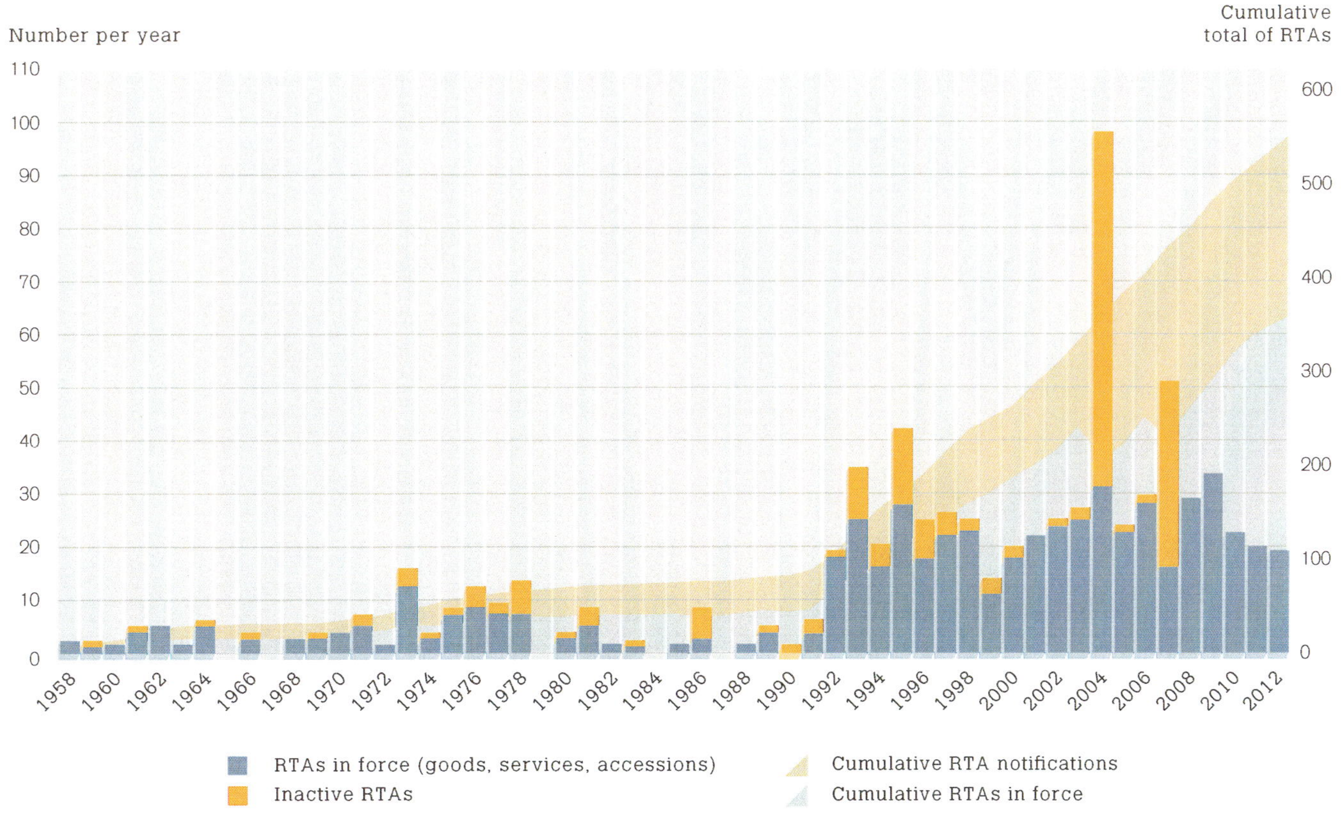

Regional trade agreements
www.wto.org/rta

Trade Policy Reviews

During 2012, the Trade Policy Review Body (TPRB) reviewed 26 WTO members: Bangladesh, Burundi, China, Colombia, Côte d'Ivoire, Guinea-Bissau, Iceland, Israel, Kenya, the Republic of Korea, the State of Kuwait, Nepal, Nicaragua, Norway, the Philippines, Rwanda, the Kingdom of Saudi Arabia, Singapore, Tanzania, Togo, Trinidad and Tobago, Turkey, the United Arab Emirates, Uganda, the United States and Uruguay (see map on page 64). The country-specific reports and the Chair's concluding remarks made at the TPRB meetings are available on the WTO website. It also began implementing the recommendations of the fourth appraisal of the Trade Policy Review Mechanism (TPRM).

Follow-up to the fourth appraisal of the TPRM

The Review Body began implementing the results of the fourth appraisal of the TPRM on a provisional basis in 2012. The appraisal, undertaken in 2011, is required under Annex 3 of the Marrakesh Agreement establishing the TPRM. Among other things, the appraisal led to three WTO members (the Philippines, Singapore and Norway) volunteering to apply alternative timelines for the question and answer process, which produced a more timely distribution of written answers ahead of the TPRB meetings.

Improvements in the organization and structure of TPRB meetings resulted in these meetings being more interactive and the discussion more fruitful. Follow-up activities to the reviews of those developing countries held every six years, especially least-developed countries (LDCs), were organized for four members under review, and digital audio files (podcasting) were introduced on a pilot basis. The fifth appraisal of the TPRM will be prepared in 2013 for the WTO's Ninth Ministerial Conference, which will take place in December.

Background on Trade Policy Reviews

The objective of the Trade Policy Review Mechanism is to encourage all WTO members to adhere to WTO rules, disciplines and commitments, and thus to contribute to the smoother functioning of the multilateral trading system. Through its regular Trade Policy Reviews, the mechanism enables WTO members to examine collectively the trade policies and practices of individual members in all areas covered by WTO agreements. Reviews are carried out by the Trade Policy Review Body, a full-membership body of equal ranking to the General Council and the Dispute Settlement Body.

Frequency of reviews

Under the TPRM, the four largest trading entities (currently the European Union, the United States, China and Japan) are reviewed every two years. The next 16 largest trading partners undergo reviews every four years and the remaining members every six years, with a longer interval envisaged for LDCs. These intervals can be extended by up to six months. Reviews take place against the background of members' wider economic and developmental needs, policies and objectives as well as the external trading environment. They are not intended to serve as a basis for the enforcement of obligations, for dispute settlement procedures, or to impose new policy commitments.

By the end of 2012, 364 reviews had been conducted, covering 145 of the 157 WTO members. The United States had been reviewed 11 times, Japan and the European Union ten times, Canada nine times, Australia, Hong Kong (China), the Republic of Korea, Norway, Singapore and Thailand six times, six members (Brazil, India, Indonesia, Malaysia, Switzerland and Turkey) five times, 15 members four times and 31 members three times.

Over the past few years, greater focus has been placed on reviews of LDCs. By the end of 2012, reviews had covered 31 of the 33 LDCs that are WTO members. TPRs of LDCs have helped to enhance understanding in these countries of WTO agreements, enabling better compliance and integration into the multilateral trading system. In some cases, better interaction between government agencies has been facilitated by the reviews. The reports' wide coverage of policies also enables members to identify any shortcomings in policy and specific areas where further technical assistance may be required.

Cost-saving

Informal consultations took place during the year on possible ways in which the documentation costs of the TPRB can be reduced. Based on the results of those consultations, some positive steps have been taken. The cost-saving improvements were mainly in the area of distribution of documents (TPR reports, minutes, questions and answers, etc), which are now only distributed electronically.

Transparency

Documents distributed for reviews are made available in electronic format to all members. The summary observations of the WTO Secretariat report, the concluding remarks by the Chair and the full reports by the member under review and the WTO Secretariat are available immediately on the WTO website. Printed versions of Trade Policy Reviews are also available for sale. Press briefings are occasionally held by the Chair, senior WTO Secretariat staff and/or the member under review.

Programme for 2013

The programme for 2013 includes 18 review meetings of 23 members (counting the European Union as one), including four LDCs and Japan and the European Union (which will be reviewed for the 11th time). However, in view of the difficulty of scheduling TPRB meetings in December 2013 (due to the WTO Ministerial Conference), it has been agreed that the TPRs of Mongolia and Tonga will take place in early 2014.

The Trade Policy Review (TPR) of the United States was the 20th TPR undertaken by the WTO in 2012.

Trade Policy Reviews in 2012

The WTO conducted 20 Trade Policy Reviews in 2012 to examine the trade policies and practices of 26 WTO members. The dates of the reviews and the countries covered are shown on the map. Further information, including the Chair's concluding remarks for each review, can be found on the WTO website: www.wto.org/tpr.

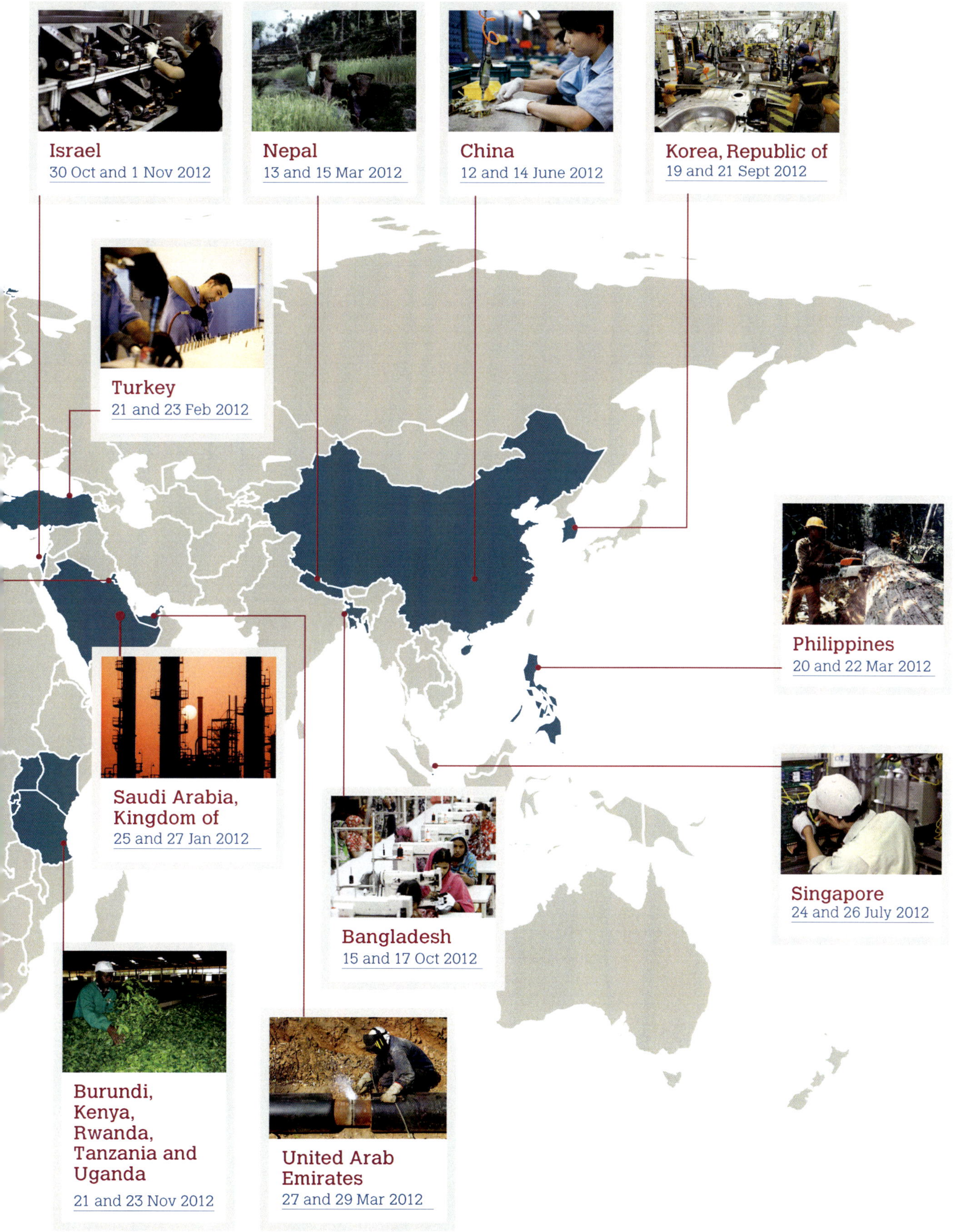
Israel
30 Oct and 1 Nov 2012
Nepal
13 and 15 Mar 2012
China
12 and 14 June 2012
Korea, Republic of
19 and 21 Sept 2012
Turkey
21 and 23 Feb 2012
Philippines
20 and 22 Mar 2012
Saudi Arabia, Kingdom of
25 and 27 Jan 2012
Singapore
24 and 26 July 2012
Bangladesh
15 and 17 Oct 2012
Burundi, Kenya, Rwanda, Tanzania and Uganda
21 and 23 Nov 2012
United Arab Emirates
27 and 29 Mar 2012

Trade monitoring reports

Countries generally resisted domestic pressures to erect trade barriers during 2012, although some of them put in place new trade-restrictive measures. Economic uncertainties and high levels of unemployment continued to feed domestic protectionist pressures. The global economy encountered increasingly strong headwinds during 2012 that hampered world trade and output growth. The WTO Secretariat revised downward its forecast for world trade growth in 2012 to 2.5 per cent from its forecast of 3.7 per cent early in the year.

The reports on global trade developments prepared by the WTO Secretariat during 2012 showed that WTO members and observers had by and large continued to resist domestic protectionist pressures and kept markets open overall. However, they also warned of potential dangers in the near future because of uncertainties in the global economy, persistently high levels of unemployment, and increasing trade tensions. The reports showed a slight declining trend in the imposition of new trade restrictions, in particular in the second half of the year. During this period, there were more trade facilitating measures than restricting ones.

Two of the reports, covering trade and investment measures taken by the Group of 20 (G20) leading developed and developing economies, were prepared jointly with the secretariats of the Organisation for Economic Co-operation and Development (OECD) and the United Nations Conference on Trade and Development (UNCTAD). The other two covered trade measures taken by WTO members and observers, and were discussed at meetings of the Trade Policy Review Body (TPRB).

The global crisis and the WTO's trade monitoring exercise underline the importance of increased transparency for the smooth functioning of the multilateral trading system. The WTO's Eighth Ministerial Conference held in December 2011 called on the TPRB to continue discussing the strengthening of the trade monitoring exercise. Following consultations held in the TPRB and suggestions made by members, some changes were introduced in the structure and coverage of the WTO reports.

Background on trade monitoring reports

In early 2009, the WTO began regular monitoring of global trade developments, covering all trade and trade-related measures implemented by WTO members and observers. Initially launched in the context of the global financial and economic crisis, the trade monitoring exercise has become a regular function in the WTO that further strengthens the transparency aims of the Trade Policy Review Mechanism by providing comprehensive information on recent trade policy changes. The continuation and strengthening of the trade monitoring exercise was confirmed by Ministers at the WTO's Eighth Ministerial Conference in December 2011. The trade monitoring is overseen by the Trade Policy Review Body, which also conducts detailed reviews of members individually (see page 62).

The Director-General's "Annual Report on the Overview of Developments in the International Trading Environment" was discussed at the TPRB meeting on 17 December 2012. At the meeting, the Director-General noted that, on the whole, most governments continued to resist domestic pressures to erect new trade barriers, although some government did put in place new restrictions which were adding to the measures implemented over the past four years, and to the stock of restrictions and distortions that have existed for a long time. He also noted that the world economy was still surrounded by many uncertainties and important global risks. The temptation to find easy solutions by closing down borders was always there, even if all knew that these measures would only aggravate the problems.

The Director-General called for a renewed firm commitment to revitalize the multilateral trading system which can restore economic certainty at a time when it was badly needed.

Transparency and surveillance

Transparency and surveillance of national trade policies are vital components of the multilateral trading system. The strengthened surveillance provided by the regular monitoring of trade and trade-related measures during the crisis has not only enhanced transparency but also helped governments faced with scrutiny by their peers to resist domestic protectionist pressures. It has thereby increased trust in the multilateral trading system.

Members and observer governments recognized the role played by the WTO in helping to mitigate the impact of the global crisis and in providing increased transparency on trade policy developments. At various summit meetings, in particular at G20 summits, world leaders welcomed the role played by the WTO.

Reports on notification activities of most WTO committees and councils show that significant work took place during the year aimed at improving the timeliness and completeness of notifications through an improvement and simplification of procedures. However, progress is still slow and compliance with formal notification obligations could be further improved.

Monitoring summary for 2012

The global economy has encountered increasingly strong headwinds over the second half of 2012 that have set back world trade and output growth. The outlook is worse than at the time of the previous report in June 2012 due, among other things, to budget developments and the persistent debt crises in some major economies.

Output and employment trends in many countries have continued to be negative, despite the many measures implemented to contain the slowdown in economic growth. The forecast for world trade growth in 2012 was revised to 2.5 per cent down from the 3.7 per cent forecast in April 2012. Trade growth in 2013 is now expected to be at 4.5 per cent, still below the long-term annual average of 5.4 per cent for the last 20 years.

The trade monitoring exercise and the Trade Policy Reviews for individual countries undertaken in 2012 show that, on the whole, governments have continued to resist domestic pressures to erect trade barriers, although some of them have put in place trade-restrictive measures. There has been a slowdown in the imposition of new trade-restrictive measures over the review period compared with last year. This time, 51 per cent of the total number of recorded measures can be considered as facilitating trade.

The new restrictive measures continue to add to the stock of old trade restrictions and distortions. Governments need to redouble their efforts to promptly address this situation and to advance trade opening as a way to counter slowing global economic growth. Trade restrictions and inward-looking policies only aggravate global problems and risk generating tit-for-tat reactions. The difficulties and concerns generated by the persistence of the global economic crisis, with its many facets, are fuelling the political and economic pressures put on governments to raise trade barriers. This is not the time to succumb to these pressures.

Measures to facilitate trade

During the review period, some countries have adopted measures to facilitate trade. Around three-quarters of the 162 trade facilitating measures recorded represent either a decrease or elimination of import tariffs. Some of these measures were taken on a temporary basis. The second most important type of facilitating measure was the streamlining of customs procedures. A number of measures were also aimed at facilitating exports.

Other trade measures

During the same period, 164 other trade and trade-related measures were recorded, out of which 132 were applied on imports. The main measures were tariff increases and new customs procedures. On exports, 32 measures were applied, comprising mainly restrictions or bans on some food products and raw materials.

Regarding trade remedy trends, anti-dumping activity overall is on the rise, due to a significant increase in new investigations. It would seem that the declining trend in anti-dumping initiations, which started in 2009, could be reversed in 2012. As far as countervailing and safeguard initiations are concerned, there have not been significant changes in patterns.

Members are increasing their notifications of sanitary and phytosanitary (SPS) measures and technical barriers to trade (TBT) measures. This may be a reflection of more active adoption of new measures for a variety of reasons, but also more systematic efforts by members to notify them. The discussion of specific trade concerns related to SPS and TBT measures provides members with an opportunity to address their differences in a multilateral framework.

Developments concerning trade in services were reported for several members. Most of the new measures can be considered as opening the services sector to foreign participation.

A few governments put in place new general economic support measures. The regular monitoring of government-support measures continues to be a challenge because of difficulties in obtaining relevant information.

The evaluation of agricultural support as well as any comparison across members or regions is difficult due to differences in methodologies used in notifications to the WTO as well as delays in notifications from many members. Based on available notifications, domestic support levels have been following an upward trend during the last decade. However, the general trend appears to be that support notified under the "Green Box" (domestic support for agriculture that is allowed without limits because it does not distort trade, or at most causes minimal distortion) is increasing while, for developed countries, support under the other "boxes" has been decreasing (triggered by higher international prices and, in some cases, domestic reforms).

For some developing countries, support under the "Amber Box" (domestic support for agriculture that is considered to distort trade and therefore subject to reduction commitments) and Article 6.2 (i.e. some development programmes in developing countries) has been increasing. In absolute terms, the levels of support still remain far higher in developed countries. The OECD data confirm that structural reforms have been taking place in some developed countries as they move away from market price support towards, according to the OECD, less trade-distorting support. On the other hand, OECD and WTO data show that at least in the years up to 2010, the trend in market price support in some OECD countries and some developing countries has been increasing despite higher world prices.

Conclusions

The world needs a renewed and stronger commitment from all governments to revitalize the multilateral trading system and restore economic certainty at a time when it is badly needed. The policy determination to resist inward-looking policies seems to be faltering in some countries, just when the world economy needs more trade to stave off recession. Due to the rapidly changing patterns of world trade, restrictions on imports will inevitably be felt in reduced export competitiveness. The last thing the world economy needs is indulgence in trade-restrictive practices. In this context, even if it is clear that the goal of achieving a Doha Development package encompassing all 20 topics is out of reach in the short term, the possibility still exists of advancing in smaller steps. This possibility should not be lost.

Trade monitoring reports
www.wto.org/trademonitoring

Trade, debt and finance

In 2012, the trade and finance agenda moved forward, in line with the deep interest of the international community in this matter. For example, the WTO Working Group on Trade, Debt and Finance continued its examination of the relationship between exchange rates and trade by holding a high-level seminar in March involving key policy-makers and academics.

Lack of trade finance impairs the ability of countries to trade. With the support of WTO members, Director-General Pascal Lamy has been a driving force behind a number of initiatives over the years aimed at closing some of the structural gaps in trade finance markets.

Director-General Lamy has been working in particular with the multilateral development banks (the European Bank for Reconstruction and Development, the Asian Development Bank, the International Finance Corporation, the Inter-American Development Bank, the Islamic Development Bank and the African Development Bank) to boost the global network of trade finance facilitation programmes that help to reduce the risk of financing trade in developing countries. These programmes have expanded considerably during the Director-General's tenure.

In line with the priorities set out at the G-20 meetings in Seoul and Cannes in 2012, the Board of Directors and senior management of the African Development Bank agreed at the beginning of 2013 to start a trade finance programme for African traders, helping to close gaps in the global support network. As a result of these global programmes, the international community is able to support billions of trade transactions by small and medium-sized enterprises (SMEs) in poor countries, which would not have necessarily received support from private markets.

Background on trade, debt and finance

WTO ministers decided in Doha in 2001 to establish a Working Group on Trade, Debt and Finance to look at how the WTO could contribute to finding a durable solution to the external debt problems of many developing countries and to avoid having WTO members' trade opportunities undercut by financial instabilities. In this framework, the Working Group has been focusing its attention on a range of financial issues with an impact on trade, including the provision of trade finance, and more recently, the relationship between exchange rates and trade.

The Director-General continued in 2012 his dialogue with the Basel Committee on Banking Supervision on achieving fair prudential regulation for the trade finance industry. In parallel with this, he sought the support of the International Chamber of Commerce, which collected data on millions of trade finance transactions. These data established that the average default rate on short-term trade finance was a mere 0.2 per cent. Accordingly, the Basel Committee took a number of positive steps, reducing prudential cost for the industry (see below).

Working Group on Trade, Debt and Finance

The Working Group on Trade, Debt and Finance's main focus at its three meetings in 2012 was to improve understanding of the links between exchange rates and trade, in particular the economic impact of exchange rates on trade. To deal with the different dimensions of the topic, the Working Group held a two-day seminar in March, with the participation of the private sector, governments, international agencies and academia. In an introductory statement, Director-General Pascal Lamy said that the international monetary system must facilitate trade. "The international community needs to make headway on the issue of reform of the international monetary system. Unilateral attempts to change or retain the status quo will not work," he declared.

The Working Group also asked the WTO Secretariat for an update on the recent economic literature on the subject. Brazil introduced a submission looking at some of the institutional and legal aspects of the impact of exchange rate fluctuations on trade. Members offered initial reactions and will be reverting to the issue in 2013.

Members continued to support the work of the Expert Group on Trade Finance and of the WTO Director-General on improving the availability of trade finance for low-income countries. In this regard, they welcomed the creation of a trade finance facilitation programme by the African Development Bank and recent moves by the Basel Committee on Banking Supervision aimed at reducing regulatory obstacles to trade finance.

Expert Group on Trade Finance

Some 80–90 per cent of world trade relies on trade finance (trade credit and insurance/guarantees) and during the worst of the financial and economic crisis in 2008-09 many companies, especially smaller enterprises in both developed and developing countries, found it impossible or prohibitively expensive to obtain the credit they needed to trade. In a context of contraction of the financial sector, the availability and affordability of trade finance for small and medium-sized enterprises in both developed and developing countries remain an issue of concern.

Against this backdrop, the Expert Group on Trade Finance continued to meet in 2012, with a view to filling the remaining gaps in the trade finance markets, especially in the poorest countries. One tool to boost the supply of trade finance in these countries has been the expansion by multilateral development banks of trade finance facilitation programmes in the regions where they operate. The Director-General advocated the creation of such a programme by the African Development Bank, with the support of the Bank's President, Mr Donald Kaberuka. The new programme was adopted at the beginning of 2013 by the Bank's Board of Directors.

The programme of the African Development Bank extends the global network of trade finance facilitation programmes already established by all major multilateral development institutions. A report to the G-20 in 2010 had concluded that only one-third of least-developed countries benefited from meaningful trade finance support. With the beefing up of multilateral development programmes, the international community is financing several billions of dollars of trade transactions in the most challenging countries in the world, from Sierra Leone to Nepal. As evidence that financing trade in such regions is no more risky than anywhere else, very few losses have been incurred by multilateral development banks in their operations.

The Director-General continued his dialogue with prudential regulators in 2012, with a view to clarifying potential regulatory obstacles to the supply of trade finance in developing countries. As a result, the Basel Committee made a number of positive adjustments to guidelines affecting trade finance in the area of capital and liquidity requirements. The main decisions were made by the Committee in autumn 2011 (removal of the maturity floor on letters of credit and the like) and at the beginning of 2013 (low liquidity coverage ratio for similar products). These measures potentially free billions of dollars of bank resources to finance more trade finance for no additional risk.

Established in the wake of the Asian financial crisis in the late 1990s, the Expert Group brings together representatives of the main players in trade finance, including the International Finance Corporation, regional development banks, export credit agencies and big commercial banks, as well as the International Chamber of Commerce and other international organizations.

Government Procurement Agreement

Further progress was achieved in 2012 on pending accessions to the Government Procurement Agreement (GPA), including those of China and New Zealand. In addition, the Committee on Government Procurement, which administers the GPA, monitored the entry into force of the revised Agreement adopted by the parties in 2012 (see page 32). Four more countries were granted observer status. Demand for technical training on the GPA continues to grow, reflecting increased interest in accession.

China submitted a third revised GPA accession offer, containing proposed additions to coverage at the sub-central government level and other improvements. Work on China's accession to the Agreement, to which the Committee attaches great importance, will continue in 2013. Moldova also submitted a revised GPA coverage offer in addition to updated information on its procurement system. Initial substantive discussions were held on New Zealand's application for accession, and there were further discussions relating to Ukraine's application for GPA accession, which was initiated in 2011.

In all, ten WTO members are in the process of acceding to the GPA, which at the end of 2012 comprised 15 parties, counting the European Union and its 27 member states as one. Commitments regarding accession to the GPA are incorporated in the WTO accession protocols of a further seven members that have joined the WTO in recent years.

The Committee granted observer status to Indonesia, Malaysia, Montenegro and Viet Nam in 2012, taking the number of observers to 26. This reflects the growing interest in learning about the GPA.

Background on the Government Procurement Agreement

The WTO Agreement on Government Procurement (GPA) ensures that signatories do not discriminate against the products, services or suppliers of other parties to the GPA with respect to the procuring agencies, goods and services that they have agreed to open to foreign competition. The Agreement also requires transparent and competitive purchasing practices in the markets covered. The GPA is a plurilateral agreement, which means that it applies only to those WTO members that have agreed to be bound by it. The Committee on Government Procurement administers the GPA.

Monitoring of implementation and legislation

In 2012, the Committee held regular roundtable sessions to monitor parties' progress towards the acceptance and bringing into force of the revised GPA adopted in March 2012. The Committee also considered modifications to parties' schedules, statistical reports, threshold levels in national currencies and changes in parties' legislation implementing the GPA.

In 2011 and 2012, the Committee, working with the WTO Secretariat, took significant steps to streamline notification processes. Procedures for the circulation of statistical reports have been greatly simplified. Furthermore, a number of the changes that are incorporated in the revised text of the GPA, e.g. with regard to the use of electronic procurement tools, are intended to simplify notification processes relating to transparency obligations.

With regard to national implementing legislation, the Committee was informed of a law adopted by a sub-federal unit of an important GPA party that, if implemented, would purportedly limit access to GPA-covered procurement. The Committee was assured that the law in question has been challenged and an injunction obtained. Other parties indicated that they are following the situation with interest and appreciate being kept informed.

Technical assistance and international cooperation

The WTO Secretariat carries out an intensive programme of technical assistance relating to the GPA, including both regional workshops and tailored national seminars that are provided on request to WTO members acceding to the Agreement and/or GPA observers. Close links are maintained with other international organizations interested in GPA accession work, notably the United Nations Commission on International Trade Law and various regional development banks.

The Committee, which is briefed regularly on relevant developments, has expressed its strong support for the Secretariat's technical assistance programme and its liaison with other interested organizations.

Figure 7: Members and observers of the Government Procurement Agreement

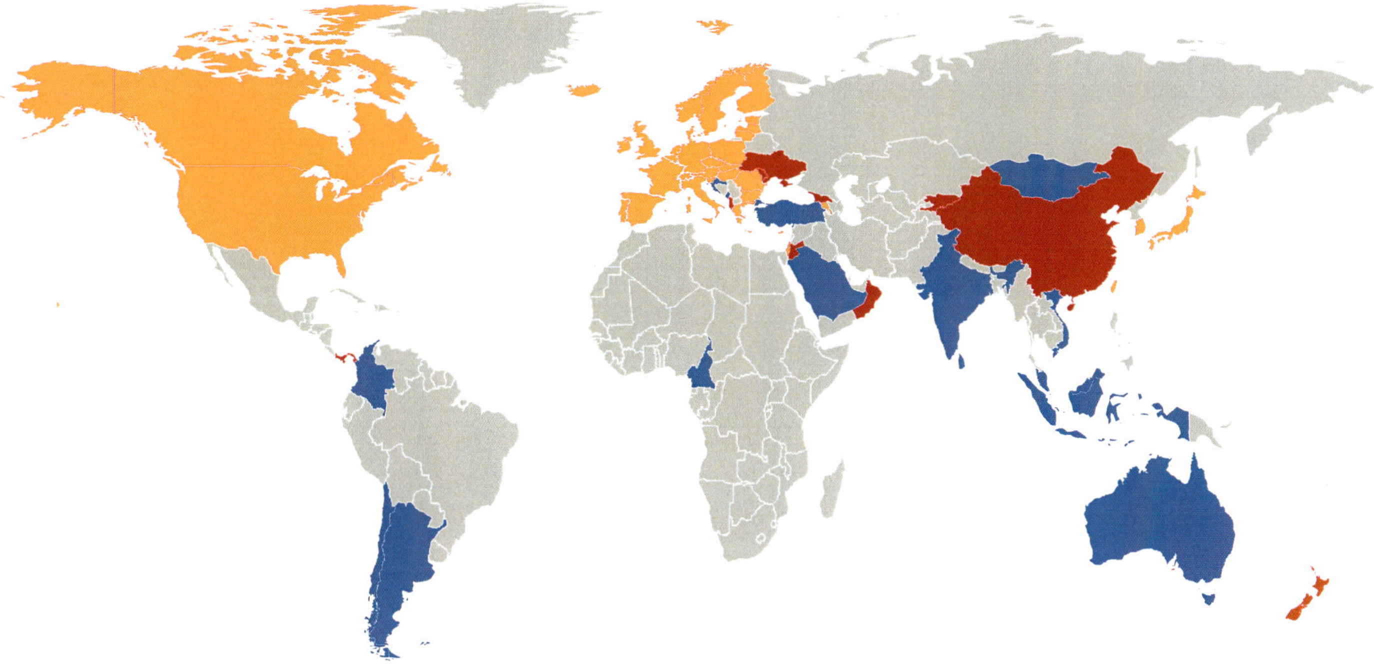

1.6

Total market access commitments under the GPA: US$ 1.6 trillion (as of 2008)

Parties to the GPA
(15 parties, comprising 42 WTO members).

WTO members negotiating GPA accession
(Albania, China, Georgia, Jordan, Kyrgyz Republic, Republic of Moldova, New Zealand, Oman, Panama and Ukraine).

Other observer countries
(Argentina, Australia, Kingdom of Bahrain, Cameroon, Chile, Colombia, Croatia, India, Indonesia, Malaysia, Mongolia, Montenegro, Kingdom of Saudi Arabia, Sri Lanka, Turkey and Viet Nam).

Integrated Trade Intelligence Portal (I-TIP)

The Integrated Trade Intelligence Portal (I-TIP) provides a single entry point for all information compiled by the WTO on trade policy measures. Containing information on over 25,000 measures, I-TIP covers both tariff and non-tariff measures affecting trade in goods as well as information on preferential trade agreements and the accession commitments of WTO members. Later in 2013, it will be expanded to cover trade in services and other areas. I-TIP was made available to the public for the first time on Trade Data Day, which took place at the WTO on 16 January 2013.

Trade in goods

I-TIP provides comprehensive information on non-tariff measures (NTMs) applied by WTO members in merchandise trade. The information includes members' notifications of NTMs as well as information on "special trade concerns" raised by members at WTO committee meetings. Areas currently covered by I-TIP include technical barriers to trade, sanitary and phytosanitary measures relating to food safety and animal/plant health, and anti-dumping, countervailing and safeguard measures.

Information on NTMs can be accessed as:

- graphs displaying summary information of trade measures, by WTO member or groupings of members
- tables showing product coverage by WTO member
- tables showing notified measures by WTO member
- summary or detailed lists of measures, as selected by the user, that can be exported into Excel.

I-TIP also provides a direct link to the WTO's extensive tariff and trade databases.

In 2013, the aim is to broaden the content available on I-TIP by including other NTMs and by improving I-TIP's functionality. The new information will include members' notifications of import licensing and quantitative restrictions as well as notifications relating to agricultural commitments. It will also include information from the WTO's Trade Monitoring Data Base (see right).

Background on the Integrated Trade Intelligence Portal (I-TIP)

I-TIP aims to serve the needs of those seeking detailed information on trade policy measures as well as those looking for summary information. Areas currently covered by I-TIP include trade in goods, WTO accession commitments, preferential trade agreements and air services. Other areas to be covered in the near future include trade across the full range of services, trade monitoring and dispute settlement.

Trade in services

The full services component of I-TIP will be made available in July 2013. This integrated database will consist of information on members' commitments under the WTO's General Agreement on Trade in Services (GATS), services commitments in preferential trade agreements, applied measures, and services statistics. A search function will allow users to access information by member, sector and mode of supply. Search results will be viewable in summary form or in more detail. Users will be able to export the information in various formats.

Air services

The WTO's Air Services Agreements Projector (ASAP) allows users to obtain information on an economy's network of bilateral air services agreements (ASAs) and associated passenger traffic flows. Based on 2011 data, it includes information on agreements available from the International Civil Aviation Organization or through WTO Trade Policy Reviews as well as scheduled passenger traffic statistics provided by the International Air Transport Association.

ASAP's Air Liberalization Index provides a measure of the openness of each ASA. Users may obtain information by signatory or groupings of signatories. The information is displayed on a world map along with the underlying data.

Trade monitoring

The Trade Monitoring Data Base (TMDB) will provide information on trade measures taken by WTO members and observers since October 2008. Drawing on data in the WTO's trade monitoring reports, the database will allow users to select information by a number of criteria, such as by country implementing the trade measures, by product(s), by countries affected by the measures, by type of measure, and by date. Information on new trade measures will be included in the TMDB only once it has been verified by the relevant countries. The database is expected to be made public in the first half of 2013. Information in the database will be updated twice a year.

Accessions

The Accession Commitments Database, launched in May 2012, provides access to all WTO accession commitments and related information contained in the working party reports and accession protocols of WTO members that have joined since 1995. Information can be extracted and exported in various ways.

On 16 January 2013, the WTO hosted Trade Data Day, an event dedicated to creating a better understanding of international trade flows and market access.

Preferential trade agreements

I-TIP provides access to information on regional trade agreements (RTAs) and preferential trade arrangements (PTAs) through its RTA and PTA databases. These databases were established as part of the Transparency Mechanism for RTAs and PTAs, which requires members to notify all such trade agreements to the WTO as soon as possible.

Dispute settlement

The Digital Dispute Settlement Registry will allow WTO members to submit dispute settlement documents online through a secure and convenient facility from anywhere in the world. The system will also serve as a storage facility for all panel and Appellate Body records dating back to 1995.

The registry will permit members and the public to search for publicly available information from past disputes, including material that has only been available in printed form up to now. Members will be able to conduct sophisticated searches - for example, searching by keywords such as "national treatment".

Dispute settlement

- WTO members filed 27 notifications of "requests for consultations" – the first stage in the dispute settlement process – in 2012, more than three times as many as in 2011.

- The Dispute Settlement Body established 11 new dispute settlement panels, adopted 18 panel reports and 11 Appellate Body reports.

- The 20-year EU-Latin America banana disputes reached a major milestone in 2012 when the European Union and Latin American countries formally settled their claims.

- The WTO's Legal Affairs Division held a conference in June 2012 to mark the 30 years since its predecessor, the GATT Office of Legal Affairs, was created.

Dispute settlement activity in 2012 76

Appellate Body 90

Background on dispute settlement

WTO members bring disputes to the WTO if they think their rights under trade agreements are being infringed. Settling disputes is the responsibility of the Dispute Settlement Body.

Dispute settlement activity in 2012

There was a sharp increase in dispute settlement activity in 2012 with both developed and developing countries active in bringing disputes to the WTO for resolution. Some WTO members, including Russia, participated for the first time. Disputes covered a wide variety of areas, including some that are less often adjudicated, such as issues under the General Agreement on Trade in Services. The European Union and Latin American countries formally settled the long-running banana disputes. Efforts to achieve efficiencies in dispute settlement processes continued. Finally, the legal affairs division celebrated an important anniversary.

Conclusion of the banana disputes

The 20-year EU-Latin America banana disputes reached a major milestone in 2012 when the European Union and Latin American countries formally settled their claims. Parties to the dispute had initially signed the Geneva Bananas Agreement in 2009. Following this, a number of legal steps were required, including each country ratifying the 2009 agreement and the European Union introducing legislation and regulations to implement it. As the WTO's membership has accepted the Bananas Agreement as part of the European Union's new scheduled commitment, it is now multilateral.

The new EU commitments to reduce its import tariffs on bananas were circulated on 27 July 2012 as a revision to the European Union's list (officially its "schedule") of commitments. WTO members were then given three months under WTO regulations to object. As there were no objections, the WTO Director-General certified the revised EU Schedule at the end of October and on 8 November 2012 the European Union and Latin American countries signed a mutually agreed solution through which they agreed to end all their pending banana disputes.

30th anniversary of Legal Affairs Division

In June 2012, the WTO's Legal Affairs Division (LAD) held a conference to mark the 30 years since its predecessor, the GATT Office of Legal Affairs, was created. The establishment of the division was an early indication of the importance that members and the Secretariat gave to a strong and clear legal framework for the conduct of international trade, including an effective and reliable dispute settlement system.

In a speech marking the event, Director-General Pascal Lamy said that initially the emphasis had been on finding politically acceptable solutions. However, over the years, procedures had evolved, moving to a dispute settlement system increasingly based on rules. Finally, he recalled the bold changes that members introduced at the end of the Uruguay Round, when they adopted the Dispute Settlement Understanding (DSU). As a result, WTO members enjoy one of the most successful systems for dispute settlement in the international sphere.

The European Union and ten Latin American countries signed an agreement on 8 November 2012 ending 20 years of EU-Latin American banana disputes.

Background on dispute settlement activity

The General Council convenes as the Dispute Settlement Body (DSB) to deal with disputes arising from any agreement contained in the Final Act of the Uruguay Round that is subject to the Understanding on Rules and Procedures Governing the Settlement of Disputes (Dispute Settlement Understanding). The DSB, which met 18 times during 2012, has authority to establish dispute settlement panels, adopt panel and Appellate Body reports, maintain surveillance over the implementation of recommendations and rulings contained in such reports, and authorize suspension of concessions in the event of non-compliance with those recommendations and rulings.

Enhancing panel efficiency

In March 2012, Deputy Director-General Alejandro Jara reported on his consultations with stakeholders on improving the efficiency of the panel in ways that do not affect the DSU itself. He grouped the proposals received into three broad categories: improving the effectiveness of the first meeting of the panel with the parties; improving the efficiency in terms of length and cost of the process, including by emulating the Appellate Body practice of setting time-limits for parties' oral statements; and improving the presentation of panel reports and reducing production costs through setting page limits for summaries of parties' arguments, and reducing the number of annexes attached to reports.

The Deputy Director-General observed that some of the innovations had already been put into place by some panels. Broader implementation would depend on WTO members working together with panellists. Members also made good progress in developing and designing a system to permit secure remote digital filing of dispute settlement documents.

At a ceremony to commemorate the 30th anniversary of the GATT/WTO Legal Affairs Division in June 2012, the WTO launched a new edition of the *Analytical Index*, a comprehensive guide to the interpretation and application of WTO agreements.

Dispute settlement activity in 2012

In 2012, the Dispute Settlement Body (DSB) received 27 notifications of "requests for consultations", the first stage in the WTO's dispute settlement process (see below). This is the highest number of requests in the last ten years. In addition, numerous disputes were already making their way through the system. Thus, in addition to the panels already under way, the DSB established 11 new panels to adjudicate 13 new cases. (Where more than one complaint deals with the same matter, the complaints may be adjudicated by a single panel.)

In 2012, the DSB also adopted 18 panel reports as well as 11 Appellate Body reports. Finally, the arbitrator established "reasonable periods of time" for implementing the DSB rulings and recommendations in two disputes.

Information about the disputes, including the reports adopted by the DSB, can be found in Table 1 on the next page.

Table 1: Panel and Appellate Body reports circulated in 2012*

Case	Document number	Complainant(s)	Respondent	Third parties	WTO Agreements covered	Date of adoption by Dispute Settlement Body
China – Raw Materials (United States)	WT/DS394/AB/R WT/DS394/R	United States	China	Argentina, Brazil, Canada, Chile, Colombia, Ecuador, European Union, India, Japan, Republic of Korea, Mexico, Norway, Chinese Taipei, Turkey, Kingdom of Saudi Arabia	China's Accession Protocol General Agreement on Tariffs and Trade (GATT) 1994 Dispute Settlement Understanding (DSU)	22 Feb 2012
China – Raw Materials (European Union)	WT/DS395/AB/R WT/DS395/R	European Communities	China	Argentina, Brazil, Canada, Chile, Colombia, Ecuador, India, Japan, Republic of Korea, Mexico, Norway, Chinese Taipei, Turkey, Kingdom of Saudi Arabia, United States	China's Accession Protocol GATT 1994 DSU	22 Feb 2012
China – Raw Materials (Mexico)	WT/DS398/AB/R WT/DS398/R	Mexico	China	Argentina, Brazil, Canada, Chile, Colombia, Ecuador, European Union, India, Japan, Republic of Korea, Norway, Chinese Taipei, Turkey, Kingdom of Saudi Arabia, United States	China's Accession Protocol GATT 1994 DSU	22 Feb 2012
Dominican Republic – Safeguard Measures	WT/DS415/R	Costa Rica	Dominican Republic	China, Colombia, El Salvador, European Union, Guatemala, Honduras, Nicaragua, Panama, Turkey, United States	Agreement on Safeguards GATT 1994 DSU	22 Feb 2012
Dominican Republic – Safeguard Measures	WT/DS416/R	Guatemala	Dominican Republic	China, Colombia, Costa Rica, El Salvador, European Union, Honduras, Nicaragua, Panama, Turkey, United States	Agreement on Safeguards GATT 1994 DSU	22 Feb 2012

Table 1: Panel and Appellate Body reports circulated in 2012* (continued)

Case	Document number	Complainant(s)	Respondent	Third parties	WTO Agreements covered	Date of adoption by Dispute Settlement Body
Dominican Republic – Safeguard Measures	WT/DS417/R	Honduras	Dominican Republic	China, Colombia, Costa Rica, El Salvador, European Union, Guatemala, Nicaragua, Panama, Turkey, United States	Agreement on Safeguards GATT 1994 DSU	22 Feb 2012
Dominican Republic – Safeguard Measures	WT/DS418/R	El Salvador	Dominican Republic	China, Colombia, Costa Rica, European Union, Guatemala, Honduras, Nicaragua, Panama, Turkey, United States	Agreement on Safeguards GATT 1994 DSU	22 Feb 2012
US – Large Civil Aircraft (2nd complaint)	WT/DS353/AB/R WT/DS353/R	European Communities	United States	Australia, Brazil, Canada, China, Japan, Republic of Korea	Subsidies and Countervailing Measures (SCM) Agreement GATT 1994 DSU	23 Mar 2012
US – Clove Cigarettes	WT/DS406/AB/R WT/DS406/R	Indonesia	United States	Brazil, Colombia, Dominican Republic, European Union, Guatemala, Mexico, Norway, Turkey	Sanitary and Phytosanitary Measures (SPS) Agreement Technical Barriers to Trade (TBT) Agreement GATT 1994 DSU	24 Apr 2012
US – Tuna II (Mexico)	WT/DS381/AB/R WT/DS381/R	Mexico	United States	Argentina, Australia, Brazil, Canada, China, Ecuador, European Union, Guatemala, Japan, Republic of Korea, New Zealand, Chinese Taipei, Thailand, Turkey, Bolivarian Republic of Venezuela	TBT Agreement GATT 1994 DSU	13 Jun 2012

Table 1: Panel and Appellate Body reports circulated in 2012* (continued)

Case	Document number	Complainant(s)	Respondent	Third parties	WTO Agreements covered	Date of adoption by Dispute Settlement Body
US – Shrimp & Sawblades	WT/DS422/R	China	United States	European Union, Honduras, Japan, Republic of Korea, Thailand, Viet Nam	Anti-Dumping Agreement GATT 1994	23 Jul 2012
US – COOL [country of origin labelling] (Canada)	WT/DS384/AB/R WT/DS384/R	Canada	United States	Argentina, Australia, Brazil, China, Colombia, European Union, Guatemala, India, Japan, Republic of Korea, Mexico, New Zealand, Peru, Chinese Taipei	Rules of Origin Agreement SPS Agreement TBT Agreement GATT 1994	23 Jul 2012
US – COOL (Mexico)	WT/DS386/AB/R WT/DS386/R	Mexico	United States	Argentina, Australia, Brazil, Canada, China, Colombia, European Union, Guatemala, India, Japan, Republic of Korea, New Zealand, Peru, Chinese Taipei	Rules of Origin Agreement SPS Agreement TBT Agreement GATT 1994	23 Jul 2012
Korea – Bovine Meat (Canada)*	WT/DS391/R	Canada	Korea	Argentina, Brazil, India, China, European Union, Japan, Chinese Taipei, United States	SPS Agreement GATT 1994	[not adopted]
China – Electronic Payment Services	WT/DS413/R	United States	China	Australia, Ecuador, European Union, Guatemala, Japan, Republic of Korea, India	General Agreement on Trade in Services (GATS)	31 Aug 2012
China – GOES [grain-oriented flat-rolled electrical steel]	WT/DS414/AB/R WT/DS414/R	United States	China	Argentina, European Union, Honduras, India, Japan, Republic of Korea, Kingdom of Saudi Arabia, Viet Nam	Anti-Dumping Agreement SCM Agreement GATT 1994	16 Nov 2012

*Appellate Body reports are the shaded rows. Further information on these reports is provided in Table 5 on page 91.

Table 1: Panel and Appellate Body reports circulated in 2012* (continued)

Case	Document number	Complainant(s)	Respondent	Third parties	WTO Agreements covered	Date of adoption by Dispute Settlement Body
Canada – Feed In Tariff Program	WT/DS426/R	Japan	Canada	Australia, Brazil, China, El Salvador, European Union, Honduras, India, Republic of Korea, Mexico, Norway, Kingdom of Saudi Arabia, Chinese Taipei, United States	SCM Agreement Trade Related Investment Measures (TRIMs) Agreement GATT 1994	[Panel Report under appeal on 5 Feb 2013]
Canada – Renewable Energy	WT/DS412/R	European Union	Canada	Australia, Brazil, China, El Salvador, India, Japan, Republic of Korea, Mexico, Norway, Kingdom of Saudi Arabia, Chinese Taipei, Turkey, United States	SCM Agreement TRIMs Agreement GATT 1994	[Panel Report under appeal on 5 Feb 2013]

DISPUTE SETTLEMENT

Sharp increase in "requests for consultations"

The number of "requests for consultations" – the first stage in dispute settlement proceedings and an obligatory step before the establishment of a panel to adjudicate a complaint – increased more than threefold in 2012 to 27, compared with eight in 2011 (see Figure 1).

However, this does not mean that 27 new disputes will necessarily be working their way through the dispute settlement system in 2013, as about half of disputes overall do not proceed beyond the consultations stage. Often, the parties reach a satisfactory settlement, or a complainant decides for other reasons not to pursue the matter. This shows that consultations are often an effective means of dispute resolution in the WTO.

Consultations are one of the key diplomatic features of the WTO dispute settlement system. They allow parties to clarify the facts involved and the claims of the complainant, possibly dispelling misunderstandings as to the true nature of the measure(s) at issue. In this sense, consultations serve either to lay the foundation for a settlement or for further proceedings under the DSU. For those disputes that are not settled at the consultations stage, which may last up to 60 days, the next step is the establishment of a panel by the DSB.

Figure 1: Number of disputes filed per year

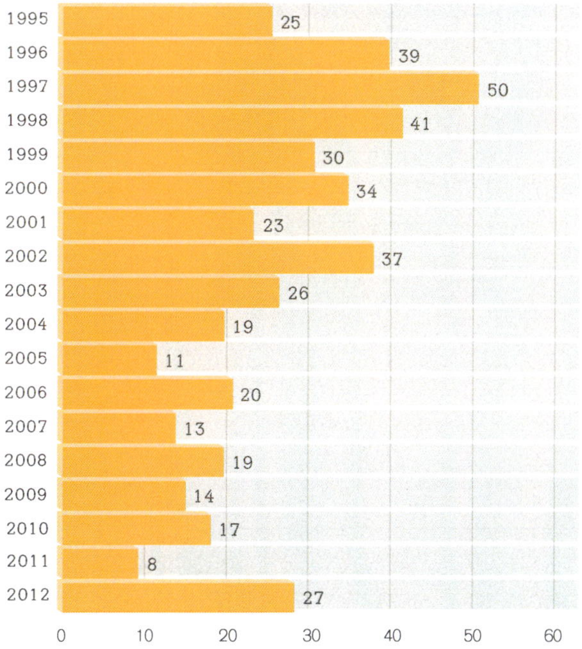

Figure 2: Requests for consultations in 2012, by complainant

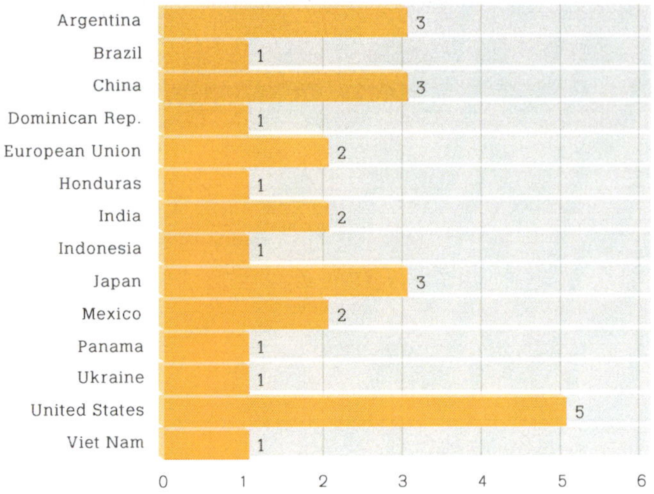

Which WTO members were active in 2012?

Of the 27 new requests for consultations, Latin American members launched nine, with Argentina the most active with three complaints. A number of Asian members, including Japan, were also active during 2012. The United States initiated five requests, with China on the receiving end of three of them, while the European Union initiated two (see Figures 2 and 3).

Overall, as the information in Table 2 shows, developing countries participated strongly in the dispute settlement system, both as complainants and respondents.

Figure 3: Requests for consultations in 2012, by respondent

Table 2: Requests for consultations in 2012

Case	Document number	Complainant	Date of initial request	WTO Agreements cited	Status as of end of 2012
Turkey – Safeguard Measures on Imports of Cotton Yarn (other than Sewing Thread)	WT/DS428	India	13 Feb 2012	GATT Safeguards Agreement	In consultations
US – Anti-Dumping Measures on Certain Shrimp from Viet Nam	WT/DS429	Viet Nam	16 Feb 2012	GATT Anti-Dumping Agreement WTO Agreement DSU Viet Nam's Accession Protocol	In consultations
India – Measures concerning the Importation of Certain Agricultural Products	WT/DS430	United States	6 Mar 2012	SPS Agreement GATT	Panel established/ panel composition pending
China – Measures related to the Exportation of Rare Earths, Tungsten and Molybdenum	WT/DS431	United States	13 Mar 2012	GATT China's Accession Protocol	Panel work has commenced

Table 2: Requests for consultations in 2012 (continued)

Case	Document number	Complainant	Date of initial request	WTO Agreements cited	Status as of end of 2012
China – Measures related to the Exportation of Rare Earths, Tungsten and Molybdenum	WT/DS432	European Union	13 Mar 2012	GATT China's Accession Protocol	Panel work has commenced
China – Measures related to the Exportation of Rare Earths, Tungsten and Molybdenum	WT/DS433	Japan	13 Mar 2012	GATT China's Accession Protocol	Panel work has commenced
Australia – Certain Measures concerning Trademarks and other Plain Packaging Requirements applicable to Tobacco Products and Packaging	WT/DS434	Ukraine	13 Mar 2012	GATT TRIPS Agreement TBT Agreement	Panel established/ panel composition pending
Australia – Certain Measures Concerning Trademarks, Geographical Indications and other Plain Packaging Requirements applicable to Tobacco Products and Packaging	WT/DS435	Honduras	4 Apr 2012	GATT TRIPS Agreement TBT Agreement	Panel request pending before the DSB
United States – Countervailing Measures on Certain Hot-Rolled Carbon Steel Flat Products from India	WT/DS436	India	12 Apr 2012	GATT SCM Agreement	Panel established/ panel composition pending
United States – Countervailing Duty Measures on Certain Products from China	WT/DS437	China	25 May 2012	GATT SCM Agreement China's Accession Protocol	Panel work has commenced
Argentina – Measures Affecting the Importation of Goods	WT/DS438	European Union	25 May 2012	GATT TRIMs Agreement Import Licensing Agreement Agriculture Agreement Safeguards Agreement	Panel request pending before the DSB
South Africa – Anti-Dumping Duties on Frozen Meat of Fowls from Brazil	WT/DS439	Brazil	25 Jun 2012	GATT Anti-Dumping Agreement	In consultations

Table 2: Requests for consultations in 2012 (continued)

Case	Document number	Complainant	Date of initial request	WTO Agreements cited	Status as of end of 2012
China – Anti-Dumping and Countervailing Duties on Certain Automobiles from the United States	WT/DS440	United States	5 Jul 2012	GATT Anti-Dumping Agreement SCM Agreement	Panel established/ panel composition pending
Australia – Certain Measures concerning Trademarks, Geographical Indications and other Plain Packaging Requirements applicable to Tobacco Products and Packaging	WT/DS441	Dominican Republic	18 Jul 2012	GATT Trade-related Aspects of Intellectual Property (TRIPS) Agreement TBT	Panel request pending before the DSB
European Union – Anti-Dumping Measures on Imports of Certain Fatty Alcohols from Indonesia	WT/DS442	Indonesia	27 Jul 2012	GATT Anti-Dumping Agreement	In consultations
European Union and a Member State – Certain Measures Concerning the Importation of Biodiesels	WT/DS443	Argentina	17 Aug 2012	GATT TRIMs Agreement	Panel request pending before the DSB
Argentina – Measures Affecting the Importation of Goods	WT/DS444	United States	21 Aug 2012	GATT Import Licensing Agreement TRIMs Agreement Safeguards Agreement	Panel request pending before the DSB
Argentina – Measures Affecting the Importation of Goods	WT/DS445	Japan	21 Aug 2012	GATT Import Licensing Agreement TRIMs Agreement Safeguards Agreement	Panel request pending before the DSB
Argentina – Measures Affecting the Importation of Goods	WT/DS446	Mexico	24 Aug 2012	GATT Agriculture Agreement Import Licensing Agreement TRIMs Agreement Safeguards Agreement Technical Barriers to Trade (TBT) Agreement	In consultations

Table 2: Requests for consultations in 2012 (continued)

Case	Document number	Complainant	Date of initial request	WTO Agreements cited	Status as of end of 2012
United States – Measures Affecting the Importation of Animals, Meat and Other Animal Products from Argentina	WT/DS447	Argentina	30 Aug 2012	GATT SPS Agreement WTO Agreement	Panel request pending before DSB
United States – Measures Affecting the Importation of Fresh Lemons	WT/DS448	Argentina	3 Sep 2012	GATT Sanitary and Phytosanitary Measures (SPS) Agreement WTO Agreement	Panel request pending before the Dispute Settlement Body (DSB)
United States – Countervailing and Anti-Dumping Measures on Certain Products from China	WT/DS449	China	17 Sep 2012	GATT SCM Agreement Anti-Dumping Agreement	Panel established/ panel composition pending
China – Certain Measures Affecting the Automobile and Automobile-parts Industries	WT/DS450	United States	17 Sep 2012	GATT SCM Agreement China's Accession Protocol	In consultations
China – Measures Relating to the Production and Exportation of Apparel and Textile Products	WT/DS451	Mexico	15 Oct 2012	GATT SCM Agreement China's Accession Protocol	In consultations
European Union and Certain Member States – Certain Measures Affecting the Renewable Energy Generation Sector	WT/DS452	China	5 Nov 2012	GATT Subsidies and Countervailing Measures (SCM) Agreement Trade in Investment Measures (TRIMs) Agreement	In consultations
Argentina – Measures Relating to Trade in Goods and Services	WT/DS453	Panama	12 Dec 2012	GATT General Agreement on Trade in Services (GATS)	In consultations
China – Measures Imposing Anti-Dumping Duties on High-Performance Stainless Steel Seamless Tubes from Japan	WT/DS454	Japan	20 Dec 2012	General Agreement on Tariffs and Trade (GATT) Anti-Dumping Agreement	In consultations

Table 3: WTO members involved in disputes, 1995 to 2012*

Member	Complainant	Respondent
Antigua and Barbuda	1	0
Argentina	18	22
Armenia	0	1
Australia	7	13
Bangladesh	1	0
Belgium	0	3
Brazil	26	14
Canada	33	17
Chile	10	13
China	11	30
Colombia	5	3
Costa Rica	5	0
Croatia	0	1
Czech Republic	1	2
Denmark	0	1
Dominican Republic	1	7
Ecuador	3	3
Egypt	0	4
El Salvador	1	0
European Union (formerly EC)	87	73
France	0	4
Germany	0	2
Greece	0	3
Guatemala	8	2
Honduras	8	0
Hong Kong, China	1	0
Hungary	5	2
India	21	21
Indonesia	6	5
Ireland	0	3
Italy	0	1
Japan	17	15
Korea, Republic of	15	14
Malaysia	1	1
Mexico	23	14
Moldova, Republic of	1	1
Netherlands	0	3
New Zealand	7	0
Nicaragua	1	2
Norway	4	0
Pakistan	3	2
Panama	6	1
Peru	3	4
Philippines	5	6
Poland	3	1
Portugal	0	1
Romania	0	2
Singapore	1	0
Slovak Republic	0	3
South Africa	0	4
Spain	0	3
Sri Lanka	1	0
Sweden	0	1
Switzerland	4	0
Chinese Taipei	3	0
Thailand	13	3
Trinidad and Tobago	0	2
Turkey	2	9
Ukraine	3	1
United Kingdom	0	3
United States of America	104	119
Uruguay	1	1
Venezuela, Bolivarian Republic of	1	2
Viet Nam	2	0

*This table indicates notifications of "requests for consultations" received by the WTO.

What issues are being litigated?

The DSB established a single panel to consider complaints by the European Union, Japan and the United States relating to China's alleged restrictions on the export of rare earths. Complaints brought by Canada and Norway against the European Union for banning the importation and marketing of seal products entered into the panel phase.

A panel was established to examine Ukraine's complaint against Australia's requirements concerning plain packaging on tobacco products. Honduras and the Dominican Republic also have pending requests before the DSB on a similar subject. Also pending before the DSB are requests from the European Union, the United States and Japan to establish a panel to look at their complaints concerning Argentina's measures that allegedly restrict the importation of goods.

Figure 4: WTO agreements referred to in requests for consultations, 1995-2012 (number of times)

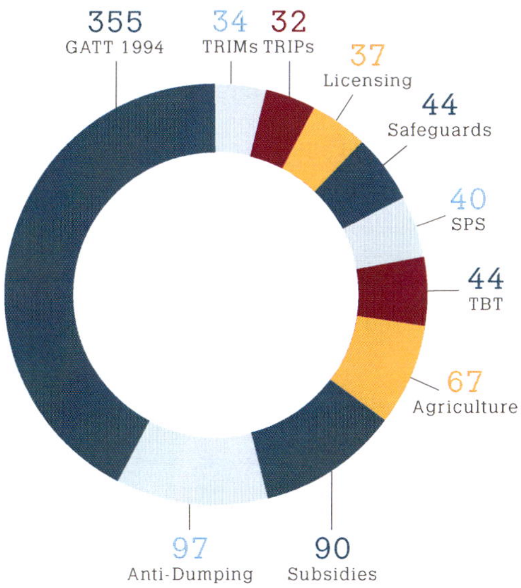

The DSB set up seven panels in 2012 to examine complaints in the area of trade remedies; these disputes concern anti-dumping measures (to deal with export products sold at prices lower than those charged in the home market), countervailing duties (subsidies) and safeguard actions (to guard against import surges). Trade remedies allow governments to take remedial action in situations where the domestic industry is being injured. The recent trend of increasing numbers of disputes in the trade remedies area continued in 2012.

Table 2 shows the variety of WTO agreements that were raised in the disputes initiated in 2012. All disputes initiated in 2012 included challenges under the GATT 1994; since 1995, 355 of the 428 requests for consultations have included a claim under this agreement. Disputes under the Agreement on Trade-Related Aspects of Intellectual Property Rights (TRIPS) and the Technical Barriers to Trade (TBT) Agreement occur much less often than do disputes under the Sanitary and Phytosanitary Measures (SPS) Agreement, the Subsidies and Countervailing Measures (SCM) Agreement, and the Anti-Dumping Agreement. Chart 3 shows the number of times an agreement has been referred to in requests for consultations from 1995 to 2012.

Reports issued

Of the reports issued by panels and the Appellate Body during 2012, four addressed claims under the TBT Agreement and three addressed export restrictions. A long report dealt with subsidies relating to large civil aircraft, and another report on the case "China-GOES" (grain oriented flat-rolled electrical steel) addressed claims under the Anti-Dumping Agreement and the SCM Agreement.

Also issued in 2012 were reports addressing claims under agreements that have not recently been the subject of disputes: "China – Electronic Payment Services", which concerns US claims under the General Agreement on Trade in Services (GATS), and "Canada – Renewable Energy" and "Canada – Feed-in Tariff Programs", where the European Union and Japan raised claims under the Trade-Related Investment Measures (TRIMS) Agreement.

Findings of the reports

In 2012, the Appellate Body issued a number of reports on technical regulations: "US – Clove Cigarettes", "US – Tuna II" and "US – COOL" (country of origin labelling).

"US – Clove Cigarettes" concerns a tobacco control measure adopted by the United States that prohibited the sale and production of flavoured cigarettes, including clove cigarettes, other than menthol-flavoured cigarettes. "US – Tuna II (Mexico)" concerns the use of a "dolphin-safe" label for tuna products sold on the US market. "US-COOL" concerns country of origin labelling requirements for meat products derived from both domestic and imported livestock.

One of the basic principles of the WTO is non-discrimination; thus, a country should not discriminate without justification between trading partners and it should not discriminate between its own and foreign products, services, service providers, or

DISPUTE SETTLEMENT

nationals. In other words, these disputes concern how members deal with non-trade concerns under the TBT Agreement, which sets specific rules for technical regulations, standards and conformity assessment procedures.

Such regulations and standards may be drawn up by governments to address various policy concerns, including animal life or health, human health or safety, or the environment. All three recent disputes concerned technical regulations, which are mandatory measures laying down product characteristics, their related processes and production methods, or labelling requirements.

In "US – Clove Cigarettes", "US – Tuna II" (Mexico) and "US – COOL", the Appellate Body first explained that this non-discrimination principle is also found in the TBT Agreement. It added that technical regulations will, by their very nature, establish distinctions between products according to their characteristics or production methods, and it explained that any detrimental impact of the regulations on imports that stemmed exclusively from "legitimate regulatory distinctions" would not amount to discrimination.

In these three disputes, the Appellate Body was not persuaded that the detrimental impact of the technical regulations stemmed from legitimate regulatory distinctions and therefore found all three technical regulations at issue inconsistent with the TBT Agreement provision on non-discrimination (Article 2.1).

Another aspect of the TBT Agreement examined in these three disputes was the requirement under Article 2.2 that technical regulations not be more trade-restrictive than necessary to fulfil a legitimate objective, taking into account the risks that non-fulfilment would create. The complainant bears the burden of demonstrating that the technical regulation is "more trade-restrictive than necessary" and, for this purpose, in most cases it will present possible alternative measures that are less trade-restrictive and can achieve to the same degree the same objective as the challenged measure. It is for the member whose measure is challenged to explain its policy justifications.

In all three of the TBT disputes, the panel or Appellate Body accepted the policy aims identified as legitimate objectives. Those objectives were the protection of human health, animal life or health, or the environment, and the provision of consumer information. The ban on flavoured cigarettes in "US – Clove Cigarettes" was found by the panel to be not more trade-restrictive than necessary to fulfil the objective of protecting human health, although the measure was struck down on other grounds.

In "US – Tuna II", the Appellate Body reversed the finding that the labelling requirements at issue were inconsistent with Article 2.2. However, the Appellate Body could not ultimately determine the consistency with Article 2.2 of the labelling requirements at issue in "US – COOL" because there were insufficient factual findings.

During 2012, export restrictions were also the subject of WTO dispute settlement. The GATT 1994 requires members, with certain exceptions, to eliminate all prohibitions and quantitative restrictions on exports (Article XI). However, it does not prevent members from imposing duties or taxes on their exports. Although this is the general rule, some recently acceded WTO members have undertaken commitments in their accession protocols to reduce or limit the export tariffs or export duties they apply to certain goods.

In "China – Raw Materials", the European Union, the United States and Mexico challenged a number of export restrictions that they alleged China placed on the exportation of certain raw materials. In 2012, the Appellate Body issued its report in this dispute. The Appellate Body agreed with the panel that there is no basis in China's Accession Protocol to allow the application of Article XX of the GATT 1994 to China's obligations under the relevant paragraph of the Accession Protocol.

Furthermore, the Appellate Body upheld the panel's finding that China did not demonstrate that its export quota on refractory-grade bauxite was "temporarily applied" to either prevent or relieve a "critical shortage", within the meaning of Article XI: 2(a) of the GATT 1994. The Appellate Body agreed with the panel that such a restriction must be of a limited duration and not indefinite. Moreover, the Appellate Body found that the term "critical shortages" refers to those deficiencies in quantity that are crucial and of decisive importance, or that reach a vitally important or decisive stage.

The question of export restrictions will be considered again by a WTO dispute panel in 2013 as the DSB established in September 2012 a panel to consider complaints about export restrictions that China allegedly imposes on a number of rare earths.

In March 2012, the DSB adopted the panel and Appellate Body reports in the dispute brought by the European Union over aircraft subsidies provided by the United States ("US – Large Civil Aircraft", often referred to as the Boeing dispute).

In the Boeing dispute, the Appellate Body upheld the panel's findings that certain US subsidies enabled Boeing to launch its 787 plane (known as the "Dreamliner") in 2004, thereby causing serious prejudice to the interests of the European Communities with respect to 200-300 seat large civil aircraft. The Appellate Body also found that certain subsidies had price effects and thus cause serious prejudice to the interests of the European Communities with respect to 100-200 seat large civil aircraft. No serious prejudice was found with respect to 300-400 seat large civil aircraft.

This was the second of the large and complex cases brought to the WTO dispute settlement system concerning subsidies given by governments to the civil aircraft industry. An earlier case concerned European subsidies provided to Airbus.

Dispute settlement activity relating to these cases is nevertheless continuing. According to the DSU, once a panel and/or Appellate Body report has been adopted, the dispute moves to the compliance stage where parties must bring into conformity the measures found not to be consistent with WTO rules.

The United States has alleged that the steps taken by the European Union have failed to bring its measures into compliance with the DSB's recommendations and rulings. A compliance panel has been set up to examine this issue. In the parallel dispute, the United States has notified the DSB that it has fully complied with the DSB recommendations and rulings. The European Union disagreed and a compliance panel was established to address this dispute.

Conclusions

In sum, WTO dispute settlement activity increased markedly in 2012. It is clear that WTO members, both developed and developing, continue to have a high degree of confidence in the WTO dispute settlement mechanism to resolve their disputes in a fair and efficient manner. It is also evident that members are confident that the system is capable of adjudicating a wide variety of disputes covering significant questions and complex issues.

Appellate Body

The Appellate Body's workload remained intense in 2012, although the number of new appeals levelled off. The Appellate Body circulated reports in nine disputes during 2012, four of which concerned appeals filed in 2011. New appeals were filed in five disputes, all of which were concluded in 2012. One Article 21.3(c) arbitration proceeding concerning the reasonable period of time for implementation was carried out in 2012. In June, a new member was appointed to the Appellate Body.

A full list of appeals filed and Appellate Body reports circulated in 2012 is provided in Tables 4 and 5. Further information on circulated reports is provided in Table 1 on pages 78-80.

Table 4: Appeals filed in 2012

Panel reports appealed	Date of appeal	Appellant	Document number	Other appellant	Document number
US – Clove Cigarettes	5 Jan 2012	United States	WT/DS406/6	-	-
US – Tuna II (Mexico)	20 Jan 2012	United States	WT/DS381/10	Mexico	WT/DS381/11
US – COOL [Certain Country of Origin Labelling] (Canada)	23 Mar 2012	United States	WT/DS384/12	Canada	WT/DS384/13
US – COOL (Mexico)	23 Mar 2012	United States	WT/DS386/11	Mexico	WT/DS386/12
China – GOES [Grain Oriented Flat-Rolled Electrical Steel]	20 Jul 2012	China	WT/DS414/5	-	-

Table 5: Appellate Body (AB) reports circulated in 2012

Panel reports appealed	Date of appeal	Appellant	Document number	Other appellant(s)	Document number	Circulation date of AB report
China – Raw Materials (United States)*	31 Aug 2011	China	WT/DS394/11	United States	WT/DS394/12	30 Jan 2012
China – Raw Materials (European Union)*	31 Aug 2011	China	WT/DS395/11	European Union	WT/DS395/12	30 Jan 2012
China – Raw Materials (Mexico)*	31 Aug 2011	China	WT/DS398/10	Mexico	WT/DS398/11	30 Jan 2012
US – Large Civil Aircraft (2nd Complaint)	1 Apr 2011	European Union	WT/DS353/8	United States	WT/DS353/10	12 Mar 2012
US – Clove Cigarettes	5 Jan 2012	United States	WT/DS406/6	-	-	4 Apr 2012
US – Tuna II (Mexico)	20 Jan 2012	United States	WT/DS381/10	Mexico	WT/DS381/11	16 May 2012
US – COOL (Canada)**	23 Mar 2012	United States	WT/DS384/12	Canada	WT/DS384/13	29 Jun 2012
US – COOL (Mexico)**	23 Mar 2012	United States	WT/DS386/11	Mexico	WT/DS386/12	29 Jun 2012
China – GOES	20 Jul 2012	China	WT/DS414/5	-	-	18 Oct 2012

* These three Appellate Body reports were circulated in a single document.

** These two Appellate Body reports were circulated in a single document.

DISPUTE SETTLEMENT

Details of the Appellate Body's findings are set out on pages 87-89. By the end of 2012, the Appellate Body had circulated 117 reports since its establishment in 1995.

One Article 21.3(c) arbitration proceeding concerning the reasonable period of time for implementation was carried out in 2012. Further information about the arbitration is provided below in Table 6.

Table 6: Article 21.3(c) arbitration awards circulated in 2012

Dispute	Parties	Document number	Circulation date of arbitration award
US – COOL	Canada Mexico United States	WT/DS384/24 WT/DS386/23	4 Dec 2012

Members of the Appellate Body, from left to right: David Unterhalter, Ujal Singh Bhatia, Peter Van den Bossche, Yuejiao Zhang, Ricardo Ramírez-Hernández, Thomas R. Graham, and Seung Wha Chang

Appellate Body members

The first term of office of Ms Yuejiao Zhang expired on 31 May 2012. The DSB reappointed Ms Zhang for a second four-year term beginning on 1 June 2012.

Mr Shotaro Oshima resigned from the Appellate Body effective 6 April 2012. On 24 May 2012, the Dispute Settlement Body appointed Mr Seung Wha Chang (Republic of Korea) to serve for four years as Appellate Body member commencing on 1 June 2012. Mr Chang was sworn in on 13 June 2012. His biography is provided below.

As of 1 June 2012, the seven Appellate Body members are:

- Ujal Singh Bhatia (India) (2011-15)
- Seung Wha Chang (Republic of Korea) (2012-16)
- Thomas R. Graham (United States) (2011-15)
- Ricardo Ramírez-Hernández (Mexico) (2009-13)
- David Unterhalter (South Africa) (2006-13)
- Peter Van den Bossche (Belgium) (2009-13)
- Yuejiao Zhang (China) (2008-16).

Ms Yuejiao Zhang served as Chair of the Appellate Body from 11 December 2011 to 31 May 2012. Ms Zhang was re-elected to serve as Chair for the period 1 June to 31 December 2012.

Background on the Appellate Body

The Appellate Body consists of seven members appointed by the Dispute Settlement Body. Each member is appointed for a term of four years, with the possibility of being reappointed for one further four-year term. Three members of the Appellate Body hear an appeal of a panel's ruling. Any party to a dispute may appeal the panel report to the Appellate Body. The appeal is limited to issues of law covered in the panel report and legal interpretations developed by the panel.

Seung Wha Chang (Republic of Korea)

Born in the Republic of Korea on 1 March 1963, Seung Wha Chang is currently Professor of Law at Seoul National University, where he teaches international trade law and international arbitration.

He has served on several WTO dispute settlement panels, including "US – FSC [foreign sales corporations]", "Canada – Aircraft Credits and Guarantees", and "EC – Trademarks and Geographical Indications". He has also served as chairman or member of several arbitral tribunals dealing with commercial matters. In 2009, he was appointed by the International Chamber of Commerce as a member of the International Court of Arbitration.

Professor Chang began his professional academic career at the Seoul National University School of Law in 1995 and was awarded professorial tenure in 2002. He has taught international trade law and, in particular, WTO dispute settlement at more than ten foreign law schools, including Harvard Law School, Yale Law School, Stanford Law School, New York University, Duke Law School and Georgetown University. In 2007, Harvard Law School granted him an endowed visiting professorial chair title, Nomura Visiting Professor of International Financial Systems.

In addition, Professor Chang previously served as a Seoul District Court judge, handling many cases involving international trade disciplines. He also practised as a foreign attorney at an international law firm in Washington D.C., handling international trade matters, including trade remedies and WTO-related disputes.

Professor Chang has published many books and articles in the field of international trade law. In addition, he serves as an editorial or advisory board member of the Journal of International Economic Law (Oxford University Press) and the Journal of International Dispute Settlement (Oxford University Press).

Professor Chang holds a Bachelor of Laws degree (LL.B.) and a Master of Laws degree (LL.M.) from Seoul National University School of Law and a Master of Laws degree (LL.M.) as well as a doctorate in international trade law (S.J.D.) from Harvard Law School.

Mr Seung Wha Chang of the Republic of Korea was sworn in as a member of the Appellate Body on 13 June 2012.

Building trade capacity

- New guidelines were introduced in 2012 to streamline the accession process of least-developed countries.

- The Fourth Global Review of Aid for Trade will take place on 8-10 July 2013, focusing on the role that Aid for Trade can play in helping connect developing countries to national, regional and global value chains.

- The WTO launched a new publicly available database on preferential trade arrangements – schemes under which developed countries grant preferential tariffs to imports from developing countries.

- The WTO undertook 343 technical assistance activities in 2012 to help government officials from developing countries gain a better understanding of the multilateral trading system.

- Over 5,400 people participated in the WTO's e-learning courses in 2012.

Trade and development 96

Small economies 97

Least-developed countries 97

Aid for Trade 99

Enhanced Integrated Framework 101

Standards and Trade Development Facility 103

Technical cooperation and training 105

Background on building trade capacity

The WTO aims to help developing countries build their trade capacity and allows them a longer time to implement trade agreements. Hundreds of training courses are organized each year for officials from developing countries.

Trade and development

In 2012, the Committee on Trade and Development (CTD) pressed ahead with implementing the work programme on electronic commerce. Other issues discussed by the CTD and its Sub-Committee on Least-Developed Countries (LDCs) included accelerating and easing LDC accessions, capacity-building initiatives, market access for LDCs and technical assistance.

The Committee responded to the call by the WTO's Eighth Ministerial Conference to continue reinvigorating the WTO work programme on electronic commerce (e-commerce). Based on a proposal from Cuba and Ecuador, it agreed that a workshop on "e-commerce, development and small and medium-sized enterprises" will be held in 2013. A number of other proposals from members were considered in the context of the mandate from ministers to undertake focused work on the link between trade and development. Duty-free and quota-free market access for LDCs remained a standing item on the agenda of the CTD at its three formal regular sessions in 2012.

The Committee received reports on the 45th and 46th sessions of the Joint Advisory Group on the International Trade Centre (ITC), which is the policymaking body of the ITC, the trade promotion agency for developing countries jointly sponsored by the WTO and the United Nations Conference on Trade and Development (UNCTAD). The ITC's work focuses on small and medium-sized enterprises in developing countries and on the private sector.

Notifications under the Enabling Clause

In 2012, the Committee received a notification, under the Enabling Clause, concerning the entry into force for Brunei Darussalam, Cambodia, Indonesia, the Lao People's Democratic Republic (PDR) and the Philippines of the Agreement establishing the free trade area between the Association of Southeast Asian Nations (ASEAN) and India.

Background on trade and development

The Committee on Trade and Development serves as the focal point for the coordination of all work on trade and development issues in the WTO. The Committee deals with a variety of issues, such as technical cooperation and training and notifications under the Enabling Clause, which allows developed countries to give more favourable treatment to developing countries.

Also with regard to regional trade agreements, a notification was received concerning the accession of Rwanda and Burundi to the Protocol on the Establishment of the East African Community Customs Union. Notifications under the Enabling Clause concerning Generalized System of Preferences (GSP) schemes – which allow developed countries to grant preferential tariffs to imports from developing countries – were made by the United States and Switzerland.

Preferential trade arrangements

After four years of negotiations and a year of work by WTO members on implementation measures and data collection, the WTO launched in March 2012 a new publicly available database on preferential trade arrangements (http://ptadb.wto.org).

Preferential trade arrangements (PTAs) are schemes in which the beneficiaries of trade concessions do not have to provide concessions in return. They include GSP schemes under which developed countries grant preferential tariffs to imports from developing countries as well as other non-reciprocal preferential schemes granted a waiver by the General Council.

The database contains information on PTAs being implemented by WTO members. This information includes the legal nature, history and background of each PTA, the range of products covered and the types of treatment offered. The database reflects the continuing efforts of the WTO to enhance transparency in trade policy.

The database was set up following negotiations in the CTD that led to the establishment of the transparency mechanism for PTAs. A notification under the mechanism was made in 2012 by the Republic of Korea outlining preferential treatment offered to LDCs.

Technical cooperation and training

The WTO's technical assistance and training activities (see page 105) were discussed. The Committee took note of the 2011 annual report on technical assistance and training, providing an overview of activities in the previous year, and the technical cooperation audit report, which evaluated those activities.

Small economies

In 2012, the Committee on Trade and Development held two formal dedicated sessions to look at the wide range of proposals by small, vulnerable economies (SVEs) in the WTO, with the aim of achieving their fuller integration into the multilateral trading system.

The Committee's work focused on carrying out instructions by ministers at the Eighth Ministerial Conference that the Committee, with the assistance of the WTO Secretariat, continue examining the impact of WTO rules on small economies and the trade-related constraints they face and analyse the effects of trade opening and non-tariff measures (such as sanitary regulations and product standards) on small economies.

The Committee discussed a Secretariat background paper on the impact of non-tariff measures and heard presentations on recent research conducted on the subject by representatives from the ITC and UNCTAD. The Committee will continue to hold dedicated sessions on SVEs to monitor the situation in the Doha Round negotiations, to further examine the impact of non-tariff measures on small economies and, where possible, to make recommendations to the General Council.

Background on small economies

The Committee on Trade and Development – in dedicated session – oversees work on small economies and monitors the progress of proposals from small, vulnerable economies (SVEs) in the various WTO bodies and Doha Round negotiating groups. SVEs – mostly but not exclusively small island states – do not constitute a defined group in the WTO but associate on specific issues.

Least-developed countries

In 2012, the Sub Committee on Least Developed Countries (LDCs) mainly focused on the accession of LDCs, following the decision to streamline LDC accessions taken by ministers at the WTO's Eighth Ministerial Conference. The Sub-Committee also took up subjects under the WTO work programme for LDCs, such as reviewing market access conditions for LDC products and the delivery of trade-related technical assistance and capacity-building initiatives for LDCs. In addition, it discussed a possible update of the WTO work programme for LDCs.

Market access for LDCs

Discussion on the issues relating to market access for LDC products continued to receive priority attention by the Sub-Committee. As mandated, the WTO Secretariat prepared a comprehensive note covering trends in merchandise and services trade during 2000-11. The note examined the market access conditions faced by LDCs in both developed and developing countries, including the status of duty-free and quota-free access for LDC products.

The WTO Secretariat reported that the value of LDCs' total exports (goods and commercial services) grew by 23.9 per cent in 2011 to reach USD 229.8 billion. Major product categories contributing to the rise included fuels and mining products as well as agricultural products, which experienced price hikes. Although many WTO members welcomed the figures, they agreed with Haiti, the LDC coordinator in the WTO, that "a lot remains to be done".

The Sub-Committee also considered four notifications concerning preferential treatment for LDC products, made by China, India, the Republic of Korea and Chinese Taipei.

Technical assistance and capacity building

The Sub-Committee regularly monitors the progress of trade-related technical assistance for LDCs and other capacity-building initiatives in which the WTO is involved, such as the Enhanced Integrated Framework (EIF – see page 101) and the Standards and Trade Development Facility (STDF – see page 103). The secretariats of both these assistance mechanisms provided detailed briefings to the Sub-Committee on their respective activities.

Background on least-developed countries (LDCs)

The Sub-Committee on Least Developed Countries (LDCs) looks at systemic issues of importance to LDCs. These include market access, trade-related technical assistance and capacity building, accession of LDCs to the WTO and trade-related commitments undertaken by the international community to help LDCs, such as the Programme of Action for LDCs adopted in 2011 by the United Nations.

Following General Council approval of its membership on 26 October 2012, Laos became the latest least-developed country to join the WTO in early 2013.

As of October 2012, 47 LDCs were at various stages of the EIF process. Total pledges to the EIF Trust Fund stood at USD 240 million, of which USD 165 million had been secured. With regard to the STDF, as of October 2012, 32 project preparation grants (PPGs) had exclusively benefited LDCs, representing more than 60 per cent of all PPGs. In addition, LDCs have benefited from one-third of all STDF project grants approved. The importance and the synergies between the EIF and the STDF were again emphasized by the Sub-Committee.

Accession of LDCs to the WTO

Of the 49 countries designated by the United Nations as LDCs, 34 are WTO members. The Lao People's Democratic Republic (PDR) became the newest LDC member on 2 February 2013 following the Government's ratification of its accession package which had been adopted by the General Council in October 2012.

One of the important achievements of the Sub-Committee in 2012 was work on the strengthening of the LDC accession guidelines initially adopted in 2002. Following up on the ministerial mandate of 2011, the Sub-Committee focused in the first half of the year on strengthening and streamlining guidelines to further accelerate and ease the accession process of LDCs.

The new guidelines introduced some new flexibility and parameters to help acceding LDCs integrate into the multilateral trading system consistent with their development, trade and financial needs. Most importantly, it established benchmarks for acceding LDCs' market access negotiations (see page 36). "These improved guidelines provide a simpler framework for the entry of LDCs into the WTO family. It is another example of positive action in favour of the world's poorest countries," said WTO Director-General Pascal Lamy.

At present, nine LDCs (Afghanistan, Bhutan, Comoros, Equatorial Guinea, Ethiopia, Republic of Liberia, São Tomé and Príncipe, Sudan and Yemen), representing more than a third of those negotiating to join the WTO, are at various stages of the accession process.

Work programme for LDCs

In the latter half of the year, the Sub-Committee sought progress in updating the work programme for LDCs, which was adopted in 2002. It was put on the agenda in October 2011 when the LDC Group made a submission indicating changes that were needed. A number of WTO members have reiterated their willingness to work on the update and have underlined that it should be technical and non-substantive. In 2013, the Chair may convene informal consultations to advance this work.

An LDC retreat took place from 18 to 20 October 2012. The retreat was intended to review areas of priority and interest to LDCs and to formulate their positions in preparation for the WTO's Ninth Ministerial Conference to be held in Indonesia in December 2013.

Aid for Trade

In 2012, Aid for Trade continued to mobilize resources. Commitments rose in 2010 to USD 45 billion, according to the latest figures, up from some USD 40 billion in 2009. This is 82 per cent more than the 2002-05 baseline period. The Committee on Trade and Development worked on implementing the 2012-13 work programme, with its main theme of "deepening coherence", and prepared for the Fourth Global Review of Aid for Trade due in 2013, which will centre on global value chains. Four thematic workshops were held.

The Committee on Trade and Development (CTD) held four formal sessions on Aid for Trade in 2012 at which WTO members discussed progress in the implementation of the 2012-13 work programme, and partners and organizations reported on their Aid for Trade work.

Four thematic workshops were also held. On Aid for Trade and sustainable development and the green economy, the workshop, attended by WTO members and representatives of other international organizations, concluded that Aid for Trade contributes to sustainable development but much more needs to be done to make green growth a reality. At a workshop on Aid for Trade and services, participants shared the view that services are an important catalyst for economic growth, employment and poverty alleviation. Aid for Trade helps to address the various factors that hold back the participation of developing countries in trade in services, including lack of access to export financing. The workshop also noted that tourism is a key services sector and an important source of revenue for developing and least-developed countries (LDCs), and yet it is still a largely untapped resource.

Access to financing was the central theme of a workshop on Aid for Trade and trade finance. Between 80 to 90 per cent of world trade relies on commercial financing, mostly of a short-term nature. But only a third of the poorest countries benefit regularly from the services offered by trade finance programmes. And even where trade finance is available, it does not mean that access is universal. Finally, a workshop on Aid for Trade and intellectual property (IP) examined how developing countries, and in particular LDCs, can use IP in support of economic growth and development – and how development partners can support this process through Aid for Trade.

The WTO hosted a workshop on Aid for Trade and services on 11 July 2012.

Background on Aid for Trade

The Aid for Trade initiative was launched at the WTO's Sixth Ministerial Conference in Hong Kong in 2005. It aims to help developing countries, and particularly least-developed countries (LDCs), enjoy the opportunities offered by the multilateral trading system. Aid for Trade assists them in developing the trade-related skills and infrastructure needed to implement and benefit from WTO agreements and to expand their trade.

Fourth Global Review

At the CTD meeting on Aid for Trade in November, the Director-General announced that the Fourth Global Review will take place on 8-10 July 2013 and that its theme will be "connecting to value chains". With a focus on private sector development, the review will cover – among other things – the role that Aid for Trade can play in helping connect developing countries – and LDCs – to national, regional and global value chains. Underpinning the review is a monitoring and evaluation exercise conducted by the WTO and the Organisation for Economic Co-operation and Development (OECD). The monitoring exercise is based on self-assessment questionnaires addressed to developing and least-developed countries, donors (bilateral and multilateral agencies) and South-South partnerships (between developing countries).

A complementary monitoring exercise – undertaken together with the New Partnership for Africa's Development's "Grow Africa" initiative, the International Chamber of Commerce, the International Trade Centre, the International Telecommunication

Union and the United Nations World Tourism Organization – was addressed to the private sector to survey five sectors of particular importance to developing countries. These sectors are agri-food, information and communication technologies, textiles and apparel, tourism, and transport and logistics. Responses to the questionnaires will be analysed and conclusions drawn in a joint publication by the OECD and the WTO, and policy implications will be discussed at the review in July 2013. In parallel, the African Union (AU) and the United Nations Commission for Africa carried out a separate monitoring exercise on the AU action plan on boosting intra-African trade.

The Aid for Trade initiative continues to mobilize resources. The most recent figures available show that Aid for Trade commitments reached approximately USD 45 billion in 2010, representing an 82 per cent increase from the 2002-05 baseline period, with an average yearly growth rate of 13 per cent. This increase was "additional" and not at the expense of other sectors. Figures 1 and 2 provide a breakdown of regional and category-specific Aid for Trade commitments.

WTO Director-General Pascal Lamy, speaking at the OECD Policy Dialogue on Aid for Trade in Paris on 16 January 2013, warned that Aid for Trade financing could be harder to come by in the future. "We have made significant progress in securing additional financial resource" for Aid for Trade for developing countries. But "sustaining financing flows in the continued tight fiscal environment is going to be tough".

Figure 1: Aid for Trade commitments by category

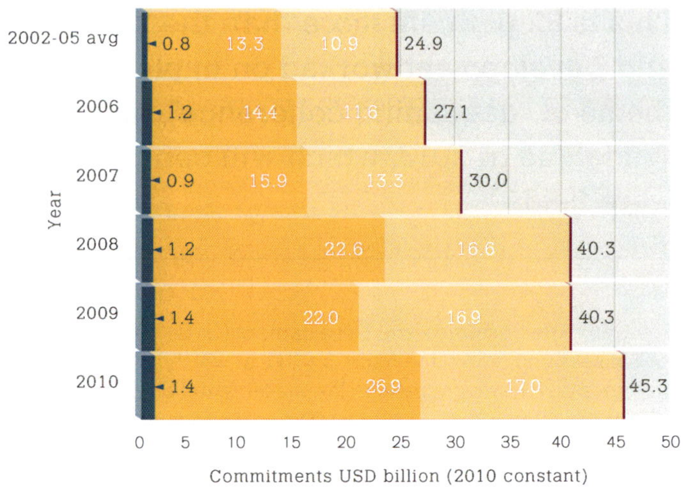

Source: OECD-DAC Aid Activity Database

Figure 2: Aid for Trade commitments by region

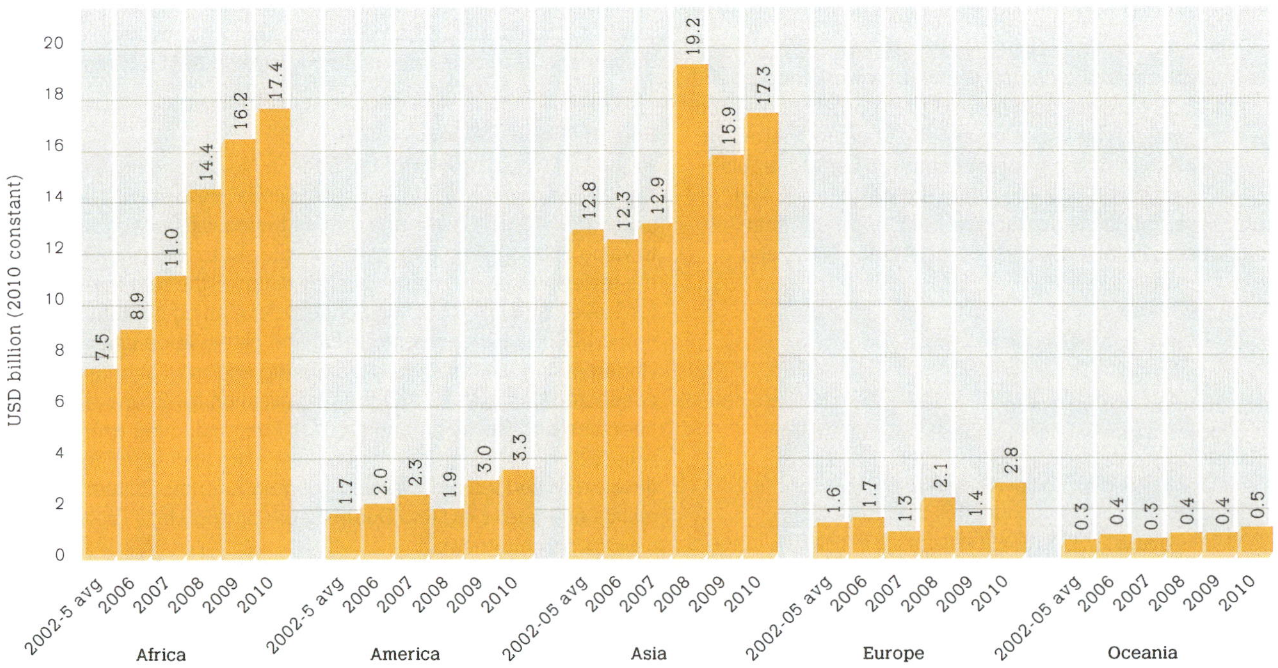

Source: OECD-DAC Aid Activity Database

Enhanced Integrated Framework

In 2012, the Enhanced Integrated Framework (EIF) – the Aid for Trade programme for least-developed countries (LDCs) – was independently rated as "highly relevant" to the trade and development priorities of LDCs. As a result, the EIF Steering Committee extended the EIF mandate until end-2015, with an additional operational period for project implementation up to 2017. Forty-three countries have so far received assistance, up from 40 at the end of 2011, to build stronger trade institutions and to address trading challenges. The EIF is supported by donor pledges of USD 240 million and contributions of approximately USD 178 million (up from USD 155 million in 2011) as of 31 December 2012.

The EIF, an Aid for Trade "partnership in action" programme for LDCs, is making headway in helping the poorest countries integrate into the global trading system. Its role is to strengthen trade institutions and foundations and roll out priority projects in areas such as adding value to agriculture, trade facilitation, export promotion and productive capacity building. The EIF operates within the framework of the Paris Declaration on Aid Effectiveness and the Accra Agenda for Action (which monitor how donors and recipients are doing against their commitments).

An independent mid-term review (MTR), conducted between July and November 2012, concluded that the EIF programme, which became operational in 2009, is highly relevant to the trade and economic priorities of LDCs. It said that the EIF had contributed to building capacity for trade-related strategies, to mainstreaming trade into national development strategies and to ensuring a coordinated delivery of trade-related assistance in line with country priorities. The MTR also indicated that the EIF had supported countries in market development, enhancing productivity, improving programme quality, addressing supply-side capacity constraints and trade integration. Following the MTR, the EIF Steering Committee accepted at its December 2012 meeting the proposal by the EIF Board to extend the programme mandate to the end of 2015, with an additional operational period for project implementation up to 2017.

Background on the Enhanced Integrated Framework

The Enhanced Integrated Framework (EIF) for trade-related assistance to least-developed countries (LDCs) is a multi-donor programme that helps LDCs become more active players in the multilateral trading system. The EIF combines the efforts of LDCs with those of 23 donors and six core international partner agencies, including the International Monetary Fund (IMF), the International Trade Centre (ITC), the United Nations Conference on Trade and Development (UNCTAD), the United Nations Development Programme (UNDP), the World Bank and the WTO. Other development partners, such as the United Nations Industrial Development Organization (UNIDO), act as observers.

Rise in funded projects

The programme provides funding to countries through two separate "windows", Tier 1 and Tier 2. Prior to receiving Tier 1 funds, recently admitted countries can also access funds for projects to lay the groundwork for EIF implementation. Tier 1 projects, comprising institutional capacity-building support and diagnostic trade integration studies (DTIS), are intended to help countries identify, address and prioritize bottlenecks and other constraints to trade, economic growth and sustainable development. DTISs provide a common basis for action by governments, civil society, the private sector and development partner stakeholders. Tier 2 projects are designed to build supply-side capacity to trade and provide start-up finance for activities identified as priorities in the first phase.

During 2012, the number of approved Tier 1 projects rose to 43, from 29 at the end of 2010. This includes 31 projects providing multi-year support for plans to mainstream trade and ensure coordinated implementation of priority activities, identified through the DTIS process, and 12 pre-DTIS projects. A total of 14 DTIS updates were approved in 2012. The number of Tier 2 projects approved for implementation rose to 12 from one at the end of 2011. There is currently a pipeline of over 28 Tier 2 projects across a variety of sectors targeting compliance with standards, enhancing the services sector, value addition, export growth and income generation for the poor.

Approved Tier 2 projects in 2012 include enhancing the sesame sector with a strong focus on private sector collaboration in Burkina Faso, institutional capacity building in sanitary and phytosanitary (SPS) standards in Burundi, feasibility studies on developing an existing export processing zone and the identification of tourism sites in Burundi, and increasing exports of milled rice and high-value silk in Cambodia. Other projects include improving the varieties of sesame, corn and palm seeds and plants in the Central African Republic, adding value in agriculture with a focus on cashew nuts, groundnuts and sesame in The Gambia, promoting fresh fruit and vegetables production for domestic and export markets in Lesotho, promoting the gum arabic sector in Mali, improving quality and adding value to ginger exports in Nepal, supporting eco-tourism in Sierra Leone, and improving the productivity and quality of honey in Yemen.

Enhanced Integrated Framework
www.enhancedif.org

EIF funding has supported the development of the silk sector in Cambodia.

Monitoring and capacity building

The EIF has been helping countries set up monitoring and evaluation (M&E) programmes to evaluate their national projects. Following an anglophone M&E workshop in 2011, a francophone one was hosted by Burkina Faso in 2012. To enhance the EIF's reporting capacity and information sharing, the EIF Database, also known as the EIF Knowledge Hub, was launched in 2012.

Tailored capacity building programmes rolled out in 2012 include a project development module jointly developed with the Standards and Trade Development Facility (STDF) and piloted in a training workshop in Senegal. The EIF also jointly organized, with the United Nations Development Programme, a trade-mainstreaming module with pilots in Burkina Faso, Cambodia and Zambia. This has resulted in the adoption of a trade road map with recommendations in Burkina Faso, the development of trade strategies in Cambodia and the start of a dialogue to reform policy implementation in trade ministries and agencies in Zambia.

New appointments

H.E. Minelik Alemu Getahun, Ambassador and Permanent Representative of the Federal Democratic Republic of Ethiopia, was elected the new Chair of the EIF Board, succeeding H.E. Mothae Anthony Maruping of Lesotho, who had chaired the Board since its inception in 2007. H.E. Päivi Kairamo, Ambassador and Permanent Representative of Finland in Geneva, was elected as the new Chairperson of the EIF Steering Committee, taking over from H.E. Hannu Himanen of Finland, who had chaired the EIFSC since its first meeting in 2010.

In March 2013, the WTO launched the process for recruiting a new Executive Director to succeed Ms Dorothy Tembo, whose term of office ends on 30 September 2013.

The EIF partnership also welcomed South Sudan as one of the new entrants to the programme following the EIF Board decision, increasing the number of EIF countries to 48.

At the international level

At the 13th session of the United Nations Conference on Trade and Development (UNCTAD XIII) in April, the EIF hosted an LDC ministerial working breakfast on the theme "Integrating Trade into National Development Strategies: Accelerating Delivery of Results in the New Global Economic Landscape". The EIF also joined the WTO in hosting an International Women's Day event, which focused on how the EIF was supporting the drive for women's economic empowerment in the poorest countries worldwide.

At the third annual meeting of the Steering Committee, one of the eight film chapters from the EIF "Trading Stories" project was premiered. The project focuses on disseminating information on good practices and lessons learnt and showcasing country results. The Cambodia Trading Stories film chapter featured national trade voices from the community perspective, the private sector and civil society as well as the government, showing the real impact of the programme in Cambodia.

For more information, go to www.enhancedif.org.

Standards and Trade Development Facility

The Standards and Trade Development Facility (STDF) – the Aid for Trade vehicle to help developing countries implement sanitary and phytosanitary (SPS) standards – continued to increase awareness, mobilize resources, strengthen collaboration and identify and disseminate good practice to enhance the effectiveness of SPS-related technical cooperation. It also focused on providing support and funding for the development and implementation of projects that promote compliance with international SPS requirements. Contributions to the STDF totalled USD 4.7 million in 2012.

The STDF began implementing a new five-year medium-term strategy (2012-16) in 2012 setting out the principles and strategic priorities that will guide its work and the use of its resources. The strategy is built on the need to promote increased collaboration and interaction among providers of SPS-related technical cooperation and continue strengthening the STDF as a "knowledge platform" for the exchange of information, sharing experiences and the identification and dissemination of good practices.

In collaboration with the Secretariat of the International Plant Protection Convention and the World Organization for Animal Health (OIE), the STDF organized a seminar on international trade and invasive alien species in Geneva on 12-13 July 2012. Invasive alien species are those that have crossed borders into new habitats, where they can survive, reproduce and outgrow local species and potentially cause environmental damage. The seminar, attended by 110 participants, was successful in:

- raising awareness about the mutually supportive objectives of the SPS Agreement and the Convention on Biological Diversity (CBD), and the contribution of effective SPS control systems to help protect against the entry of harmful species, including pests, diseases and other invasive alien species
- fostering increased collaboration between the SPS and the CBD "communities" at both regional and national levels
- reviewing initiatives that aim to build national and/or regional capacities to manage the entry and spread of invasive alien species, including pests and diseases, and highlighting common challenges, good practices and additional capacity building efforts required.

The STDF organized a seminar on 12-13 July 2012 at the WTO on international trade and invasive alien species.

The STDF continued its work on the application of multi-criteria decision analysis (MCDA) to inform SPS decision-making and improve resource allocation. The STDF facilitated the application of the MCDA tool in Viet Nam in September 2012 and organized a regional workshop for selected experts in food safety, animal and/or plant health and trade from Asian and Pacific countries in Bangkok, Thailand, on 12-13 November 2012. The workshop provided practical skills to enable them to apply the tool in their own countries. Following the workshop, several SPS experts expressed interest in using the MCDA framework.

The STDF and the Inter-American Development Bank jointly published "Public-Private Partnerships to enhance SPS capacity: What can we learn from this collaborative approach?". Building on an STDF seminar on this topic held in October 2010, the paper analyses the emergence, operation and performance of selected SPS-related partnerships between SPS government

Background on the Standards and Trade Development Facility

The Standards and Trade Development Facility is a global partnership that helps developing countries build their capacity to implement international sanitary and phytosanitary (SPS) standards, guidelines and recommendations and improve their human, animal and plant health status in order to gain and maintain access to markets. This work contributes to sustainable economic growth, poverty reduction, food security and environmental protection in developing countries. Established by the UN Food and Agriculture Organization, the World Organization for Animal Health (OIE), the World Bank, the World Health Organization and the WTO, the STDF is financed by voluntary contributions. The WTO provides the secretariat.

Figure 3: Location of STDF projects and project preparation grants*

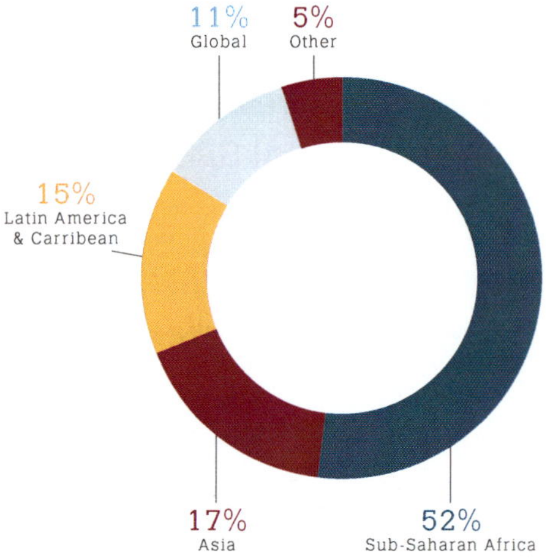

Figure 4: Coverage of STDF projects and project preparation grants*

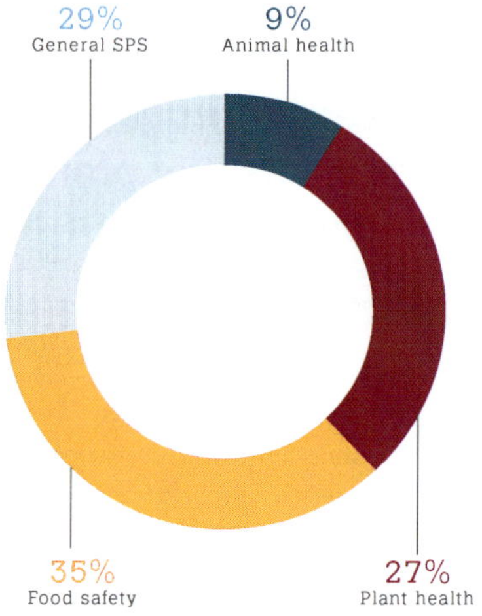

*The total may not add up to 100% due to rounding.

agencies and the private sector, raises awareness about the potential value and role of such partnerships in enhancing SPS capacity and provides practical guidance to facilitate and promote their use for SPS capacity development.

The STDF launched a virtual library containing SPS-related capacity-building documentation, including SPS needs assessments, action plans, training materials, evaluations of projects funded by the STDF and other donors, research papers and articles from various publishers and sources. The library will assist beneficiaries, international organizations, stakeholders, researchers and consultants in the development and implementation of SPS-related capacity-building initiatives and further facilitate the dissemination of relevant experiences and good practices.

The STDF initiated research on the implementation of SPS measures in the context of trade facilitation. This work will be pursued in 2013 and seeks to raise awareness about the synergies between the implementation of SPS measures and trade facilitation. It will also identify key needs, opportunities and good practices to improve the implementation of SPS measures in a way that ensures the appropriate level of health protection while minimizing trade transaction costs. Finally, it will develop recommendations to strengthen future work and technical cooperation focused on SPS and trade facilitation.

The STDF actively participated in a series of conferences, training workshops and other information sessions and meetings at international, regional and national levels, including the WTO SPS Committee. This work included the STDF's involvement in and collaboration with other Aid for Trade programmes, mechanisms and initiatives (such as the Enhanced Integrated Framework or EIF) aimed at ensuring that SPS issues and priorities are properly addressed. A joint EIF/STDF training workshop in Senegal resulted in a practical guide on project development and results-based management tools (in collaboration with the Centre for International Development and Training at the University of Wolverhampton, United Kingdom).

Three project preparation grants (PPGs) and eight project grants were approved in 2012, bringing the total number of PPGs and projects funded by the STDF to 53 and 63, respectively. Of the total number of grants, 52 per cent have been awarded to sub-Saharan Africa, 17 per cent to Asia and 15 per cent to Latin America and the Caribbean. In addition, 11 per cent of projects and PPGs can be classified as global (see Figure 3).

On a thematic basis, 35 per cent of projects and PPGs were dedicated to food safety issues, 27 per cent to plant health and 9 per cent to animal health, while 29 per cent could be classified as SPS general (see Figure 4).

Overall, the STDF has devoted 44 per cent of project resources to least-developed countries and other low-income countries.

Technical cooperation and training

The Institute for Training and Technical Cooperation (ITTC) strengthened both content and delivery of WTO technical assistance and training programmes in 2012, reinforced its capacity to interact with beneficiaries in all regions and bolstered its coordinating role for trade capacity building. The WTO undertook 343 technical assistance activities in 2012, the vast majority aimed at government officials. Results-based management was further consolidated in the design, management, delivery and evaluation of capacity-building programmes.

The work programme on technical assistance in 2012 was guided by the WTO's biennial Technical Assistance Plan 2012-13, which built on lessons learned from the implementation of previous biennial plans (2008-09 and 2010-11). The ITTC continued to institute measures to improve its own institutional capacity and to enhance the efficiency and impact of its trade-related technical assistance.

The ITTC strengthened the progressive learning strategy (PLS) for trade-related technical assistance. PLS makes maximum use of e-learning (Internet-based training) to deliver technical assistance across all products, from basic to intermediate levels. This approach ensures that when participants attend the more advanced training, they have acquired a minimum level of knowledge.

A critical element of the PLS is the selection of candidates using pre-determined criteria. This has ensured a consistent learning path for all trainees across all WTO members. It has strengthened linkages between programmes and has promoted more coherence and cost-effectiveness in the delivery of technical assistance. Geneva-based courses are now attended by participants with the same level of WTO knowledge and this approach is gradually being extended to national and regional activities.

Background on technical cooperation and training

The trade-related technical assistance programme is the WTO's contribution to the Aid for Trade initiative (see page 99). In the WTO Secretariat, this assistance is coordinated by the Institute for Training and Technical Cooperation. Its activities include e-learning, global and regional training courses, academic programmes and workshops at national and regional level. The technical assistance programme helps WTO members better understand their rights and obligations in the multilateral trading system, which strengthens countries' capacity to deal with the challenges and attain the benefits of participation in this system.

The newly upgraded WTO Reference Centre in Santo Domingo, Dominican Republic, was inaugurated on 10 April 2012.

The WTO Secretariat re-affirmed its commitment to delivering technical assistance with regional partner institutions. The regional approach to addressing capacity constraints complements the work and initiatives undertaken by bilateral donors as well as other agencies offering trade-related technical assistance. Coordination of technical assistance has been enhanced within the Secretariat and with partner agencies.

The Secretariat continued to pursue its outreach programmes in 2012, including its work with parliamentarians (see page 116), the private sector (see page 121), academics and universities. One other branch of outreach is the WTO Chairs Programme (see page 126), which has greatly improved coordination and cooperation by concentrating WTO support on academic courses, research activities, academic networking and public outreach.

The results-based management initiative, which requires the use of appropriate indicators to measure the impact and results of WTO's technical assistance programmes, was further refined after being formally introduced in 2011. It covers the design, management and delivery of WTO's trade capacity-building programmes and will become fully operational in 2013.

The WTO undertook 343 technical assistance activities in 2012 to help government officials gain a better understanding of the WTO.

Overview of activities

In 2012, the WTO undertook 343 technical assistance activities, both in Geneva and in various WTO members. The majority of these activities were organized in partnership with other international organizations and regional and sub-regional organizations. At the national level, the activities most in demand were multi-topic briefing sessions on issues relating to WTO agreements or the Doha negotiations. These included non-agricultural market access, rules, trade in services, trade-related aspects of intellectual property rights (TRIPS), and sanitary and phytosanitary (SPS) measures.

The immediate goal of these activities was to give participants a better understanding of fundamental WTO principles on the topics covered. However, on some specific Doha negotiating issues, an objective was to give participants the factual and analytical information necessary for meaningful participation in the negotiations.

Subject-specific regional seminars were conducted in all regions. These continued, as in recent years, within the framework of a strengthened role for ITTC regional desks. This approach reinforces the Secretariat's interaction with beneficiaries and regional partners, and enhances the WTO's coordinating role in the field of trade capacity building.

Activities by region

The technical assistance programme continued to place particular emphasis on providing assistance to Africa and to least-developed countries (LDCs), whose integration into the multilateral trading system remains a priority for the WTO.

Activities held for the benefit of Africa during 2012 constituted 24 per cent of the total number, followed by Latin America with 14 per cent, Asia and the Pacific with 13 per cent, 9 per cent for Central and Eastern Europe and Central Asia, 5 per cent for Arab and Middle Eastern countries and 3 per cent for the Caribbean. Global events represented 31 per cent of trade-related technical assistance in 2012. For a full breakdown of activities by region, see Table 1.

There has been a gradual, but marginal, decline of overall activities conducted by the Secretariat mainly because of increased use of e-training and better filtering of requests to ensure consistency with assessed needs.

LDCs benefited from approximately 41 per cent of all technical assistance activities, including national activities held in LDCs and regional and global activities in which LDCs were invited to participate. Several products have been specifically created for LDCs, or have LDCs as a priority. Examples are the three-week introduction courses for LDCs and a new course, the advanced LDCs course, which follows the PLS approach.

Other programmes give LDCs priority in determining beneficiaries. For example, the reference centres programme (see below) specifically focuses on the installation/upgrade of reference centres for LDC members.

Taking into account field-based activities only, the regional spread of events in which LDCs were involved shows that a majority of courses were targeted at Africa (58 per cent), followed by Asia-Pacific economies (22 per cent), Arab and Middle East countries (8 per cent) and the Central and Eastern European and Caucasus and the Caribbean regions (6 per cent each). Global events, including e-learning and Geneva-based courses, accounted for 42 per cent of activities involving LDCs in 2012.

Figure 5: Participants by region, 2012

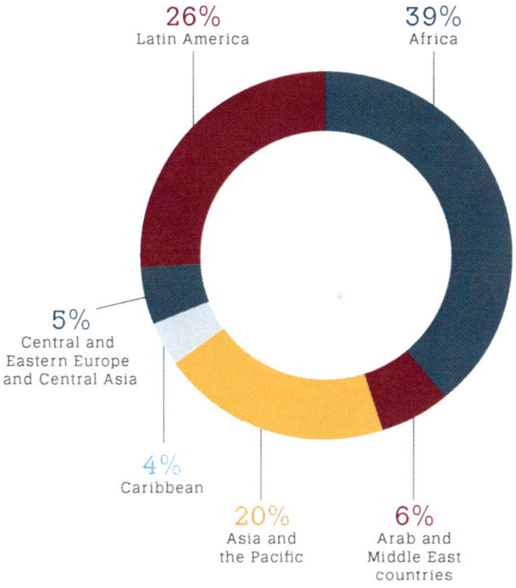

Figure 6: Participants by course language in 2012

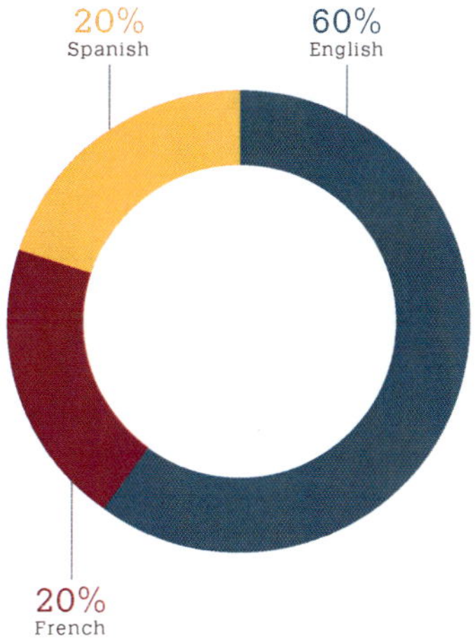

The Netherlands Trainee Programme, which assists in the economic and social development of low-income countries and comparable poor small, vulnerable economies in trade policy, and the WTO mission internship programme both give priority to applicants from African and LDC countries.

In 2012, six out of 18 candidates admitted to the internship programme, which was developed for Geneva-based missions, were from LDCs and half of these were from Africa. In the Netherlands Trainee Programme, 12 out of the 16 candidates were from Africa, and seven of the candidates were from LDCs. In addition, the Enhanced Integrated Framework (see page 101) is entirely focused on LDCs.

The high proportion of activities at national level reflects continued demand and allows the Secretariat to tailor its technical assistance to the particularities of each country. Most activities held at national level are meant to address those aspects of the WTO agreements that pose specific challenges for the country in question.

At PLS level 2 (intermediate), five regional trade policy courses were held: in Swaziland for English-speaking Africa, in Colombia for Latin American countries, in India for the Asia-Pacific region, in Kuwait for Arab and Middle-East countries and in Turkey for Central and Eastern Europe and Central Asia.

At PLS level 3, two three-month advanced trade policy courses for government officials were held in Geneva, one each in English and in French. In addition, a range of shorter, intensive advanced thematic courses were delivered, addressing such topics as dispute settlement, trade and environment, agriculture, sanitary and phytosanitary measures, LDC-specific issues, regionalism and intellectual property (the latter jointly with the World Intellectual Property Organization).

Twenty-eight technical assistance activities were held at the WTO, including the advanced trade policy course, an introduction course, two introduction days, nine thematic courses, nine Geneva symposia, three Standards and Trade Development Facility (STDF) and trade facilitation activities, and the twice-yearly "Geneva Weeks". The purpose of the Geneva Week is to inform non-resident WTO members about recent developments in the WTO's work programme and the Doha negotiations. The last Geneva Week was held from 10 to 14 December 2012.

E-learning

The WTO e-learning programme continued its growth in 2012, with a total of 33 online courses in English, French and Spanish, available on the e-learning website (https://etraining.wto.org) and through the WTO website.

Over 6,500 applicants from all regions applied for enrolment in e-learning courses, including more than 1,110 from LDCs. Out of the total applications, some 5,442 candidates met the criteria of being government officials and were selected to take the course (see Figure 7). Around 60 per cent of participants enrolled for the online courses in English, with the remainder split evenly between French and Spanish.

E-learning will continue to enhance its outreach, both regionally and academically, through partnerships. The objective is to strengthen partnerships and consolidate an already good geographical coverage, which would increase the value-added of technical assistance.

The regional distribution of participants taking the courses continued to be comprehensive, covering all regions, with Africa (39 per cent), Latin America (26 per cent) and Asia and Pacific (20 per cent) having the highest rates of participation.

Table 1: Trade-related technical assistance by region in 2012[1]

Trade-related technical assistance by region	National technical assistance		Regional		Global[2]		Other (conferences, etc.)		Total	
Africa	47	35%	13	22%	0	0%	22	33%	82	24%
Arab and Middle East countries	7	5%	6	10%	0	0%	4	6%	17	5%
Asia and the Pacific	26	19%	16	28%	0	0%	4	6%	46	13%
Central and Eastern Europe and Central Asia	19	14%	6	10%	0	0%	7	10%	32	9%
Caribbean	4	3%	6	10%	0	0%	0	0%	10	3%
Latin America	31	23%	11	19%	0	0%	6	9%	48	14%
Sub-total	134	100%	58	100%	0	0%	43	64%	235	69%
Global	0	0%	0	0%	84	100%	24	36%	108	31%
Total	**134**	**100%**	**58**	**100%**	**84**	**100%**	**67**	**100%**	**343**	**100%**

[1] Percentage columns do not always add up to 100 due to rounding.

[2] Activities under the "global" category are not targeted at a specific region, but include, for example, the Geneva-based courses and topic-specific workshops and symposia, distance learning, internship programmes and the advisory role on legal issues – Dispute Settlement Understanding (DSU).

Changes introduced in the delivery of the courses in 2012 gave participants more flexibility to register at any time. As of 22 January 2013, around 740 participants were in the process of finishing a 2012 course. This new approach has been key to the successful implementation of the PLS, in which e-learning functions both as a training and selection tool, ensuring that only successful participants in the online prerequisite courses are eligible to apply for higher level activities.

New courses on trade and development, WTO trade economics and the WTO market access database were finalized and opened for registration in 2012. In addition, a new type of course ("My Course") was made available to guide participants in identifying gaps in their WTO knowledge, and to select the appropriate training material accordingly. The catalogue of courses will continue to be expanded to include specialized courses. The aim is to cover all the main WTO subjects at level 2. New courses also continued to be made available in French and Spanish.

The number of online interactive activities in English, French and Spanish, as well as the number of multimedia and audio-visual components on specific WTO topics, was boosted to increase the quality of WTO e-learning courses and increase knowledge transfer.

Figure 7: Number of participants selected for WTO e-learning courses, 2010-2012

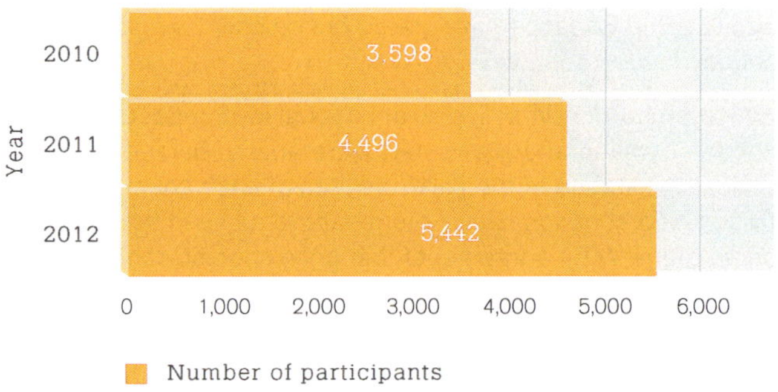

Source: WTO

Figure 8: Relative share of reference centres by region in 2012

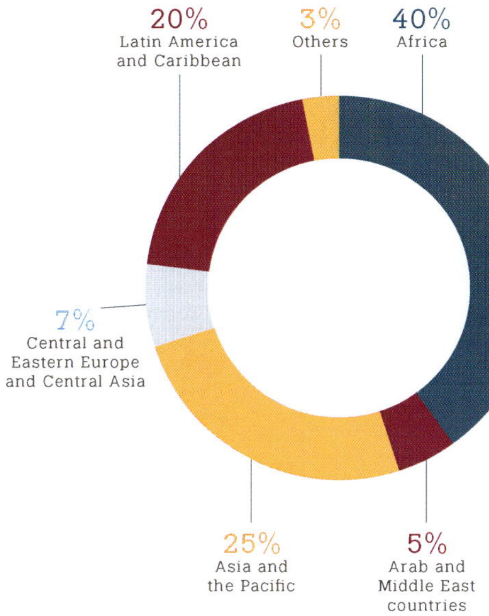

WTO reference centres

WTO reference centres (RCs), located primarily in LDCs, are open to government officials, business representatives, academics, and the general public to allow them to access WTO-related information. RCs are equipped with IT equipment, books, CDs, DVDs, and any relevant WTO-related documentation. RCs have full access to WTO databases, publications and WTO training material. In 2012, new RCs were established/upgraded in nine countries, taking the total number in operation to 108.

The programme was first launched in 1997 and has evolved considerably since then, turning RCs into effective learning centres. The RC programme has been refined, ensuring that it responds adequately, primarily to the needs of LDCs and countries without a resident mission in Geneva. The RCs enable these countries to follow WTO developments. In addition, the RCs serve as an effective means of undertaking WTO e-learning activities.

RCs can also be established in regional/sub-regional organizations to improve their collaboration with their member states and other agencies. They can be established within a government, i.e. at a ministry, at an academic institution or within business organizations, for example, a chamber of commerce.

Each RC has an RC manager, who is responsible for its daily operation. In order to operate the RC programme in the most effective way, the WTO Secretariat provides RC managers with full training to acquire the technical knowledge and skills required. These training events are organized both in Geneva and in the field.

RCs narrow the geographical distance between capitals and the WTO Secretariat, thus easing lines of communication and enabling participation in WTO discussions and decision-making. There are currently 108 working RCs located in 92 countries (See Figure 8).

Financing the technical assistance programme

One of the continuing challenges for the trade-related technical assistance programme is the need to ensure timely and adequate levels of funding. The programme is financed mainly from the Doha Development Agenda Global Trust Fund, which is a voluntary funding window provided by WTO members.

Donors provided CHF 24,669,734 in new funds in 2012, down from CHF 25,977,529 in 2011. Contributing countries have continued their support for the trust fund and funding levels for 2012 were sufficient to meet the minimum level of assistance required by eligible countries.

Outreach

- The WTO Public Forum, whose theme in 2012 was "Is Multilateralism in Crisis?", attracted about 1,200 participants.

- The WTO organized two regional technical assistance events in Ghana and Colombia for African and Latin American non-governmental organizations and two regional workshops for parliamentarians in Singapore and Laos.

- The WTO published two joint reports with the United Nations Conference on Trade and Development and the Organisation for Economic Co-operation and Development (OECD) on trade and investment measures in the G20 countries.

- Over 300 businesses replied to a WTO survey asking for their views on the work of the WTO and on how to improve cooperation between business and the WTO.

- The WTO and the (OECD) developed a database on trade in value-added terms that was launched in early 2013.

Relations with non-governmental organizations 112

Youth Ambassador Programme 114

Contact with parliamentarians 116

Cooperation with other international organizations 118

Contact with the media 120

Contact with the business community 121

Contact with the public 123

- WTO website 123
- Social media 123
- Visiting groups 123
- WTO publications 124

Cooperation with academic institutions 126

- WTO Chairs Programme 126
- Academic Support Programme 127

WTO Essay Award for Young Economists 128

Economic research activities 129

"Made in the World" 130

Background on outreach

The WTO maintains regular dialogue with non-governmental organizations, parliamentarians, other international organizations, the media and the general public to enhance cooperation and raise awareness of trade issues.

Relations with non-governmental organizations

The 2012 WTO Public Forum, whose theme was "Is Multilateralism in Crisis?", attracted many representatives of non-governmental organizations (NGOs). The WTO continued to hold briefings on trade issues for NGOs, and NGO representatives were able to attend two dispute panel hearings, which have been open to the public since 2005.

WTO Public Forum

The 2012 Public Forum, held in Geneva on 24-26 September, provided participants with the opportunity to express views and voice concerns on all aspects of the multilateral trading system. Since its launch in 2001, the Forum has become one of the most important meeting grounds for dialogue between relevant stakeholders of the multilateral trading system.

This year, the Forum addressed the question "Is Multilateralism in Crisis?", taking into account both the Doha Round deadlock and WTO activities that continue to work well. It took a close look at the factors shaping 21st-century trade in a fast-changing world, with a view to identifying solutions to the challenges that lie ahead. The new world order in which the WTO operates was also among the topics for discussion.

The programme featured 44 sessions, including three high-level panels, 31 regular panels, three ideas workshops, three book launches and one youth panel, besides the opening and closing sessions. New approaches to multilateral trade opening and the role of non-state actors in strengthening the multilateral trading system were also widely debated. The Forum also allowed participants to provide valuable guidance on how the WTO can face today's challenges and contribute to greater cooperation across all areas of global governance.

The Public Forum attracted about 1,200 participants from a wide variety of backgrounds and organizations (see Figure 1).

New features at the Forum

This year, the Forum included a number of new features. In the run-up to the event, a discussion forum was launched on the WTO's website, allowing stakeholders to submit short articles on the Public Forum's themes and to give their views on articles submitted by others.

At the Forum, ideas workshops were organized in parallel to the various formal sessions – one for each day of the Forum. These provided an opportunity for participants to share their ideas on a number of key trade topics (environment and dispute settlement among others) in an informal and interactive environment.

By using specially adapted USB sticks, participants were able to collect digital information about the event and to download background information from smart tags displayed at various points within the WTO.

A cartoon exhibition provided a humorous insight into how the WTO has been portrayed. In total, over 100 cartoons were on display from prominent international newspapers, including *Le Monde, Le Temps, The International Herald Tribune, The Financial Times, China Daily, The Washington Post* and *The Economist*.

Figure 1: Public Forum participation in 2012

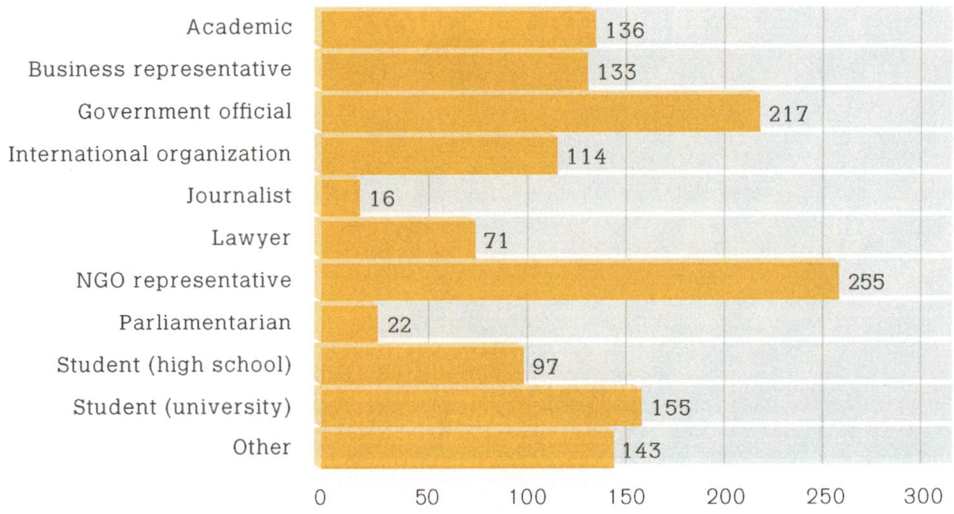

Source: WTO on-line registration figures for the 2012 Public Forum.

Micheline Calmy-Rey, Former President of the Swiss Confederation, gave the inaugural speech at the 2012 Public Forum.

At the Social Media Corner, participants were invited to record a video message in response to the question "Is Multilateralism in Crisis?". Their videos were subsequently posted on the WTO website.

Outreach activities

Two regional technical assistance events were organized in Ghana and Colombia, reaching out to African and Latin-American NGOs.

NGOs from Benin, Burkina Faso, Cameroon, Congo, Democratic Republic of Congo, Côte d'Ivoire, Gabon, Ghana, Guinea, Mali, Niger, Nigeria, Senegal and Togo attended a regional dialogue session in Accra, Ghana, on 29-31 October 2012. The meeting was entitled "Current and future challenges for the multilateral trading system – perspectives from Western Africa".

From 7 to 8 November, a group of Latin American trade-related NGOs met in Bogotá, Colombia, to participate in a roundtable discussion on trade and sustainable development in Latin America. The focus was on the evolving global trade landscape and protectionism in Latin America, trade disputes at the regional and multilateral level, perspectives for new preferential trade agreements, with an emphasis on the Trans-Pacific Partnership Agreement, policies and strategies to better integrate the Latin American region into global value chains and the importance of trade facilitation for the region.

Background on relations with non-governmental organizations

The WTO maintains regular dialogue with civil society organizations on various aspects of the WTO and the ongoing Doha Round negotiations, with the aim of enhancing cooperation and increasing public awareness of WTO activities and the role and value of the rules-based multilateral trading system.

NGO briefings

The WTO Secretariat undertook ten NGO briefings in 2012, reporting on the General Council and Trade Negotiations Committee meetings, the World Trade Report, the Rio+20 agenda and a seminar on exchange rates. Overall, a total of nearly 200 briefings have been organized since 2000.

NGO papers

NGOs can submit their position papers and studies to the WTO Secretariat and have them posted on the WTO website. A monthly list of available NGO papers is sent to WTO members. In 2012, only one contribution was received. Submitted by the International Chamber of Commerce, it addressed "Cross-Retaliation under the WTO Dispute Settlement Mechanism involving TRIPS Provisions".

Public hearings

Since 2005, a number of panel meetings, Appellate Body hearings and arbitration proceedings have been open to the public, including NGOs. As a result, registered NGOs have been able to follow the open hearings through video links. In 2012, two dispute panel meetings and one Appellate Body hearing were opened to the public (DS412 – "Canada – Renewable Energy", DS426 – "Canada – Feed In Tariff Program" and DS384/DS386 – "US – COOL" – see pages 80-81).

Youth Ambassador Programme

In 2012, the WTO named its first two Youth Ambassadors, students Ankita Mishra from India and Karina Hehs from Brazil, who were appointed after winning a contest to produce the best essay and video, respectively, on the theme of "How can trade promote development?".

The WTO Youth Ambassador Programme, launched in 2011, aims to raise awareness of trade issues among young people, encourage their engagement in policy discussions and bring new perspectives to trade debates.

Ankita is an MBA student at the Institute of Business Management in Pune, India, while Karina is studying Agricultural Engineering at the University of São Paulo, Brazil. Ankita's essay and Karina's video were chosen from 116 essays and 20 videos submitted to the selection panel for the inaugural contest, whose prize was the ambassadorships.

Ankita plans to get young Indians, particularly in the universities, thinking more about trade matters. "India enjoys the asset of a huge young population … (I plan to) … organize discussion forums and debates to get their views on how India can contribute to global development," she said shortly after being named one of the ambassadors by WTO Director-General Pascal Lamy.

Karina will launch a blog and a website in Brazil to discuss trade issues. She has already begun work on setting up the website, which she will use to act as a channel between society, especially young people, and the WTO, so that the views of young people get heard, she said. "Everyone has to play their role; you cannot expect the WTO or another country to do your share. So if everyone does their share, we can have global trade that helps people instead of promoting more segregation," she said. "I think it is really important to be a Youth Ambassador because… all the ideas I am going to present here are sort of in representation of all other young people around the world," she said.

Since September 2012, the WTO has remained in contact with the two Youth Ambassadors to follow their progress and assist them in implementing their projects.

The two young people kicked off their ambassadorships by attending the 2012 WTO Public Forum in Geneva where they attended a session on the topic tackled by their competition entries, along with other students with a proven interest in international trade issues. The Forum, held at WTO headquarters in September (see page 112), is an annual event that provides a platform for public debate and discussion across a wide range of WTO issues and activities.

Karina reminded the audience of how important it is for the idealistic voice of youth to be part of the trade debate. All voices need to be heard in the process of developing new ideas for promoting trade and development, she said. As she declared in her prize-winning video: "With a few changes in attitude, everyone can contribute to the process of building a fair global trading system and can promote development along the way."

Ankita explained the concept of "soft trade", which was a key part of her winning essay. She believes that the driving forces of trade should be changed. Instead of being driven solely by materialistic motives, trade should be a tool to promote the advancement of developing nations. Knowledge sharing and capacity building could be the way to accomplish this. Ultimately, bridging the gap between change-loving youths and decision-makers is a good way to achieve progress, she said.

The theme for the 2013 Youth Ambassador contest will be announced in the spring.

116 20 videos and 116 essays and were submitted for the contest.

Contact with parliamentarians

In 2012, the annual Parliamentary Conference on the WTO, organized by the Inter-Parliamentary Union (IPU) and the European Parliament, was held at the WTO. The WTO Secretariat continued the distribution of its regular newsletter to a growing number of parliamentarians. It also organized two regional workshops for parliamentarians in cooperation with regional and international partners.

Parliamentary Conference on the WTO

For the second time, the Parliamentary Conference was held at WTO headquarters, this time under the overall theme of "Back to basics: connecting politics and trade". It attracted some 300 legislators, who debated international trade and WTO issues, with a particular focus on the challenges of the role of trade in creating jobs.

Participants met WTO Director-General Pascal Lamy and some ambassadors to the WTO as well as members of the Director-General's Panel on Defining the Future of Trade (see page 121). In his welcoming remarks, Mr Lamy said: "We believe we are accountable to parliamentarians … We believe that this accountability and your own engagement and involvement in our trade issues is a good way to strengthen the multilateral trading system, providing legitimacy for what we do."

The main themes of the Conference debates were "Trade as a tool of economic growth, job creation and poverty alleviation" and "Trade in services: time for political decisions". The Conference produced a document listing the challenges for job creation in the current crisis. In this document, WTO agreements and negotiations are identified as particularly important, given the potential of trade to contribute to economic growth, job creation and poverty alleviation.

Background on contact with parliamentarians

Parliamentarians have constitutional responsibility to consider and ratify WTO agreements negotiated by their governments. The WTO seeks to maintain an open dialogue with parliamentarians and help them gain a deeper understanding of the organization and its work. The WTO participates in the meetings of ad hoc parliamentary bodies and organizes workshops for parliamentarians at national and regional levels.

Formal meetings of parliamentary bodies

The Steering Committee of the IPU on WTO matters met twice in 2012, in Geneva on the sidelines of the WTO Public Forum, and in Brussels at the European Parliament.

WTO Deputy Director-General Alejandro Jara represented the WTO at the Brussels Steering Committee meeting and spoke at a workshop organized by the European Parliament on the "Future of the WTO and the international trading system". He briefed both meetings on the current situation at the WTO and the state of play in the Doha negotiations. The workshop attracted almost 400 participants, including representatives of European industries and many Members of the European Parliament (MEPs) and their staff.

The Steering Committee is made up of around 30 parliamentarians. The WTO Director-General, senior staff, the Chair of the WTO General Council and Geneva-based ambassadors regularly participate in its meetings to brief legislators on important issues facing the multilateral trading system.

WTO Public Forum

At the WTO Public Forum (see page 112) in Geneva, the Assemblée Parlementaire de la Francophonie organized a well-attended session entitled "Is a multilateral approach to fair trade possible? The parliamentarian point of view". Food sovereignty was one major concern raised, particularly by African countries, which feared that rapid liberalization of agricultural markets can make it difficult for countries to meet their own food needs.

The annual Parliamentary Conference on the WTO, organized by the Inter-Parliamentary Union and the European Parliament, was held on 15-16 November 2012 at the WTO.

Regional workshops

In 2012, the WTO held two regional workshops for parliamentarians:

- in Singapore, for parliamentarians of the ASEAN-plus countries (the ten member countries of the Association of South-East Asian Nations plus Australia, China, Japan, the Republic of Korea and New Zealand), organized in collaboration with the Temasek Foundation, a non-profit philanthropic organization based in Singapore
- in Vientiane, Lao People's Democratic Republic (PDR), for Francophone members of parliament from Asia Pacific, attended by representatives from Viet Nam, Cambodia and Laos. Deputy Director-General Valentine Rugwabiza participated in this meeting.

The WTO regularly cooperates with regional parliamentary associations, such as the Commonwealth Parliamentary Association, the Assemblée Parlementaire de la Francophonie and the Inter-Parliamentary Forum of the Americas as well as the Temasek Foundation to organize outreach activities at the regional level.

Regional initiatives complement the national workshops for parliamentarians, which are carried out as part of the WTO's regular technical assistance work. Through these initiatives, the WTO has been able to enhance working relations with national parliaments as well as with parliamentary organizations.

Newsletter

In 2012, the WTO published four issues of the "WTO Newsletter for Parliamentarians", which is distributed to parliamentarians and made available on the WTO website.

Cooperation with other international organizations

In 2012, the WTO participated in the Rio+20 Earth Summit and the XIIIth UNCTAD Ministerial Conference. It continued cooperation with a variety of intergovernmental organizations, including the United Nations, the Organisation for Economic Co-operation and Development (OECD), the International Monetary Fund (IMF) and the World Bank. Together with the United Nations Conference on Trade and Development (UNCTAD) and the OECD, the WTO published reports on trade and investment developments in the Group of 20 (G20) countries.

United Nations

In 2012, the WTO Director-General participated actively in the Rio+20 Earth Summit, held in Rio de Janeiro, Brazil. He told the meeting that "we must strive to take the multilateral trading system forward so it may help us place the global economy on a sustainable development pathway".

The Director-General also took part in the XIIIth UNCTAD Ministerial Conference in Doha, Qatar. On the sidelines of this event, he delivered a speech to an International Trade Centre (ITC) seminar on the Arab region, where he outlined the need to "unlock trade for job creation". In Qatar, he also joined a ministerial breakfast bringing together ministers of least-developed countries (LDCs) and Enhanced Integrated Framework (EIF) partner agencies, organized by the WTO, UNCTAD and the EIF Executive Secretariat.

The Director-General attended the two regular meetings of the United Nations Chief Executives Board (CEB) – a high-level body composed of heads of UN agencies, funds and programmes as well as the Bretton Woods institutions and the WTO. The UN Secretary-General chairs the CEB. The role of the CEB is to enhance international cooperation on global issues. WTO Secretariat officials participate in meetings of the Board's subsidiary bodies dealing with programme and management issues.

The WTO participated in the Rio+20 Earth Summit, held in Rio de Janeiro, Brazil on 20-22 June 2012.

The WTO Secretariat is represented at the high-level United Nations Coordination Committee, which monitors progress in achieving the United Nations Millennium Development Goals, as well as at meetings of the UN Economic and Social Council, which deals with development issues.

United Nations Conference on Trade and Development (UNCTAD)

In 2012, the WTO published two joint reports with UNCTAD and the OECD on trade and investment measures in the G20 group of leading developed and developing countries. The latest report showed that there had been a slowdown in the imposition of new trade-restrictive measures by G20 economies, but that trade frictions seemed to be increasing. Presenting the report, WTO Director-General Pascal Lamy urged G20 governments "to redouble their efforts to keep their markets open, and to advance trade opening as a way to counter slowing global economic growth".

With UNCTAD, the WTO also co-published a book on trade policy analysis. Written by experts with practical experience in the field, A Practical Guide to Trade Policy Analysis outlines the major concepts of trade policy analysis and contains practical guidance on how to apply them to concrete policy issues.

The WTO continued its close cooperation with UNCTAD on training and technical assistance to developing countries and LDCs. UNCTAD is a major partner of the WTO in programmes such as the EIF (see page 101) and the Joint Integrated Technical Assistance Programme. The two organizations jointly sponsor the ITC, the trade promotion body for developing countries.

The WTO and UNCTAD organize various inter-regional information sessions and training activities to help representatives from developing countries learn more about the WTO and trade negotiations. These activities usually involve staff from both the WTO and UNCTAD. The WTO also cooperates with UNCTAD within the framework of the UN interagency "cluster" on trade and productive capacity, which aims to coordinate trade and development operations throughout the UN system.

International Trade Centre

The WTO works closely with the International Trade Centre (ITC) to build supply-side capacity and trade-related infrastructure that developing countries need to implement and benefit from WTO agreements. Some of the joint initiatives include the Joint Integrated Technical Assistance Programme, the EIF and the Business for Development initiative.

Together with UNCTAD, the WTO and ITC have made important commitments to strengthening their interagency cooperation. One area of successful collaboration is within the interagency cluster on trade and productive capacity (see left).

The WTO/UNCTAD co-publication *A practical guide to trade policy analysis* was launched at the WTO on 26 June 2012.

Organisation for Economic Co-operation and Development

The WTO and the OECD have a long-standing and close working relationship at all levels, with WTO Secretariat officials participating in many OECD meetings. The two organizations have recently developed a new database for measuring trade in value-added terms rather than the traditional customs returns. The database was formally launched in January 2013 (see page 130). The WTO also continued to publish joint reports with the OECD on trade and investment developments (see above). The Director-General also participated in the annual OECD Forum and Ministerial Meeting.

Other intergovernmental organizations

The WTO cooperated on trade issues and the needs of developing countries with a number of intergovernmental organizations, such as the United Nations Development Programme (UNDP), the IMF and the World Bank. The WTO also has longstanding working relationships with organizations such as the UN Food and Agriculture Organization (FAO), the World Customs Organization, the World Intellectual Property Organization (WIPO) and the United Nations Educational, Scientific and Cultural Organization (UNESCO).

The WTO worked with the World Health Organization (WHO) and WIPO in 2012 on preparing a study of the linked roles that public health policies, intellectual property and trade can play in advancing medical technology and ensuring it is available equitably to all who need it. The co-publication – *Promoting access to medical technologies and innovation: Intersections between public health, intellectual property and trade* – was launched at the WTO on 5 February 2013.

G20

The WTO participated actively, and at the highest level, in the work of the G20 during 2012, providing input on trade and on protectionism. The Director-General attended the G20 Summit in Los Cabos, Mexico, in June 2012.

Background on cooperation with other international organizations

The WTO works closely with other intergovernmental organizations and regional bodies, especially those involved in trade-related issues. This cooperation helps to ensure coordinated action and a coherent approach to international trade policies.

Cooperation with other international organizations
www.wto.org/otherorgs

Contact with the media

In 2012, the WTO continued to have regular contact with journalists, through press briefings, press conferences and e-briefings. The number of journalists registered to use the "media newsroom" on the WTO website rose 16 per cent to 2,702. The WTO also held a number of training activities for journalists.

The WTO's Information and External Relations Division held 22 press briefings and two press conferences in 2012 covering various aspects of the WTO's work, including dispute settlement, the Doha Round negotiations and the work of the General Council (see Figure 2). In addition, around 130 e-mail briefings on various WTO meetings were sent to journalists.

The WTO also maintained regular contact with 2,702 journalists in many countries, up from 2,330 in 2011, who have registered to use the "media newsroom" on the WTO website. This allows them to receive regular email bulletins on developments at the WTO and to access information under embargo. Journalists were also regularly invited to WTO events, including book launches and seminars.

Training activities

In 2012, the WTO held four training activities for journalists: a seminar at the WTO for French-speaking journalists, a regional workshop in Ghana, and two national workshops, held in Colombia and the Dominican Republic, respectively.

The fifth seminar for French-speaking journalists was organized in conjunction with the Friedrich Ebert Stiftung Institute. The three-day seminar (30 April-2 May) at the WTO was attended by journalists from Benin, Burkina Faso, Cameroon, Côte d'Ivoire, Democratic Republic of the Congo, Mali, Senegal and Togo. The seminar provided the opportunity for journalists to learn more about the WTO through presentations by experts on specific issues combined with interactive sessions and the use of various media tools (videos and social media). The participants also undertook a field trip to a Swiss customs post where they had a first-hand look at examples of trade facilitation.

The regional workshop in Accra, Ghana (29-31 October), was attended by journalists from Benin, Burkina Faso, Cameroon, Congo, Democratic Republic of the Congo, Côte d'Ivoire, Gabon, Ghana, Guinea, Mali, Niger, Nigeria, Senegal and Togo. The workshop provided an introduction to the WTO, an update on the Doha Round, a briefing on WTO disputes of interest to West Africa, and a comprehensive guide on how to access WTO information. The Friedrich Ebert Stiftung Institute helped to cover the costs of the workshop.

A regional workshop for journalists was organized by the WTO and the Friedrich Ebert Stiftung Institute in Accra, Ghana, on 29-31 October 2012.

National media workshops were held in Santo Domingo, Dominican Republic (29-31 October) and Bogotá, Colombia (6 November). They are part of the WTO technical assistance programme, which invites governments to request WTO training missions for media workshops in their respective countries. Both seminars provided comprehensive introductions to the WTO and a forum for discussion of national and international trade issues.

Figure 2: Meetings/subjects covered by WTO briefings/press conferences in 2012

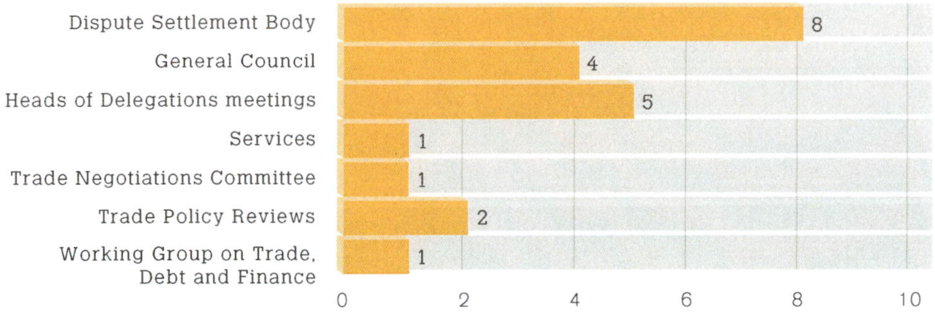

Journalists
www.wto.org/media

Contact with the business community

In 2012, the WTO took a number of initiatives to bring the WTO and the business community closer together. The Director-General launched a panel of eminent persons, with a strong business presence, to analyse challenges to trade opening. The WTO also carried out a survey among business leaders on how to improve cooperation between business and the WTO.

Panel on Defining the Future of Trade

The Director-General established in April 2012 a panel of eminent persons to analyse challenges to global trade opening in the 21st century.

The panel has a strong business presence, recognizing the role and responsibilities the private sector has in driving trade and the trading system in support of growth, development, jobs and the fight against poverty. The panel's analysis will be published in 2013 and should make an important contribution to debate between WTO members on the best way to tackle these challenges.

ICC World Trade Agenda Launch

In March 2012, the WTO hosted a meeting of over 80 business leaders and trade experts to launch the ICC Business World Trade Agenda, an initiative of the International Chamber of Commerce (ICC). It aims at involving global business leaders in defining the multilateral trade negotiation priorities for the private sector and helping governments set a trade policy agenda for the 21st century that contributes to economic growth and job creation.

In the presence of the ICC leadership, the Qatar Chamber of Commerce, the WTO Director-General and many representatives of the WTO membership, the WTO held an in-depth briefing on the state of play in the World Trade Agenda consultations in December 2012. "The WTO is not only business-friendly but business-like in the way we address our work," Director-General Pascal Lamy told the gathering.

WTO business survey

The WTO launched a survey in November 2012 of businesses from various sectors and different regions to get their views on the work of the WTO and on how cooperation with the business community can be improved. Over 300 businesses replied.

The survey found that 95 per cent see the work of the WTO as vital for businesses, 97 per cent believe that trade plays a role in generating growth and creating jobs and 72 per cent think that the WTO has been successful in ensuring that governments comply with their commitments. In addition, 62 per cent believe that the Doha Round can deliver benefits to businesses. Allowing business representatives at WTO meetings and involving them more in technical assistance programmes were two of the recommendations made in the survey.

The International Chamber of Commerce and the Qatar Chamber of Commerce and Industry held a briefing on the ICC's World Trade Agenda initiative at the WTO on 6 December 2012.

Background on contact with the business community

Business, trade and the WTO have always been closely connected. The biggest beneficiary of transparent and predictable trade rules and obligation is the private sector. Without business, there would be no trade and no WTO. Business is an important interlocutor for both governments and the WTO. It is actively involved in the multilateral trading system and participates in public activities of the WTO.

OUTREACH

The survey also sought the business community's opinions on how the WTO communicates with business. It found that 89 per cent of businesses considered the information provided on the WTO website to be relevant to their international activities, 82 per cent would like to have a dedicated web area for the business community, 95 per cent were interested in receiving an electronic newsletter containing WTO news and information, and 80 per cent expressed satisfaction with WTO efforts to reach out to them via social media, the website, the Public Forum, and WTO briefings.

The WTO will provide more detailed findings from the survey later in 2013.

Figure 3: Key findings of the WTO business survey

Ways of improving cooperation between the WTO and business

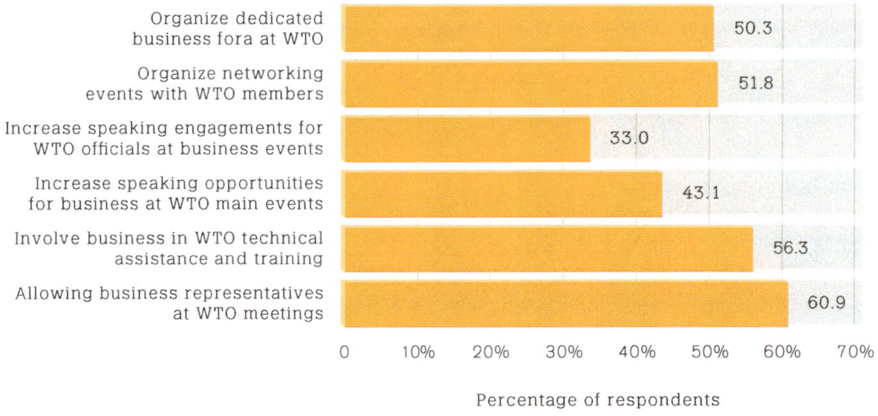

Contact with the public

Visitors to the WTO website continue to grow, with the site currently attracting almost 1.4 million visits a month. In addition, over 151,000 people have registered to receive email alerts when website updates are published. The WTO is also attracting an increasing number of followers on its social media pages, such as Facebook, Twitter and YouTube. The WTO receives numerous public email enquiries and comments (over 40,000 in 2012) and welcomed over 180 visiting groups to its offices in 2012. Over 100 new titles were published by the WTO during the year.

WTO website

The WTO website currently attracts almost 1.4 million visits a month. The number of people who have registered to receive email updates now stands at over 151,000. The largest categories for email alerts are university students (29 per cent) and business representatives (14 per cent). The countries with the largest total number of registrations are India and the United States. Over 2,000 pages were created or updated during the course of the year.

One of the new features launched on the website in 2012 is the "Information Centre", which provides a weekly round-up of WTO news and a preview of events in the weeks to come. Another new feature is the "International Trade and Market Access" tool, which provides a new dynamic presentation for all WTO data on merchandise and commercial services trade. The data is presented in the form of interactive maps, charts and data tables, using arrows and pop-up boxes to depict trade flows and to provide additional information.

Social media

In 2012, the WTO continued to make extensive use of social media, such as Facebook, Twitter and YouTube, to convey information about its work and its membership. The number of fans and followers of the WTO on Facebook and Twitter more than doubled in 2012 due to more active use of these media. The WTO's main Facebook page currently has over 16,000 fans while the WTO's publications page on Facebook has 5,076 followers. On Twitter, the WTO has over 13,000 followers. The WTO's channel on YouTube has over 1,500 subscribers.

Social media are used in particular to promote WTO events, such as the Public Forum (see page 112). The information provided is geared specifically for Facebook and Twitter. Fans and followers can access information that is not on the WTO website, such as a daily summary of WTO coverage in the media and interviews with the WTO Director-General. In September 2012, a virtual "Open Day" was created on Facebook to present the work of WTO members through videos and other sources of information.

Visiting groups

The WTO welcomed 183 visiting groups in 2012, totalling approximately 5,700 people. Most of the presentations covered the history, functions and current work of the organization. Some visiting groups were given presentations on specific WTO topics, primarily dispute settlement, agriculture, development and trade-related aspects of intellectual property rights (TRIPS).

The majority of the presentations (74 per cent) were given in English. A total of 12 per cent were given in French while 4 per cent were in German. The remaining 10 per cent of the presentations were given in Chinese, Dutch, Italian, Korean, Portuguese and Spanish.

Figure 4: Individuals registered with the WTO website's contacts database, as of end 2012

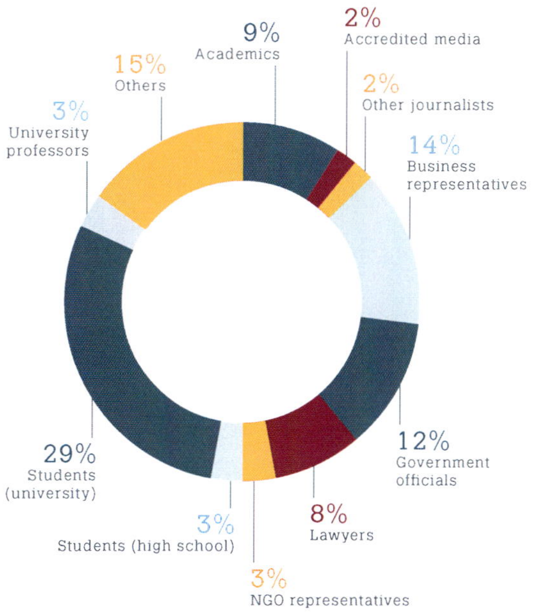

WTO website
www.wto.org

WTO publications

In 2012, the WTO produced over 100 publications in the WTO's three working languages: English, French and Spanish. Most of these publications can be downloaded free of charge from the WTO website. Printed copies can be purchased from the WTO online bookshop at http://onlinebookshop.wto.org.

Flagship publications

Annual Report 2012

ISBN 978-92-870-3825-8 | CHF 55

The 2012 WTO Annual Report is divided into two parts: 1) a brief summary of the organization, with an overview of 2012; and 2) a detailed review of the WTO's main areas of activity.

World Trade Report 2012 Trade and public policies: A closer look at non-tariff measures in the 21st century

ISBN 978-92-870-3815-9 | CHF 60

Regulatory measures for trade in goods and services raise challenges for international cooperation in the 21st century. The World Trade Report 2012 examines why governments use these non-tariff measures and to what extent such measures may distort international trade.

International Trade Statistics 2012

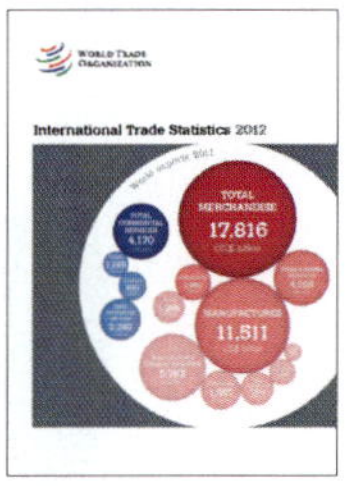

ISBN 978-92-870-3840-1 | CHF 50

International Trade Statistics provides comprehensive statistics on the world's leading exporters and importers, with information broken down by region, country, product and commercial service. Major trends are illustrated with numerous charts and maps.

Other annual publications

Trade Profiles 2012

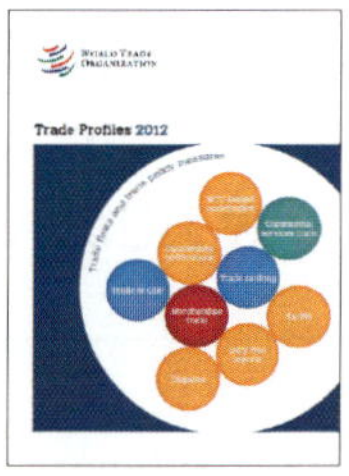

ISBN 978-92-870-3846-3 | CHF 40

Presented in a handy format, with one page devoted to each country, Trade Profiles provides a country-by-country breakdown of trade flows and trade policy measures for WTO members and those seeking to join the WTO.

World Tariff Profiles 2012

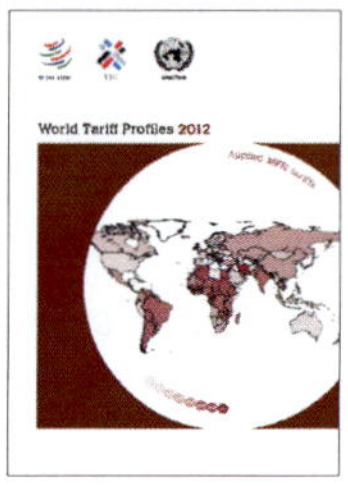

ISBN 978-92-870-3843-2 | CHF 50

World Tariff Profiles provides a listing of the tariffs imposed by each WTO member on its imports and an analysis of the market access conditions it faces in its major export markets. Co-published by the WTO, the United Nations Conference on Trade and Development (UNCTAD) and the International Trade Centre (ITC).

Boxed set of WTO statistical titles 2012

ISBN 978-92-870-3849-4 | CHF 100

The set comprises the WTO's three annual statistical publications: International Trade Statistics 2012, World Tariff Profiles 2012 and Trade Profiles 2012. (Available in English only.)

WTO Public Forum 2011: Seeking answers to global trade challenges

ISBN 978-92-870-3786-2 | Online only

The 2011 WTO Public Forum publication provides a round-up of the discussions that took place at the 2011 event, for which the special theme was "Seeking answers to global trade challenges".

Trade Policy Reviews 2012

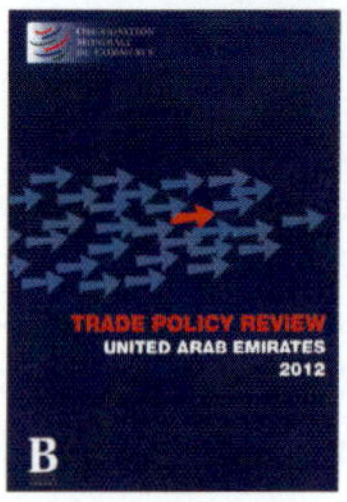

The Trade Policy Reviews provide detailed coverage of WTO members' trade policies and practices. Fourteen reviews were published in 2012 covering Bangladesh, Norway, Republic of Korea, Singapore, Colombia, China, Uruguay, United Arab Emirates, the Philippines, Nepal, Trinidad and Tobago, Turkey, the State of Kuwait, and the Kingdom of Saudi Arabia. Co-published with Bernan Press.

Dispute Settlement Reports 2011

The Dispute Settlement Reports include dispute settlement panel and Appellate Body reports as well as arbitration awards in disputes concerning the rights and obligations of WTO members under the provisions of the Marrakech Agreement. Ten volumes were published in 2012 covering reports issued in 2011. Co-published with Cambridge University Press.

New publications

15 years of the Information Technology Agreement: Trade, innovation and global production networks

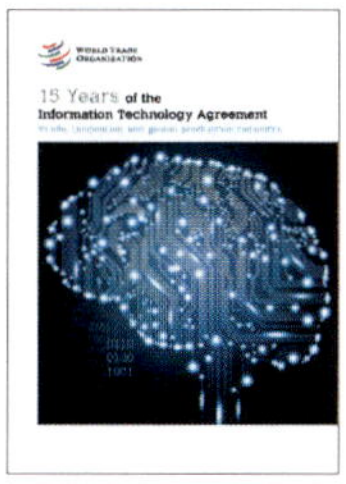

ISBN 978-92-870-3826-5 | CHF 40

To mark the 15th anniversary of the Information Technology Agreement, this publication charts the history of the Agreement and the effect it has had on the global trade in information technology products.

A Handbook on the WTO TRIPS Agreement

ISBN 978-1-107-62529-7 | CHF 80

The Handbook provides a comprehensive explanation of the WTO Agreement on Trade-related aspects of Intellectual Property Rights (TRIPS), later legal instruments, current policy issues and the relationship between TRIPS and public health. Co-published with Cambridge University Press.

A Practical Guide to Trade Policy Analysis

ISBN 978-92-870-3812-8 | CHF 50

This publication provides the main tools for the analysis of trade policy. It outlines the major concepts of trade policy analysis and contains practical guidance on how to apply them to policy questions. An accompanying DVD contains data required for the exercises. Co-published with the United Nations Conference on Trade and Development (UNCTAD).

WTO Dispute Settlement: One-Page Case Summaries (1995-2011): 2012 edition

ISBN 978-92-870-3828-9 | CHF 35

The publication provides a summary of the key findings of every dispute panel report up to the end of 2011 and, where applicable, the subsequent Appellate Body report.

WTO Analytical Index: Guide to WTO Law and Practice – 3rd edition

ISBN 978-1-107-02525-7 | CHF 400

The WTO Analytical Index is a comprehensive guide to the interpretation and application of the WTO agreements by the Appellate Body, dispute settlement panels and other WTO bodies. This edition covers cases from January 1995 to September 2011. Co-published with Cambridge University Press.

The WTO Dispute Settlement Procedures: A Collection of the Relevant Legal Texts – 3rd edition

ISBN 978-1-107-68415-7 | CHF 60

This fully updated edition collects together the treaty texts, decisions and agreed practices relating to the procedures that apply in the settlement of WTO disputes. Co-published with Cambridge University Press.

Status of WTO Legal Instruments (2012 edition)

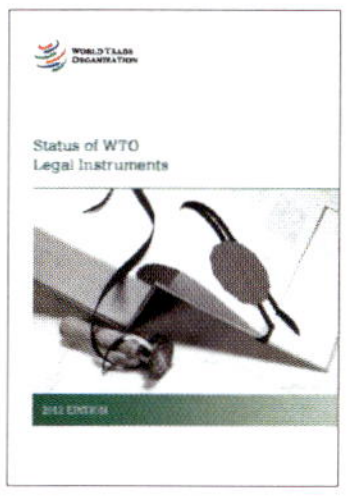

ISBN 978-92-870-3853-1 | CHF 20

This publication covers the legal instruments drawn up by WTO members in relation to the Marrakesh Agreement Establishing the World Trade Organization and the plurilateral trade agreements annexed to that agreement. For each legal instrument, information is provided regarding signature, acceptance, ratification, accession and entry into force.

10 things the WTO can do

ISBN 978-92-870-3831-9 | Unpriced

This new publication highlights some of the benefits of the trading system, but it does not claim that everything is perfect – otherwise there would be no need for further negotiations and for the system to evolve and reform continually. The publication replaces "10 Benefits of the WTO Trading System" and "10 Common Misunderstandings about the WTO".

Cooperation with academic institutions

In 2012, cooperation with academic institutions focused on three main activities: the mid-term review of the WTO Chairs Programme (WCP), the annual meeting of the stakeholders of the WCP and the sponsoring of projects by universities not covered by the WCP. Fifty-four activities were carried out in support of academic institutions from developing and least-developed countries, including lectures, sponsoring of academic projects, regional and national seminars, attendance at academic conferences, study visits to the WTO and the donation of WTO publications to universities.

WTO Chairs Programme

Launched in 2010, the WTO Chairs Programme (WCP) currently supports 15 universities from developing countries. The programme provides financial and substantive support for a period of up to four years. An external advisory board consisting of 23 eminent scholars assists in decisions regarding its operations.

The programme helps academic institutions provide students with a deeper understanding of trade policy issues and enhance the contribution of these institutions to the analysis, formulation and implementation of national trade policies.

The mid-term review assessed progress in the implementation of the Chair's respective projects and the overall functioning of the programme, notably with regard to the quality of results, the management of the projects and the sustainability of the projects after the conclusion of the four-year memorandum of understanding.

The review provided numerous comments and recommendations. In general, it seems clear that the WCP has been a catalyst in generating a significant amount of activity in the areas of curriculum development and teaching, research and outreach. It is felt that the programme has significantly contributed to enhancing the visibility of partner institutions and their relationship with the respective national governments.

Recommendations made to the WTO and the Chairs are being implemented. In a speech in June 2012, the Director-General Pascal Lamy noted that areas for improvement highlighted by the review include the development of new and/or clearer guidelines in relation to some administrative aspects of the programmes and better and more detailed reporting. There is also a question whether some Chairs would like more active participation by Secretariat counterparts in their programmes. Secretariat officials have volunteered to be available to assist in any way the Chairs consider appropriate, but it is for the Chairs to let their counterparts know if they think they can be of assistance, he said.

The annual meeting of the WCP was held in June 2012 to review the work undertaken by the Chairs, to discuss the findings of the mid-term review and to discuss several research papers completed by the Chairs. Opening the conference, the Director-General noted that the Chairs are strengthening their roles as reference points on trade-related matters vis-à-vis

Universities participating in the WTO Chairs Programme

their respective communities. He said that the 15 Chairs have produced more than 100 pieces of research, including four books, many working papers, articles, case comments and one database.

Academic Support Programme

The Academic Support Programme aims at supporting academic institutions from developing countries and least developed countries (LDCs) outside the scope of the WCP. It also supports existing or new academic projects through lecturing arrangements, donation of publications, research collaboration and a fellowship programme for doctoral students.

A new feature was introduced in 2012, adding a sponsoring mechanism for small projects in the fields of research, curriculum development and outreach. Seven projects were initially selected from Ecuador, Fiji, Haiti, Iran, Madagascar, South Africa and Tunisia. This mechanism will be reviewed for the purposes of determining possible improvements for 2013.

Twenty-four activities were implemented under the Academic Support Programme during 2012, including regional and national level activities. In addition, several study tours of the WTO for universities partnering with the WTO were organized while donations of publications were made to twenty-four academic institutions.

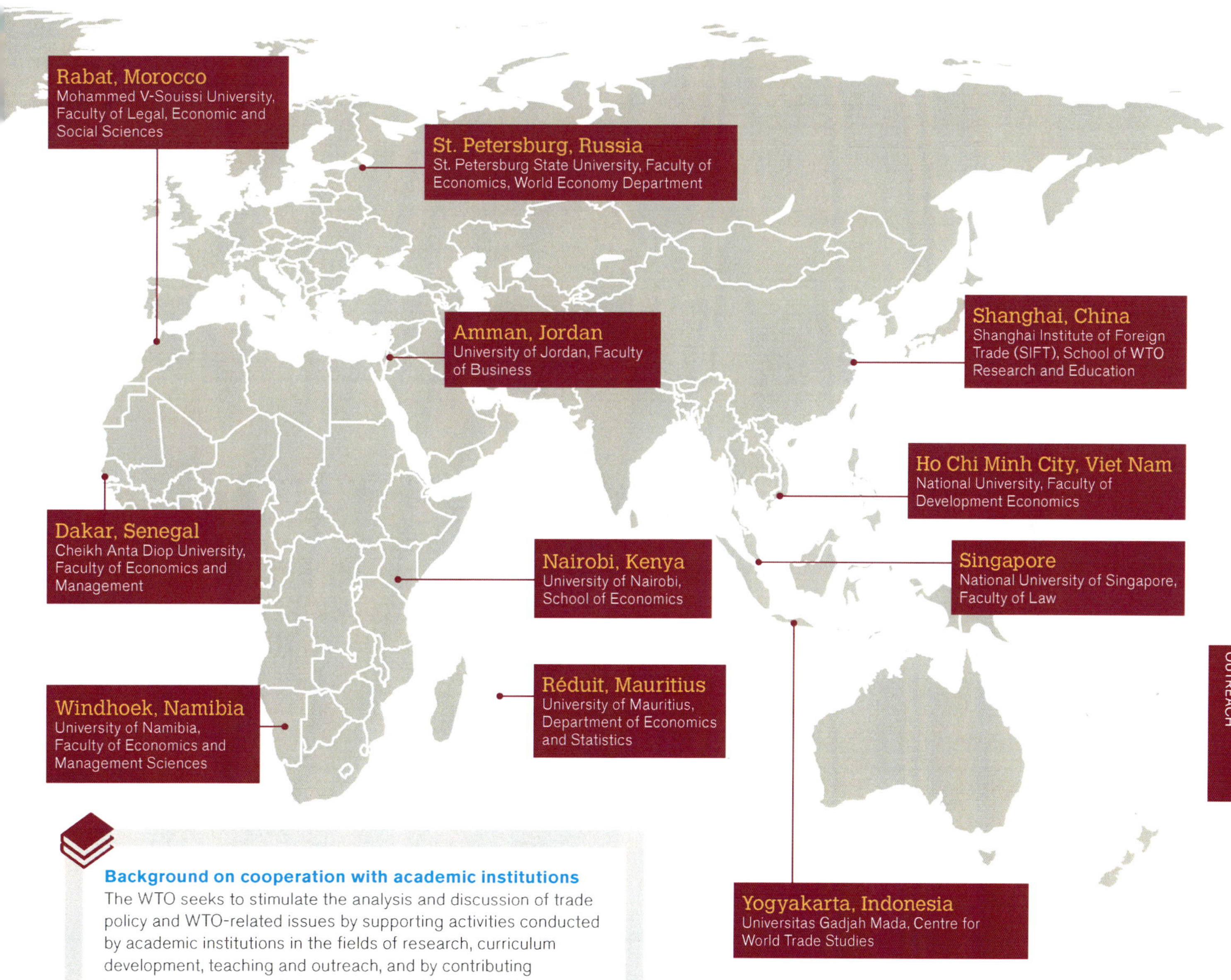

Background on cooperation with academic institutions

The WTO seeks to stimulate the analysis and discussion of trade policy and WTO-related issues by supporting activities conducted by academic institutions in the fields of research, curriculum development, teaching and outreach, and by contributing to enhancing the capacity of academic institutions in these areas. WTO support is implemented through the WTO Chairs Programme and the Academic Support Programme.

WTO Essay Award for Young Economists

The WTO Essay Award for Young Economists went in 2012 to American economist Treb Allen for a paper on information frictions in trade. The selection panel also gave a special mention to the work of Pablo Fajgelbaum, an Argentine national, on labour market institutions and international trade.

The paper by Treb Allen, currently a Fellow at the International Economics Section at Princeton University (United States), offers a framework to understand the role of information frictions in trade and to quantify their effects. Information frictions can be caused by several factors, including the growing number of regulatory standards for manufactured and agricultural goods that exporters need to meet to access export markets.

Entitled "Information Frictions in Trade", the paper finds that information frictions, more than transportation costs, account for a large part of trade costs. In the judgement of the Academic Selection Panel, the paper contributes significantly to understanding the changing nature of trade costs and their relation to trade flows.

The paper by Pablo Fajgelbaum, entitled "Labor Market Frictions, Firm Growth, and International Trade", develops a theoretical framework for studying the impact of labour market institutions on export dynamics and the gains from trade. The paper provides empirical evidence consistent with a number of the model's key predictions, including that labour market rigidities negatively affect export participation by limiting firms' growth. According to the Academic Selection Panel, this is an extremely well executed paper that offers new insights into the role of trade and labour policies on export flows.

Background on the WTO Essay Award for Young Economists

In April 2009, the WTO established the annual WTO Essay Award for Young Economists. The award, which carries a prize of CHF 5,000, aims to promote high-quality economic research on the WTO and WTO-related issues and to reinforce the relationship between the WTO and the academic community.

Treb Allen studied political economy at Williams College before obtaining a Ph.D. in Economics from Yale University (United States). He will be joining the Economics Department of Northwestern University (United States) as an Assistant Professor in 2013.

Pablo Fajgelbaum studied economics at the University Torquato di Tella in Argentina and later received a Ph.D. in economics from Princeton University. He is currently an Assistant Professor in the Economics Department at the University of California, Los Angeles (United States).

Academic Selection Panel

The Academic Selection Panel for 2012 comprised Dr Avinash Dixit (Emeritus Professor of Economics, Princeton University), Dr Patrick Low (Director, Economic Research and Statistics Division, WTO), Dr Robert Staiger (Professor of Economics, Wisconsin University, United States) and Dr Alberto Trejos (Professor of Economics, INCAE Business School). Dr Michele Ruta (Counsellor, Economic Research and Statistics Division, WTO) coordinated the work of the panel.

The WTO Essay Award for Young Economists went in 2012 to American economist Treb Allen of Yale University.

Economic research activities

In 2012, the Economic Research and Statistics Division (ERSD) organized 56 events, many in collaboration with other institutions. They included the launch of the World Trade Report 2012, a seminar on exchange rates and trade, the annual Global Trade Analysis Project (GTAP) conference, a co-publication with UNCTAD and a series of seminars in the Geneva Trade and Development Workshop programme.

In March 2012, ERSD organized a two-day seminar for the Working Group on Trade, Debt and Finance on the relationship between exchange rates and trade. The seminar brought together the private sector, governments, international agencies and academia (see page 69).

In June, it co-organized the 15th Annual Conference on Global Economic Analysis with the Global Trade Analysis Project (a global network of researchers and policymakers), UNCTAD and the International Trade Centre. The conference promotes the exchange of ideas among economists conducting quantitative analysis of global development issues. The theme for the 2012 conference was "New Challenges for Global Trade and Sustainable Development". The event attracted 250 participants from 46 countries and 150 papers were presented.

Also in June, UNCTAD and the WTO launched a co-publication entitled A Practical Guide to Trade Policy Analysis. The publication aims to help economists with an interest in the applied analysis of trade and trade policies to choose the best sources of data and the most useful tools to analyse world trade and trade policies. It explains analytical techniques, reviews the data necessary for analysis and provides illustrative applications and exercises for independent practice. The accompanying DVD contains datasets and other materials to complete the exercises.

In July 2012, the World Trade Report, "Trade and public policies: a closer look at non-tariff measures in the 21st century", was launched. The report observes that non-tariff measures (NTMs) have acquired growing importance as tariffs have been progressively reduced or ceilings set. At the same time, the variety and complexity of NTMs have grown as they have been increasingly used to attain a broad range of public policy objectives.

Background on economic research activities

The WTO's Economic Research and Statistics Division organizes regular seminars and conferences as well as online forums involving academics and researchers in Geneva and around the world. These activities include the Geneva Trade and Development Workshop programme, which is a joint project with the Graduate Institute's Centre for Trade and Economic Integration, the United Nations Conference on Trade and Development (UNCTAD) and the University of Geneva.

The 2012 World Trade Report, entitled *Trade and public policies: a closer look at non-tariff measures in the 21st century*, was launched by Director-General Pascal Lamy and Chief Economist Patrick Low (centre).

The World Trade Report explores the changes in the NTM universe and discusses the challenges they raise for the multilateral trading system. The report finds that the transparency of non-tariff measures must be improved and that the WTO has a central role to play, with its multiple transparency mechanisms. It suggests that more effective criteria may be needed to identify why a measure is used. It argues that current WTO disciplines may not always strike the right balance between policy commitments and flexibility. Finally, it suggests that addressing the adverse trade effects of public policies requires regulatory convergence, which raises the question of the role of the WTO in achieving this convergence.

In 2012, the Geneva Trade and Development Workshop programme, co-organized by the WTO, the Graduate Institute's Centre for Trade and Economic Integration, the University of Geneva and UNCTAD celebrated its fifth anniversary. The 21 events hosted during the year brought together academics and researchers in the Geneva region working in the area of trade and development. By providing a forum for discussion, the programme contributes to the exchange of ideas, supports relevant and high-quality research and facilitates outreach to policymakers and the wider Geneva trade policy community.

"Made in the World"

In 2012, the WTO and the Organisation for Economic Co-operation and Development (OECD) developed a database on bilateral trade flows measured in value-added terms rather than the traditional customs value. The "Made in the World" Initiative and its implications for trade and development policies was also the subject of several international seminars. At its Puerto Vallarta meeting in March 2012, the G20 highlighted the importance of understanding the role of global value chains in international trade and their implications for the world economy.

The need for new statistics

International supply chains are at the core of globalization in the early 21st century. They have changed the old ways of organizing international specialization and of understanding comparative advantages. Most manufacturing activities and many services industries today are characterized by supply chain production, and nearly all supply chains have an international dimension. Traditional statistics that rely on customs values cannot give a clear picture of today's way of trading and they fail to fully capture the huge role played by services in manufacturing. Most importantly, they are not sufficient for ensuring that trade policy is properly informed.

The need for adequate information on the industrial interconnection between countries increased dramatically with the 2008-09 global crisis. The role of international supply chains in leveraging the growth of international trade and the rise of emerging country economies during the two decades preceding this crisis was generally recognized. But their responsibility in synchronising the transmission of the financial crisis has since concentrated the attention of analysts on the importance of the issues at hand.

Background on economic research activities

Globalization is changing business models and increasing international fragmentation of production. Companies increasingly divide their operations across the world, from the design of the product and manufacturing of components to assembly and marketing, so creating international production chains. More and more products are "made in the world" rather than in any particular country. In this process, the nature of comparative advantages is altered, with new trade opportunities being created for emerging countries. In 2011, the WTO launched the "Made in the World" Initiative (MIWI) to support the sharing of projects, experiences and practical approaches in measuring and analysing international supply chains.

Cooperation with other international organizations

In 2012, the WTO and the OECD set out to develop statistics on trade in value added and produce a publicly available database of trade flows estimated in value-added terms. The database was launched in Paris in January 2013. Its aim is to help policymakers, academics and the public at large better understand trade in the 21st century. By measuring bilateral trade in value-added terms, the database better reflects the true nature of economic interdependencies in today's international economy, in particular the role of imports of intermediate goods and services in determining export performance.

In a similar initiative, the European Commission held a high-level conference in April, in which the WTO participated, to mark the launch of the World Input-Output Database (WIOD). This new database allows trade analysts to have a better view of the global value chains created by world trade. Also in April, the G20 meeting of leading developed and developing countries in Puerto Vallarta (Mexico) identified the incidence of global value chains in today's world economy as one of the priority issues to be considered by the international community.

China's Ministry of Commerce, the WTO, the United Nations Conference on Trade and Development (UNCTAD) and the OECD jointly organized a conference in Beijing in September 2012 that gathered national and international experts to discuss global value chains in the 21st century and their policy implications for trade, investment, statistics and developing countries.

The WTO also cooperated with a number of regional initiatives for exploring the statistical and analytical implications of "Made in the World". In March 2012, the WTO organized a workshop with the United Nations Economic Commission for Latin America and the Caribbean on measuring trade in value added. It took place during an inter-agency seminar on "Latin America's Prospects for Upgrading in Global Value Chains". Participants included experts from different agencies active in the field, including the Institute of Developing Economies, Japan External Trade Organization (IDE-JETRO), the Mexican Statistical Institute (INEGI), the US International Trade Council, the WIOD project and the OECD.

"Made in the World"
www.wto.org/miwi

In 2012, the OECD and WTO worked together to develop a database of trade in value-added terms. The launch of the database in January 2013 was attended by EU Trade Commissioner Karel de Gucht (left), OECD Secretary General Angel Gurria (centre) and WTO Director-General Pascal Lamy.

Following a WTO contribution to an Asia-Pacific Economic Cooperation (APEC) conference in Singapore in November 2011 on exploring whether international input-output tables and related models may be a practical tool for policymaking in APEC, an APEC meeting in February 2012 in Moscow analysed evidence on global value chains and trade in services. In May, a trade policy dialogue on "Facilitating Global Supply Chains" was also organized in Kazan, Russia. The WTO presented the latest developments in new statistical measures of trade in a world of global supply chains and demonstrated how new value-added indicators can provide evidence for better trade policy.

Practical implications

The focus of discussion in 2012 was also on the practical implications of "Made in the World" for public policy and trade facilitation. The Fung Global Institute (FGI) invited the WTO to co-organize the global value chain sessions in a regional meeting on "Towards a New Global Economy: Re-defining Asia's Role", which took place in Hong Kong, China, in May/June.

Similarly, the WTO sponsored a conference organized in San José in October/November by Costa Rica's Ministry of Commerce and Investment, the Inter-American Development Bank and the OECD on "Tapping into International Value-Chains: Opportunities and Challenges for Latin America". In November, the WTO, FGI and the Temasek Foundation Centre for Trade Negotiations organized a conference in Singapore to promote dialogue between private and public policymakers and to identify practical implications in terms of policymaking.

Website

The "Made in the World" website (www.wto.org/miwi) provides a discussion forum and access to relevant sources of information to address the issues raised by this initiative and to foster the development of statistical research in the field of international supply chains.

Secretariat and budget

- The WTO Secretariat has 639 staff on the regular budget.

- The WTO increased the number of nationalities represented among its staff to 77 in 2012.

- The WTO's total budget for 2013 is CHF 197,203,900.

- Work on the annex at the WTO's Geneva headquarters was completed in 2012, putting all staff under the same roof for the first time.

WTO Secretariat 134

New recruits 134
WTO Secretariat organizational chart 135
Allocation of staff by division 136
WTO staff on regular budget by grade and gender 137
WTO staff on regular budget by gender and nationality 138

Budget, finance and administration 140

Consolidated expenditure 2012 141
Consolidated budget 2013 141
Members' contributions to the WTO budget and the budget of the Appellate Body 2013 142

Background on Secretariat and budget

The WTO Secretariat has over 600 regular staff and coordinates the activities of the WTO. Most of the WTO's annual budget consists of contributions by its 159 members.

WTO Secretariat

The WTO Secretariat is based in Geneva. It has 639 staff on the regular budget and is headed by Director-General Pascal Lamy, whose term of office ends on 31 August 2013. The Secretariat has no decision-making powers as all decisions in the WTO are taken by members. The selection process for a new Director-General began at the end of 2012, with nine candidates being nominated by their respective governments.

The Secretariat's main duties are to supply technical and professional support for the various councils and committees, to provide technical assistance for developing countries, to monitor and analyse developments in world trade, to provide information to the public and the media and to organize the ministerial conferences. The Secretariat also provides some forms of legal assistance in the dispute settlement process and advises governments wishing to become members of the WTO.

Secretariat staff on the regular budget includes people from 77 WTO members (see Figure 4), one more member country than at the end of 2011. The professional staff is composed mostly of economists, lawyers and others with a specialization in international trade policy. There is also a substantial number of personnel working in support services, including informatics, finance, human resources and language services.

Women outnumber men at the WTO by 349 to 290. The working languages of the WTO are English, French and Spanish.

Background on the WTO Secretariat

The WTO's recruitment policy is based on the principle of equal opportunity for all, with the objective of ensuring the broadest possible diversification of the WTO Secretariat. The fullest regard is given to merit, qualifications and experience.

The Human Resources Division continues to respond to the evolving needs of the Secretariat. Enhancing staff performance and ultimately corporate output is the main driver behind a number of key human resources initiatives. Among the various initiatives, robust management systems have been implemented to ensure that there are collective discussions by WTO leadership regarding expectations of staff as well as an annual collective evaluation of staff performance and output to determine who best merits a reward.

The WTO Staff Council, elected by staff members, promotes the interests of all staff within the Secretariat, provides staff with a forum for issues of concern, increases staff understanding of their rights and duties, represents the interests of staff and presents staff views to senior management.

Director-General selection process

Nine candidates were nominated by their governments at the end of 2012 for the post of Director-General. The term of office of Director-General Pascal Lamy ends on 31 August 2013. The nominated candidates were Mr Roberto Carvalho de Azevêdo from Brazil, Mr Taeho Bark from the Republic of Korea, Mr Herminio Blanco from Mexico, Ms Anabel González from Costa Rica, Mr Tim Groser from New Zealand, Mr Ahmad Thougan Hindawi from Jordan, Mr Alan John Kwadwo Kyerematen from Ghana, Ms Amina C. Mohamed from Kenya, and Ms Mari Elka Pangestu from Indonesia.

New recruits Q&A

Dana Albajjali

Information Officer, Information and External Relations Division
Nationality: Jordanian   Date of joining the WTO: 1 February 2012

What prompted you to apply for a job at the WTO?
I previously worked in communications and external relations for the United Nations High Commissioner for Refugees (UNHCR). I wanted to continue in this line of work, but from a different perspective. The WTO is the perfect place to pursue my career because of the diverse and complex topics it covers. I find that this challenges me to become a better communicator.

What does your new job involve?
My new job entails briefing visiting groups on the work of the WTO and networking with media in the Middle East and North Africa (MENA) region. I am also the focal point for business relations in the Information and External Relations Division.

How well known is the WTO in your country?
The WTO is not as well known as other international organizations among the public in Jordan. The WTO's presence in the Arab media and other arenas could be strengthened, and this is an area in which I can try to help.

Figure 1: WTO Secretariat organizational chart, as of 31 December 2012

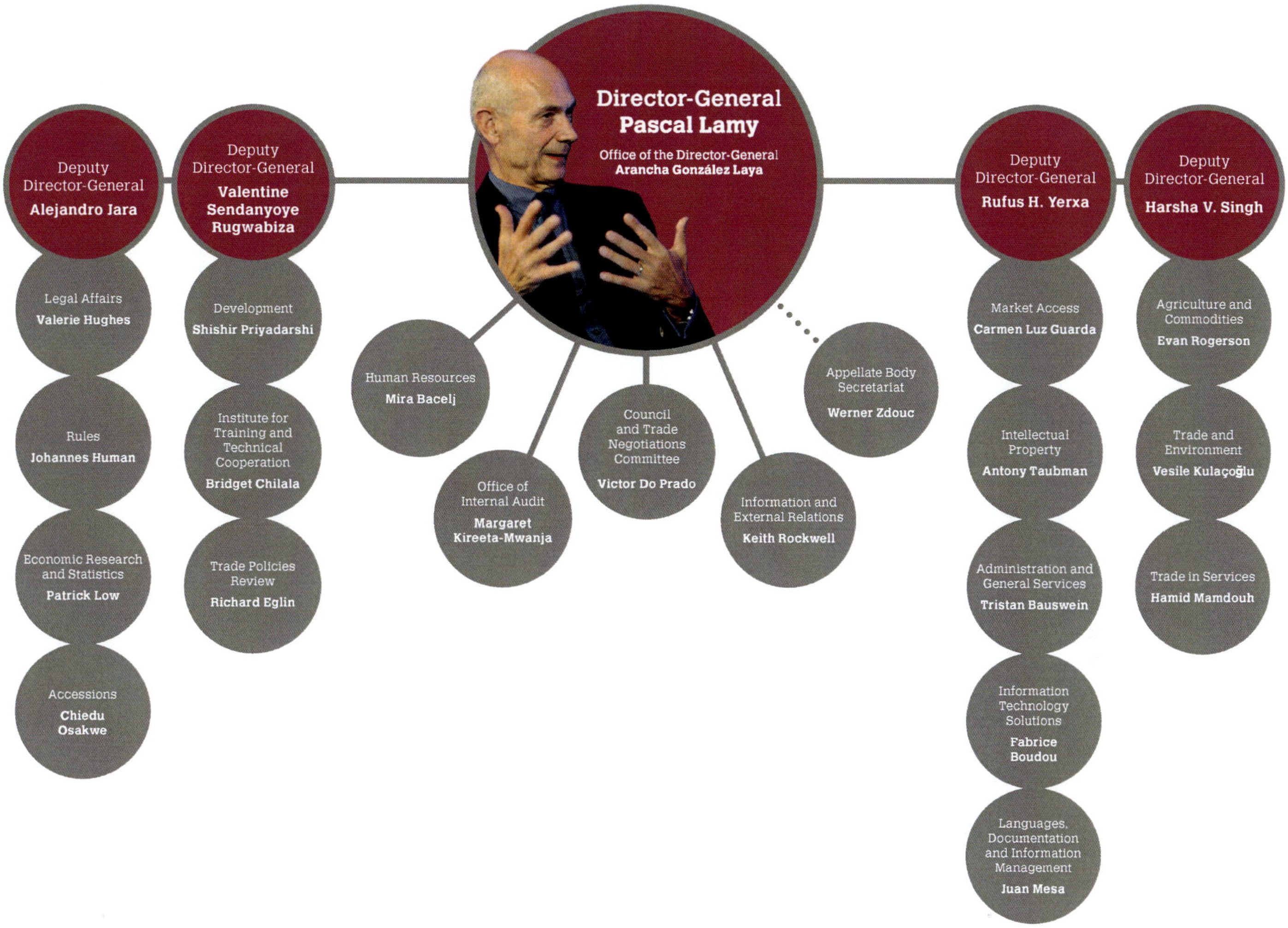

All the candidates made a presentation on their vision for the WTO at a General Council meeting in January 2013. The appointment process concludes with a General Council meeting no later than 31 May 2013, at which a decision to appoint a new Director-General must be taken.

Appellate Body

The Appellate Body, which has its own secretariat, was established by the Understanding on Rules and Procedures Governing the Settlement of Disputes to consider appeals against decisions by dispute settlement panels (see page 90). The seven Appellate Body members are individuals with recognized standing in the fields of law and international trade. They are appointed to a four-year term and may be reappointed once.

"My goal is to make a positive contribution to the activities of the Information and External Relations Division"

What were you doing before you joined the WTO?
At the UNHCR, I worked in the Jordan field office as an External Relations Officer. I was in charge of relations with the media, the general public, the refugee community and donors during the Iraqi refugee crisis.

What are your goals?
My goal is to make a positive contribution to the activities of the Information and External Relations Division and, more specifically, to raise the level of awareness of the WTO in the MENA region.

The following tables, giving a breakdown of staff membership in terms of gender and nationality, gender and divisions, and gender and grades, are provided for reasons of transparency.

Figure 2: Allocation of staff by division, as of 31 December 2012

Division	Regular Staff [1]	Senior management and directors [2]	Total
Director-General		1	1
Office of the Director-General	12	1	13
Offices of the Deputy Directors-General	4	4	8
Accessions Division	11	1	12
Administration and General Services Division	71	1	72
Agriculture and Commodities Division	15	2	17
Council and Trade Negotiations Committee Division	13	1	14
Development Division	16	1	17
Economic Research and Statistics Division	40	2	42
Human Resources Division	21	1	22
Information and External Relations Division	27	1	28
Information Technology Solutions Division	45	1	46
Institute for Training and Technical Cooperation	34	1	35
Intellectual Property Division	14	1	15
Languages, Documentation and Information Management Division	148	1	149
Legal Affairs Division	17	1	18
Market Access Division	11	1	12
Office of Internal Audit	2		2
Rules Division	18	1	19
Trade and Environment Division	9	1	10
Trade in Services Division	17	1	18
Trade Policies Review Division	53	2	55
Appellate Body	13	1	14
	611	**28**	**639**

[1] Regular budget posts, include posts not yet filled.
[2] Posts at grades 11 and 12.

New recruits Q&A

Nelnan Koumtingué

Trade Policy Analyst, Trade Policies Review Division
Nationality: Chadian Date of joining the WTO: 1 March 2012

What prompted you to apply for a job at the WTO?
I have always been interested in issues related to trade and economic integration. This position at the WTO offers me the opportunity to gain a better understanding of the multilateral trading system and the challenges countries face in trading with each other. And Switzerland, with its nice environment, is a bonus.

What does your new job involve?
My job consists of preparing reports on trade policies and practices of WTO members. The aim of these reports is to contribute to a better understanding of these policies and practices, and, ultimately, to a more transparent multilateral trading system.

How well known is the WTO in your country?
Chad is a long-standing member of the GATT/WTO and is one of the four African countries that initiated the Cotton Initiative – a call in 2003 for the elimination of cotton subsidies. This certainly raised awareness of the WTO among the population. Other aspects of the WTO mandate are not yet well known in Chad.

Figure 3: WTO staff on regular budget by grade and gender, as of 31 December 2012

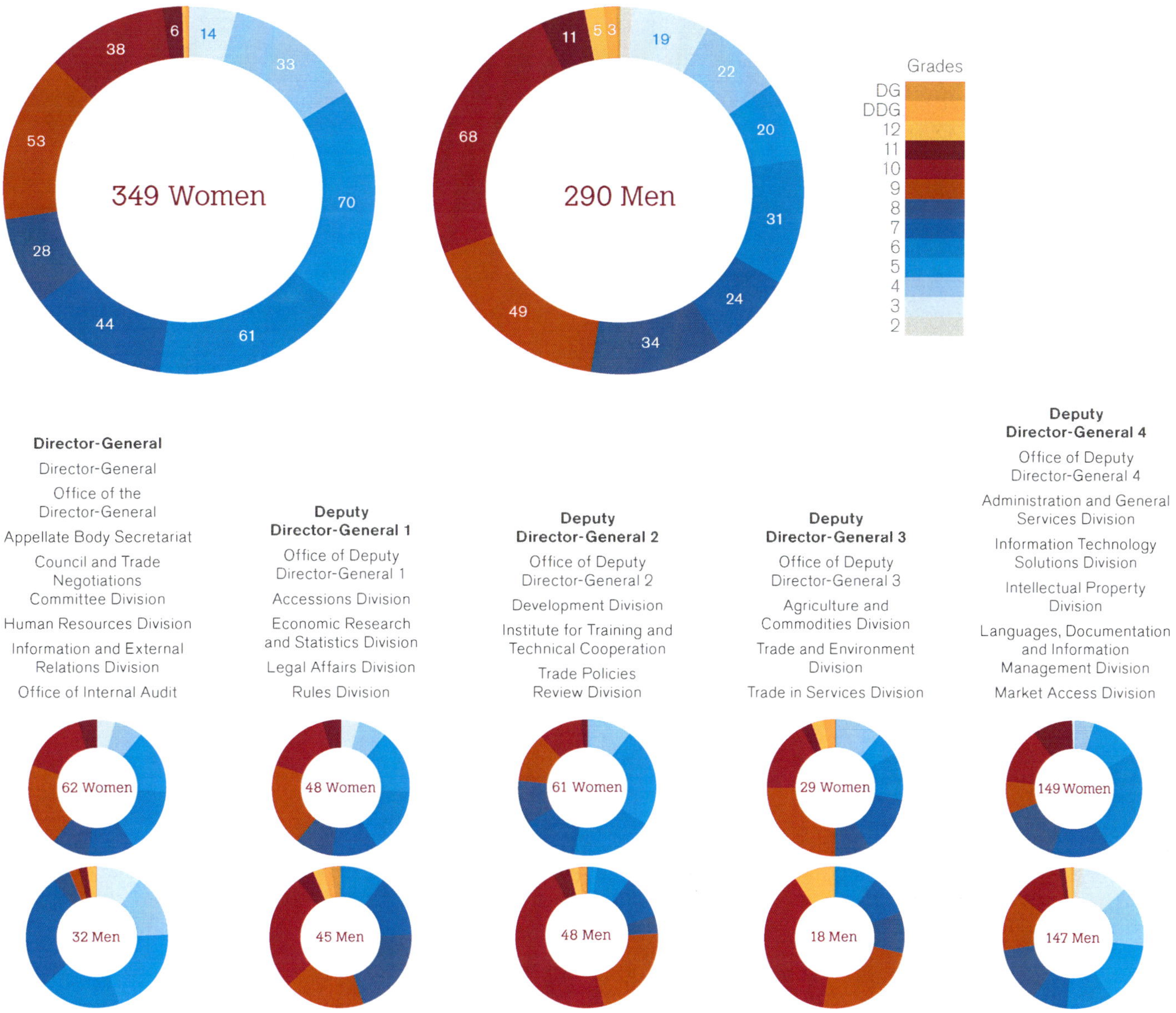

"My immediate goal is to add value to the work we do here at the Trade Policy Review Division"

What were you doing before you joined the WTO?
Prior to joining the WTO, I worked on trade statistics at the United Nations Statistics Division in New York. The experience I acquired there is quite useful in my current position, as trade policy reviews involve a lot of data analysis.

What are your goals?
My immediate goal is to add value to the work we do here at the Trade Policy Review Division and learn from my colleagues as well. I plan to grow in this field, and contribute to helping countries progress towards their development goals in a more open and transparent world trading system.

Figure 4: WTO staff on regular budget by gender and nationality, as of 31 December 2012

77 Secretariat staff includes people from 77 WTO members

North America

Member	Women	Men	Total
Canada	6	15	21
Mexico	2	4	6
United States of America	19	9	28
Grand total	27	28	55

South/Central America

Member	Women	Men	Total
Argentina	4	6	10
Barbados	0	1	1
Bolivia, Plurinational State of	1	2	3
Brazil	3	5	8
Chile	3	1	4
Colombia	4	6	10
Costa Rica	1	1	2
Cuba	1	0	1
Ecuador	1	1	2
Guatemala	1	0	1
Honduras	1	0	1
Paraguay	1	0	1
Peru	3	4	7
Trinidad and Tobago	1	0	1
Uruguay	1	6	7
Venezuela, Bolivarian Republic of	1	4	5
Grand total	27	37	64

New recruits Q&A

Florencia Mangiapane

Translator, Languages, Documentation and Information Management Division
Nationality: Argentinian Date of joining the WTO: 1 February 2012

What prompted you to apply for a job at the WTO?
My studies focused, amongst other things, on the specifics of translating for international organizations, and I was eager to work in a multicultural environment, so I applied for a post in the Spanish Translation Section.

What does your new job involve?
I translate different types of documents, such as dispute settlement communications, speeches and texts for the website. I also work closely with the revisers when the texts pose translation challenges.

How well-known is the WTO in your country?
Argentina has been a WTO member since 1995 and international trade is a topic of interest there. Personally, I remember studying the role of organizations in the area of international trade and the General Agreement on Tariffs and Trade at school.

Europe

Member	Women	Men	Total
Albania	1	0	1
Austria	2	3	5
Belgium	3	2	5
Bulgaria	0	3	3
Croatia	1	0	1
Denmark	1	1	2
Estonia	1	0	1
Finland	2	3	5
France	101	74	175
Germany	7	12	19
Greece	3	2	5
Hungary	0	1	1
Ireland	10	1	11
Italy	7	9	16
Netherlands	2	4	6
Norway	0	2	2
Poland	2	2	4
Portugal	0	2	2
Romania	2	0	2
Spain	29	14	43
Sweden	1	2	3
Switzerland	22	14	36
Turkey	3	1	4
United Kingdom	50	15	65
Grand total	250	167	417

349 Women, 290 Men

Total 639

Asia

Member	Women	Men	Total
Bangladesh	0	1	1
China	6	4	10
India	2	10	12
Japan	2	2	4
Jordan	1	0	1
Korea, Republic of	4	1	5
Malaysia	1	2	3
Pakistan	0	2	2
Philippines	5	7	12
Sri Lanka	1	2	3
Thailand	0	1	1
Grand total	22	32	54

Africa

Member	Women	Men	Total
Benin	0	1	1
Chad	0	1	1
Côte d'Ivoire	0	1	1
Democratic Republic of the Congo	0	1	1
Egypt	3	2	5
Ghana	0	1	1
Guinea	1	1	2
Kenya	1	0	1
Malawi	0	1	1
Mauritius	0	2	2
Morocco	1	2	3
Nigeria	0	1	1
Rwanda	1	1	2
Saint Lucia	1	0	1
Senegal	0	1	1
South Africa	0	1	1
Tanzania	1	0	1
Tunisia	2	3	5
Uganda	3	0	3
Zambia	1	0	1
Zimbabwe	2	0	2
Grand total	17	20	37

Oceania

Member	Women	Men	Total
Australia	5	5	10
New Zealand	1	1	2
Grand total	6	6	12

“I would like to further my knowledge of the WTO’s subject matter, its legal framework and its key documents.”

What were you doing before you joined the WTO?
I completed graduate degrees in translation and communication and obtained a Master’s degree in Translation and Intercultural Mediation. I also worked as a journalist and freelance translator.

What are your goals?
I would like to further my knowledge of the WTO’s subject matter, its legal framework and its key documents, and enhance my translation skills in the specialized texts that are translated in this division.

Budget, finance and administration

In 2012, work on the annex at the WTO's Geneva headquarters was completed, putting all staff under the same roof for the first time. The Committee on Budget, Finance and Administration regularly reviewed the budgetary and financial situation of the organization, the arrears of contributions from members and observers, the management of human resources and the WTO pension plan.

The new building is spacious enough to accommodate up to 300 staff members, who will have nine meeting rooms at their disposal. The atrium at headquarters, the Centre William Rappard, was also renovated.

The Director-General and the external auditor presented the 2011 financial performance report and the 2011 external auditor report to the Committee. The Committee examined these reports and proposed the approval of the 2011 audited accounts to the General Council.

In the area of human resources, special attention was given to the annual report on diversity, to the application of the salary indexation methodology and to reforms in the area of job profiling and internal mobility.

The Committee reviewed and recommended to the General Council to approve pro-rata contributions for four new acceding members – Montenegro, Samoa, Vanuatu and the Russian Federation.

It also reviewed and recommended to the General Council to approve payment plans proposed by the following three members subject to administrative measures and which had arrears in contributions for periods of up to 15 years – Chad, Djibouti and Sierra Leone. When a country is under administrative measures, its membership is subject to certain restrictions. The Working Group on Administrative Measures concluded its work and submitted its report and recommendations to the Committee. The Committee recommended to the General Council that a revised set of administrative measures be implemented for members and observers with arrears in contributions as from 1 January 2013.

Background on budget, finance and administration
The Committee on Budget, Finance and Administration monitors the WTO's budgetary and financial situation, including matters relating to the receipt of contributions, and undertakes any function assigned to it by WTO members. It considers issues concerning human resources management, hears progress reports on the WTO pension plan and deals with financial and administrative matters concerning the WTO Secretariat. The Committee reports to the General Council.

In 2012, work on the annex at the WTO's Geneva headquarters was completed, putting all staff under the same roof for the first time.

On building projects, the Committee examined and approved six projects to be funded from the members' transition operating fund for a total amount of CHF 13.7 million. These are the signage project, the equipment of the kitchen facilities in the Centre William Rappard, the equipping of the North Wing conference room and the equipment of the data centre, the security facilities and the accreditation facility.

Finally, the Committee examined the reports related to the 2012-2013 biennium mid-term review for the WTO and the International Trade Centre (ITC). No changes were proposed to the 2013 budget, which was approved by the General Council at the end of 2011. The Committee proposed to the General Council to approve the scale of contributions for 2013.

WTO biennium budget 2012-2013

The WTO derives its income from annual contributions from its 159 members (see Table 5) and miscellaneous income. These contributions are based on a formula that takes into account each member's share of international trade. Miscellaneous income mainly consists of contributions from observer countries and income from the sale of publications.

The WTO's budget for 2013 amounts to:

- WTO Secretariat: CHF 191,099,300
- Appellate Body and its Secretariat: CHF 6,104,600

Table 1: Consolidated expenditure 2012

Section	Budget 2012 CHF	Expenditure 2012 CHF[1]	Balance 2012[1]
Work years (including salary and pension)	127,002	119,622	7,380
Temporary assistance	15,171	16,932	-1,761
Communications (including telecommunications and postal charges)	1,780	1,376	404
Building Facilities (including rental, utilities, maintenance and insurance)	4,314	3,525	789
Permanent equipment	1,354	1,229	125
Expendable supplies	1,201	900	301
Contractual services (including reproduction, office automation and security)	9,037	7,486	1,551
Staff overheads (including training and insurance)	4,962	4,158	804
Missions	3,057	2,888	169
Trade policy courses	2,960	2,539	405
Various (including dispute settlement panels, publications, library and public information activities)	6,257	5,110	1,146
International Trade Centre	18,911	18,911	0
Total	**196,004**	**184,676**	**11,328**

[1] Unaudited accounts.

Expressed in '000 CHF

Table 2: Consolidated budget 2013[1]

Section	CHF
Work years (including salary and pension)	127,783,800
Temporary assistance	15,240,500
Communications (including telecommunications and postal charges)	1,719,700
Building facilities (including rental, utilities, maintenance and insurance)	4,529,000
Permanent equipment	1,454,000
Expendable supplies	1,201,000
Contractual services (including reproduction, office automation and security)	8,936,600
Staff overheads (including training and insurance)	5,162,000
Missions	3,157,000
Trade policy courses	2,851,300
Various (including dispute settlement panels, publications, library and public information activities)	6,258,000
International Trade Centre	18,911,000
Grand Total	**197,203,900**

[1] Consolidated statements refer to the WTO and the Appellate Body Secretariats.

TOTAL WTO BUDGET IN 2013

CHF 197,203,900

Table 3: Members' contributions to the WTO budget and the budget of the Appellate Body 2013

Member	2013 Contribution CHF	2013 Contribution %
Albania	54,740	0.028%
Angola	459,425	0.235%
Antigua and Barbuda	29,325	0.015%
Argentina	737,035	0.377%
Armenia	31,280	0.016%
Australia	2,447,660	1.252%
Austria	2,328,405	1.191%
Bahrain, Kingdom of	179,860	0.092%
Bangladesh	224,825	0.115%
Barbados	29,325	0.015%
Belgium	4,250,170	2.174%
Belize	29,325	0.015%
Benin	29,325	0.015%
Bolivia, Plurinational State of	62,560	0.032%
Botswana	58,650	0.030%
Brazil	2,209,150	1.130%
Brunei Darussalam	68,425	0.035%
Bulgaria	336,260	0.172%
Burkina Faso	29,325	0.015%
Burundi	29,325	0.015%
Cambodia	74,290	0.038%
Cameroon	70,380	0.036%
Canada	5,434,900	2.780%
Cape Verde	29,325	0.015%
Central African Republic	29,325	0.015%
Chad	41,055	0.021%
Chile	760,495	0.389%
China	15,047,635	7.697%
Colombia	453,560	0.232%
Congo	52,785	0.027%
Costa Rica	156,400	0.080%
Côte d'Ivoire	107,525	0.055%
Croatia	303,025	0.155%
Cuba	146,625	0.075%
Cyprus	123,165	0.063%
Czech Republic	1,429,105	0.731%
Democratic Republic of the Congo	78,200	0.040%
Denmark	1,802,510	0.922%
Djibouti	29,325	0.015%
Dominica	29,325	0.015%
Dominican Republic	158,355	0.081%
Ecuador	205,275	0.105%
Egypt	582,590	0.298%
El Salvador	84,065	0.043%
Estonia	181,815	0.093%
European Union[1]	0	0.000%
Fiji	29,325	0.015%
Finland	1,180,820	0.604%
France	8,156,260	4.172%
Gabon	41,055	0.021%
The Gambia	29,325	0.015%
Georgia	52,785	0.027%
Germany	16,723,070	8.554%
Ghana	103,615	0.053%
Greece	920,805	0.471%
Grenada	29,325	0.015%
Guatemala	136,850	0.070%
Guinea	29,325	0.015%
Guinea-Bissau	29,325	0.015%
Guyana	29,325	0.015%
Haiti	29,325	0.015%
Honduras	93,840	0.048%
Hong Kong, China	5,022,395	2.569%
Hungary	1,233,605	0.631%
Iceland	82,110	0.042%
India	3,520,955	1.801%
Indonesia	1,548,360	0.792%
Ireland	2,207,195	1.129%
Israel	846,515	0.433%
Italy	6,746,705	3.451%
Jamaica	72,335	0.037%
Japan	9,014,505	4.611%
Jordan	156,400	0.080%
Kenya	105,570	0.054%
Korea, Republic of	5,405,575	2.765%
Kuwait, the State of	615,825	0.315%
Kyrgyz Republic	31,280	0.016%
Latvia	156,400	0.080%
Lesotho	29,325	0.015%
Liechtenstein	46,920	0.024%

[1] Contributions from the member states of the European Union are made individually by its 27 member states.

Table 3: Members' contributions to the WTO budget and the budget of the Appellate Body 2013 (continued)

Member	2013 Contribution CHF	2013 Contribution %
Lithuania	279,565	0.143%
Luxembourg	805,460	0.412%
Macao, China	183,770	0.094%
Madagascar	29,325	0.015%
Malawi	29,325	0.015%
Malaysia	2,033,200	1.040%
Maldives	29,325	0.015%
Mali	29,325	0.015%
Malta	78,200	0.040%
Mauritania	29,325	0.015%
Mauritius	58,650	0.030%
Mexico	3,427,115	1.753%
Moldova, Republic of	37,145	0.019%
Mongolia	33,235	0.017%
Montenegro	29,325	0.015%
Morocco	369,495	0.189%
Mozambique	41,055	0.021%
Myanmar	64,515	0.033%
Namibia	48,875	0.025%
Nepal	33,235	0.017%
Netherlands	6,095,690	3.118%
New Zealand	430,100	0.220%
Nicaragua	44,965	0.023%
Niger	29,325	0.015%
Nigeria	715,530	0.366%
Norway	1,691,075	0.865%
Oman	306,935	0.157%
Pakistan	353,855	0.181%
Panama	185,725	0.095%
Papua New Guinea	48,875	0.025%
Paraguay	89,930	0.046%
Peru	349,945	0.179%
Philippines	709,665	0.363%
Poland	2,168,095	1.109%
Portugal	955,995	0.489%
Qatar	477,020	0.244%
Romania	711,620	0.364%
Russian Federation	4,066,400	2.080%
Rwanda	29,325	0.015%
Saint Kitts and Nevis	29,325	0.015%
Saint Lucia	29,325	0.015%
Saint Vincent and the Grenadines	29,325	0.015%
Samoa	29,325	0.015%
Saudi Arabia, Kingdom of	2,248,250	1.150%
Senegal	44,965	0.023%
Sierra Leone	29,325	0.015%
Singapore	4,430,030	2.266%
Slovak Republic	764,405	0.391%
Slovenia	365,585	0.187%
Solomon Islands	29,325	0.015%
South Africa	1,071,340	0.548%
Spain	4,772,155	2.441%
Sri Lanka	134,895	0.069%
Suriname	29,325	0.015%
Swaziland	29,325	0.015%
Sweden	2,412,470	1.234%
Switzerland	2,623,610	1.342%
Chinese Taipei	3,065,440	1.568%
Tanzania	72,335	0.037%
Thailand	2,140,725	1.095%
The Former Yugoslav Republic of Macedonia	58,650	0.030%
Togo	29,325	0.015%
Tonga	29,325	0.015%
Trinidad and Tobago	127,075	0.065%
Tunisia	248,285	0.127%
Turkey	1,861,160	0.952%
Uganda	43,010	0.022%
Ukraine	789,820	0.404%
United Arab Emirates	2,232,610	1.142%
United Kingdom	8,453,420	4.324%
United States of America	22,891,095	11.709%
Uruguay	95,795	0.049%
Vanuatu	29,325	0.015%
Venezuela , Bolivarian Republic of	727,260	0.372%
Viet Nam	785,910	0.402%
Zambia	58,650	0.030%
Zimbabwe	37,145	0.019%
TOTAL	**195,500,000**	**100.00%**

Abbreviations

ASEAN	Association of Southeast Asian Nations	MFN	Most-favoured nation
CTD	Committee on Trade and Development	MIWI	"Made in the World"
DDA	Doha Development Agenda	NAMA	Non-agricultural market access
DSB	Dispute Settlement Body	NFIDCs	Net food-importing developing countries
DSU	Dispute Settlement Understanding	NGO	Non-governmental organization
EIF	Enhanced Integrated Framework	NTMs	Non-tariff measures
EU	European Union	OECD	Organisation for Economic Co-operation and Development
FAO	Food and Agriculture Organization	PLS	Progressive learning strategy
FDI	Foreign direct investment	PTAs	Preferential trade arrangements
GATS	General Agreement on Trade in Services	RTAs	Regional trade agreements
GATT	General Agreement on Tariffs and Trade	SCM	Subsidies and Countervailing Measures
GDP	Gross domestic product	SMEs	Small and medium-sized enterprises
GIs	Geographical indications	SPS	Sanitary and phytosanitary measures
GPA	Government Procurement Agreement	STDF	Standards and Trade Development Facility
HS	Harmonized System	SVE	Small, vulnerable economy
ICC	International Chamber of Commerce	TBT	Technical barriers to trade
ILO	International Labour Organization	TNC	Trade Negotiations Committee
IPU	Inter-Parliamentary Union	TPR	Trade Policy Review
ISO	International Organization for Standardization	TPRM	Trade Policy Review Mechanism
ITA	Information Technology Agreement	TRIMs	Trade-related investment measures
ITC	International Trade Centre	TRIPS	Trade-related aspects of intellectual property rights
ITTC	Institute for Training and Technical Cooperation	UNCTAD	United Nations Conference on Trade and Development
ITU	International Telecommunication Union	WIPO	World Intellectual Property Organization
LDCs	Least-developed countries		
MEAs	Multilateral environmental agreements		

0 is zero or became zero due to rounding.

Billion means one thousand million.

Minor discrepancies between constituent figures and totals are due to rounding.

Unless otherwise indicated, (i) all value figures are expressed in US dollars; (ii) trade figures include the intra-trade of free trade areas, customs unions, regional and other country groupings.

Note

This report covers the WTO's activities in 2012. The word "country" is frequently used to describe WTO members whereas a few members are officially "customs territories", and not necessarily countries in the usual sense of the word.

Further information

Further information about the organization and its activities can be found on the WTO website: **www.wto.org**

General information about the WTO is available in the following publications, which may all be downloaded free of charge from the website:

WTO in Brief

WTO in Brief provides a starting point for essential information about the WTO. Concise and practical, this short brochure is an ideal introduction to the WTO.

10 things the WTO can do

This new publication highlights some of the benefits of the trading system, but it does not claim that everything is perfect – otherwise there would be no need for further negotiations and for the system to evolve and reform continually. The publication replaces "10 Benefits of the WTO Trading System" and "10 Common Misunderstandings about the WTO".

Understanding the WTO

An introduction to the WTO, what it is, why it was created, how it works, and what it does, Understanding the WTO has been written specifically for non-specialists. More comprehensive than WTO in Brief, this publication details WTO agreements, the dispute settlement process, the Doha Round of negotiations and many other issues.

Online bookshop

Printed publications can be purchased through the WTO's online bookshop: http://onlinebookshop.wto.org.

Many publications may be downloaded free of charge from the WTO website: www.wto.org.

You may register to receive free alerts when new titles become available.